MW01517526

Children of a
Child-Centered School

Children of a Child-Centered School

Don Wallis

and the children
and teachers of
the Antioch School

Photographs by

Erik and Deirdre Owen

and Dianne Collinson

OYO PRESS

© 2005 by Don Wallis. All rights reserved.

ISBN 0-9622336-1-7

Published by Oyo Press, Box 476, Yellow Springs, OH 45387
937-767-7818

Printed in Korea by Graphics International

All proceeds from sales of this book are donated to the Antioch School.

Book design by Jane Baker

Contents

Acknowledgments

Many, many thanks to all the children and adults of the Antioch School,
who opened their hearts and minds, as well as their school, to this project;
to Erik and Deirdre Owen and Dianne Collinson, for their photographs,
so wonderfully evocative of the many essences of childhood;
to Jane Baker, for her publishing expertise;
and to Mary Goode Wallis, for her understanding.

Note: The children's real names are used throughout the book,
except in the last chapter: "Michael" and "Angela" are pseudonyms.

The Meaning of the Antioch School

A child is innately wise and realistic.

—A. S. Neill, *Summerhill*

This book grew out of a conversation I had one day with the teachers at the Antioch School. The teachers were seeking ways to communicate to the parents of the children what really happens at the Antioch School—what the children actually do there, and how and why they do it. And what it *means*: the meaning of the children's experience of the school. As we talked, it became clear to us that to explore all this might take a book. I volunteered to try and write it.

The teachers were concerned that the children's parents did not fully understand what the Antioch School was about. The parents knew their children liked the school, and they knew the kids were thriving there, learning and growing and coming into their own. But they did not really understand how and why this was happening.

And it *is* hard to understand. At the Antioch School there's no "objective proof" of a child's progress—no competitive rankings, no standardized tests, no grades. Each child's incentives and rewards are self-determined; the children are free to follow their own paths of exploration and discovery.

Trust is the word the teachers use when they talk about their work with the children. The teachers trust each child's inborn love of learning, each child's capacity for personal growth and self-development. And they trust the power and wisdom of the children as a *group*, learning together, building community, creating and sustaining relationships, discovering one another and the world.

The value of trust may be hard to prove, but I have seen it work at the Antioch School and I believe in it. I have believed in it since my own children, Laura, Sarah, and Jessica, were children at the Antioch School. That was a generation ago; and even before then—ever since Laura, my first child, was born—it has been a fervent interest of mine, the wonderful ways children learn and grow and come into their own being when they are respected and trusted and free to be who they really are.

That is what goes on at the Antioch School. Children discover paths to wholeness there. To me, there is nothing in the world more important than this.

So I set out to write this book.

First I planned to interview the teachers. I made a notebook full of questions to ask them about their work with the children. But before I could begin talking with the teachers, the children began presenting themselves to me directly. They did this by just being there, living their everyday lives at the school, being themselves. I would walk into the school and notice a child, or a group of children, doing something—it would catch my eye. I'd pay attention, and I'd see a whole scene full of meaning unfolding there in front of me.

The first time this happened I was standing in the school office saying hello to Didi when I glanced through the open doorway and saw a slender young girl working hard at a difficult task—teaching herself to ride a unicycle. As I watched, she took a hard fall. I wrote in my notebook:

> She gets up, her face taut and closed in. One arm is wrapped around her back, to reach the place where it hurts most. She stands there for a long moment, not moving, staring in through the window, seeing nothing. The unicycle lies in a heap at her feet. Then she gathers it up and gets back on it and rides it . . .

This was, you see, *in this moment,* a child pursuing her own path toward wholeness. As I watched I felt blessed to witness it.

The next day, again a scene unfolded. A group of boys from the Nursery were playing with blocks in the sunny corner of the hallway. I sat on the floor near the center of the action and began taking notes. The children didn't even notice me, they were so deeply engaged in their work. I was struck by the *story* I saw being enacted, complete with a full set of characters, a developing plot, purpose and meaning. And how these very young children so fully expressed and embodied their needs and wants, their ways of being, their relationship with the world:

> Douglas's voice is even-toned, calm, serious. He's intent on his work. He is willing to respond to the others, willing to have a conversation, but it's something he does while he's doing the main thing, which is build the road. He is working furiously, constantly in purposeful motion. He has a plan. When he gets a block from the stack and lugs it back to his construction site, he knows exactly where he wants it to go, and he puts it there. Then he goes and gets another block.

These scenes kept on presenting themselves, day after day, week after week, as I became caught up in the ongoing life of the school. The children kept enacting these scenes, and I kept writing them down. In this way the children themselves wrote much of this book.

Eventually I witnessed the children engaged in the most inspiring scenes of all, when whole groups of twenty or more children came together in special meetings to work out serious conflicts among them. The children conducted these meetings with an elegant allegiance to truth and justice; with a personal, heartfelt concern for each other's well-being; and with the shared purpose of sustaining the strength and harmony of the group:

> All around the circle, all the children are absorbed in this meeting. They are listening intently; and when they speak, they speak meaningfully, with conviction, and they express themselves clearly and

directly. They are taking everything in, thinking about it, responding to it, expressing themselves to one another.

It was a wonderful thing for me, to be there in the school and observe—I want to say *receive,* as one receives a gift—the workings of childhood. Often they seemed to me to be magical workings, all the wonderful ways the children would find and create to be true to themselves.

But it is not magic. What I saw happening at the Antioch School was, yes, the natural life of children manifesting itself—*and,* all-importantly, it was the careful, skillful work of wise and dedicated teachers. The teachers of the Antioch School know each child well and love them all and possess a deep understanding of the nature of children.

The teachers spoke with me at length and in depth about the children and the school. I met with each teacher individually for interviews and conversations, and we all met together many times for a series of discussions. The teachers love to talk about the school; they especially love talking about the children, the things they do and say, the giant leaps forward they make in their lives. We laughed at a lot of the memories the teachers have saved like treasures through the years. Much of it was very moving, for the teachers and the children create deeply meaningful moments together.

The group discussions were tape-recorded and passages are presented in the book verbatim, to honor the value of hearing masterful teachers talking among themselves about their work. These passages of the teachers talking form a kind of frame for the children's scenes. In the book, as in their work at the school, the teachers support the children.

In their discussions the teachers explore the guiding principles of their teaching. At the heart of it all is: *Trust in the child.*

From trust flows the teachers' shared beliefs about education, self-discovery, growing up whole:

Learning is natural.
Play is the finest way of learning.
Choice teaches responsibility.
There is wisdom in the group.

The teachers' dedication to these beliefs, and their ability to apply them wisely to *each child,* makes the Antioch School a child-centered school. As one of the teachers, Ann Guthrie, speaking for them all, said: "Each child is seen and valued for his or her own set of gifts. Each child's personality, creativity, developmental time frame—each child's integrity—is respected."

It *works.* At the Antioch School you can *see* how well the children are doing by how they look and act, how they relate to each other, how they go about being themselves. If you get closer, and talk with them, and *listen,* you can hear their strength.

But it's hard sometimes for us to trust our own eyes and ears. All that we have been trained to believe about human nature works against our understanding of the true nature of children. We are trained not to believe that love of learning is natural to the child, an inborn quality, a birthright gift. To the Antioch School teachers, this is an obvious, basic, undeniable fact of life. In one of our of group discussions two of the teachers, Jeanie Felker and Chris Powell, spoke passionately about this:

Jeanie: Learning is natural. It's right in *here.*
   [She places her hand over her heart.]
Chris: Yes! The excitement of learning is *inside* us. It's intrinsic. Children *love* to learn!

Children love to learn. Once we accept this truth, we begin to understand what education really is. We understand that the true function of a school is to provide a nurturing environment that respects the great powers of learning children possess. We understand that the true purpose of a teacher is to help children find and follow their own paths toward wholeness. And to join the children on that path.

This is what happens at the Antioch School.

As I worked on this book I had the good fortune to become an Antioch School teacher myself, on a small scale. Chris Powell, the Older Group teacher, invited me to teach a class in creative writing. For an hour or so, two days a week, I met with some of the Older Groupers (ages nine through twelve) for what we called Writers Group.

At first, we didn't write much; we talked. We talked about words, and about our ideas and our feelings, about dreams and hopes and fears. We laughed a lot.

After a while we started writing. We'd take our pocket-sized notebooks and go outside and walk around noticing things—exploring, discovering—and writing about them. I loved their writing, so full of life and heart and wisdom. These children create meaningful poems as naturally as their bodies breathe: they'd write poems in their notebooks while swinging on the swings, tossing a football, walking in the woods, climbing a tree . . .

And they were fine poems. One cold bright December day, Nicky wandered off from the rest of us and when he came back a few minutes later he brought us this poem:

Snowflake
I could swear I see
a little snowflake falling
from the loving, overcast sky.
It flows on a wisp of air,
waiting for its friends to come.
Small, crystallized, star-shaped,
it is fragile
like a piece of glass
ready to fall
and shatter
into a layer
of magnificent snow

Anna C, swaying on a swing with her notebook on her lap, wrote a powerful poem protesting the war in Iraq, and denouncing the conflict-ridden condition of the world:

Beware
A cry I hear
not far not near
it comes without
a tag of fear
or ring of stature
merely a warning
to the immature battles
fought on earth
where the spies are blind
the negotiators mute
and the warriors numb with confusion

Hannah wrote in celebration of her childhood self:

I am a squirrel
Frolicking in the flowers
I am a single snowflake
Falling gently to the ground
I am a flute
Playing softly to the sound of bells
I am the color pink
Refreshing and bright
I am a stream
Flowing, going with the wind
I am me,
And that's all I shall be.

Being in the Writers Group was a revelation. I wasn't, of course, really a teacher, but my experience afforded me a powerful insight into what it's like to teach at the Antioch School. It is hard work. It is hard not for the usual reasons—professional and political reasons—that teaching is hard; it goes deeper than that. Teaching at the Antioch School is hard work because you are always in close, direct, dynamic relationship with children who expect and require you to be truly yourself. Always. Nothing else will do. The children are truly themselves: this is the standard they set, and you must meet it.

So it is very difficult; and it is deeply, deeply rewarding. I learned more as a member of our Antioch School Writers Group—more about being true to one's self, and about creative spirit, and about coming to know and respect and care about others—than any school setting I've ever been in, as student or teacher (and I've lived most of my life being one or the other).

And I learned what a school is. I learned from all the children, each in their own ways, what Gabe, one of the poets in our Writers Group, showed us with his poem. It is a meditation on the meaning of the sandpile in the Antioch School play-yard—and a powerful statement about the *community* of the school:

The Sand Mound
It's never the same.
Whenever a leaf falls, whenever it rains,
when a child walks on it—
it changes.
Ever shifting sand
with different shapes and sizes,
like the tumbling waters of the vast oceans,
stretching from one place to another
from thousands of miles
to just a couple hundred yards across.
Little plastic trowels and children
litter the sand mound like fish in the sea.
A kid crying
is like an underwater volcano erupting,
forming an island of teachers and children
coming to help.
That's the Sand Mound.

What happens at the Antioch School is important.

In a fearful nation plagued by anxiety about the failure of its schools, the Antioch School is a bold success. Free from the repression of penalty-based tests, free from the fear of being "left behind," the children of the Antioch School grow up gaining what they need to explore and discover their chosen paths toward wholeness.

In a world where we see every day the tragic destruction of childhood, the children of the Antioch School grow up with the nature of their child-life fully honored and trusted, and respected as their own.

In an age of cynical and fatalistic self-doubt, the children of the Antioch School affirm human nature; for the open-hearted nature of these children is our true human nature. To perceive our human *possibilities,* we need only take a careful look at these children. See how much they understand. See how deeply they care.

"They would save the world, if they could," Kit Crawford said of her Younger Group children.

They are who we used to be; and can be again—"Deep down," as Marlee, in the Older Group, said about the roots of kindness dwelling within an un-kind person. Human beings are at our best when we are children; if we can find a way to really *know* this, maybe we could save the world. Deep down.

Don Wallis
Yellow Springs, Ohio
June 2005

I dedicate this book, with love,
to Laura, Sarah, and Jessica Wallis,
who taught me the meaning of childhood.

Children of a Child-Centered School

Orientation

We conceived of ourselves as an environment for growth,
and accepted the relationships between the children and ourselves
as being the very heart of the school.
—George Dennison, *The Lives of Children*

Ann Guthrie, the teacher of the Nursery at the Antioch School, in a presentation to new parents at the beginning of the school year:

Just to give you a little historical background, the Antioch School was founded in 1921. We're one of the two pioneers of early childhood education in Ohio. We're also one of the oldest alternative schools in the country.

Many first-time visitors to the school are surprised by its size; for a school with such a big history, it's really quite small. The enrollment tends to be about seventy-five students, ages three to twelve. There are five teachers, two assistant teachers, and a school manager. That's all.

We see our small size as one of the fundamental strong points of the school; it means that there's a homelike atmosphere, and that everyone can know everyone else. It supports children in their natural desire to understand and know the others around them, and to be known and understood. It allows them to feel safe and secure in their daily environment. *All* of our children are part of this child-sized school.

There is freedom for children at the Antioch School, and along with that freedom comes responsibility. Problem solving and conflict resolution are a focus all the way through, from the Nursery to the Older Group. Children are not given the solutions or the resolutions ready made, but are given the sup-

port and the tools they need so they can become skilled in doing this for themselves.

We focus on building analytic skills. Young children possess an innate capacity for wonder and discovery, and for figuring things out. When a child asks "Why?" we will often ask "Why do you think?" The children build on their ability to think for themselves and with one another. Being able to do this is the foundation of any graceful human interaction.

There are basically two educational models in this country. The one that most of us have experienced is one in which we are asked to sit and absorb. We are spoonfed a prescribed amount of information, on a prescribed timetable and schedule. We are measured and valued according to how closely we can approximate this model.

At most schools, children see their education as something done to them. At the Antioch School, children are active learners. They are problem solvers and critical thinkers. Asking questions is encouraged. Decision making is encouraged. Self-direction is encouraged. Our assumption is that the children are active participants in their education.

We are saying to the children: "We trust you to make choices that are good for you." And we know that trust works both ways—that the children trust us to know and understand them, and to keep them safe and secure: physically, emotionally, socially, intellectually. It means respecting and supporting each child's own individual course in life, and to guide them and help them stay on course.

Our mutual trust is what makes the school a safe, secure place from which we can explore and discover, learn and grow—each in our own way.

Here I Am

The Antioch School, surrounded by trees, is on the edge of a village, a college campus, and a nature preserve. Most of the children of the school live in the village: Yellow Springs, a progressive little college town in the midst of conservative southwest Ohio. The college is Antioch, famous for its commitment to social justice; its students still take seriously the admonition of Antioch's nineteenth-century president, Horace Mann: "Be ashamed to die until you have won some victory for humanity." The Antioch School children are regular visitors at the college, a short walk away across the tree-lined campus. A short walk the other way takes you into the nature preserve: Glen Helen, a constant presence in the life of the Antioch School. In the Glen are a thousand acres of woods and hilly paths and rocky streams and limestone wonders, hawks and squirrels and white-tailed deer. The children of the school go for long walks in the Glen. They draw pictures of what they see, and write stories about being there. I like to think of Neetahnah, one of the children in an Antioch School group I walked with into the Glen one day. She looked around at everything, taking it all in. Then she opened her notebook and wrote *Here I am*—a perfect beginning.

The Antioch School has a fresh and open feeling, it's light-filled and bright, and there's an easy, free flow of movement through all the rooms. There are windows everywhere, in every room and along the length of the hallway, walls of windows reaching all the way up to the high ceilings. From anywhere inside the school the children can see outdoors, and they're always *going* outdoors, to play.

Inside, all the spaces are interconnected. The rooms of the four groups—Nursery (ages three and four), Kindergarten (ages five and six), Younger Group (ages seven through nine) and Older Group (ages nine through twelve)—are adjacent to one another in a row down the hallway, with doorways connecting the rooms each to each. At any moment a child can see and hear (and visit, if she wishes) the children in the group she used to be in, or the children in the group she'll be joining next, when she grows a little older. She can reconnect to where she's come from and look forward to where she will be. "It ties us together," says Ann Guthrie, the Nursery teacher.

Down the long hallway and around the corner is the Art/Science Room. It's a large, multi-purpose space: arts/crafts studio and science lab, kitchen and lunch room, workshop, theater, library, media center, meeting place, lounge. Here the children do their art and science work—they draw and paint, conduct experiments, make pottery and stained glass, build bird houses and model rockets—and they cook food, eat lunch, stage plays, make movies, read books, write stories, build stuff, hold meetings, have parties, wander around, and just hang out . . .

Beyond the Art/Science Room door is the big play-yard. It's on what the children call the "cycle-circle side" of the school, because that's where they ride their unicycles. The smaller play-yard is on the other side of the building, what the children call the "tire-swing side," in honor of the big, free-swinging truck tire, suspended from a tree, that can hold two or three, and even four or five, risk-taking children at a time, spinning and whirling happily around.

Tucked into the middle of the building, in the center of it all, is the office of the school manager, Dianne Collinson. All the kids call her Didi. In her tiny office Didi presides over the constant comings and goings of children and teachers and parents and visitors, and she tracks the money, keeps the books, answers the phone, writes letters, feeds the fish, buys supplies, pays bills, raises funds, publishes a newsletter every week and a journal twice a year, and answers everybody's questions all day long . . .

But right now she's got better things to do:

Down the hallway by the Kindergarten several children are playing with blocks. One of them—it is Emma Rose—suddenly lets out a cry, a quick loud tearful cry.

Jeanie, her teacher, appears in the doorway, and the child reaches up for her, her tiny arms making a circle of space that Jeanie leans down into, filling it up. She hugs the child and comforts her . . .

Jeanie walks Emma hand-in-hand down the hall to Didi's office. Emma sits down in one of the chairs by Didi's desk. She sits there calmly as Jeanie leaves Didi's office and goes back to the Kindergarten. She sits perfectly still in the chair. Her hair is brown, her eyes blue.

"Are you all right, Emma?" Didi says. "Do you want to stay here for awhile?"

"I want to call my mom," Emma says, solemnly.

"Okay," Didi says.

Didi writes down Emma's home phone number on a piece of paper. "Here you go, Emma," Didi says, as she tapes the piece of paper to the wall next to a little telephone, placed there for little children to use. She shows Emma how to dial the number. Emma does so, a bit hesitantly—it may be the first time she's ever called home like this.

A man's voice answers—it's her father—and there's a shift in Emma's composure. She wanted her mom. Emma tells her father she wants to come home. Then she listens intently to what her father says. She says thoughtfully into the phone: "Yes"—breathless pause—"Yes" again. Another pause . . .

Then Emma wails: "No! No!" and begins to cry.

Gently, Didi takes the phone, and talks to Emma's father. When Didi hangs up, Emma stops crying. She stops as suddenly as she began.

She whimpers a little. Didi comforts her; she hugs her, holds her for a moment or two.

Emma is calm now. Her eyes are dry.

"Do you want to go back to Jeanie?" Didi asks.

Emma nods yes. Didi nods yes, too, affirming Emma's decision. They walk together, hand in hand, down the hallway to the Kindergarten.

The Antioch School building is a bit worn, weathered, comfortably ragged at the edges; it's been in active service for fifty years, and it has a well-used look and feel. There's stuff all around, everywhere in view—books overcrowding shelves, cardboard boxes full of papers, drawers overflowing with tools and yarn, drawings and pictures taped to the walls, signs and messages posted on the doors . . .

The children know the building intimately. They are super-aware of everything about it. One day in Art/Science the Kindergarten children drew pictures of the school. From memory they re-created in great detail each of the four classrooms, and the rugs and the tables in all the rooms, and the lofts, and the window walls and doorways, and the rows of cubbies and coat hooks in the hallway, and the water fountain and the lost-and-found box, and the bathrooms, and the Art/Science room with the kitchen in the corner, and the play-yards (the play-yard equipment was drawn in the greatest detail of all). The children drew their pictures from an omniscient, god-like point of view, envisioning the scene simultaneously from high above, front-on and all four sides, so that *every* detail could be shown. It was a revelation to look at their drawings and realize how very much even the youngest of the children know about their school.

They like the place. They take care of it. They clean it up every day; all the children, from the Nursery schoolers to the Older Groupers, have daily chores, and most of the time they do them willingly, even proudly. The children feel the school is *theirs*. They are loyal to it. The children rarely complain about the cramped space, or the doubling up of the use of it. On the same tables where they finger-paint and build model rockets, the children gather at noon and eat their lunch. That's okay with them. They like the place just the way it is.

Recently a new door was installed in the hallway. The kids didn't like it. It was too shiny and sleek, too slow to swing open—it just wasn't right. "It just doesn't feel like an Antioch School door," one child said, and everyone knew what she meant.

The parents of the children do a lot of work for the school. They maintain the building and the grounds —they paint walls, make shelves, mow grass, plant trees, haul sand, rake leaves, shovel snow. They do fundraising in the community, run special errands, chaperone the children's field trips. They come into the classrooms and talk to the children about things they know about, special interests they have. A few of the parents occasionally help teach the children, when a teacher needs a substitute.

And the parents pay most of the costs of running the school. The tuition fee is $6,000 a year, less than at most private schools in Ohio; still, the cost is a deterrent for many families who would like to send their children to the school, and it is a hardship for some who do. The school provides financial aid scholarships for several families, but cannot afford as many as are needed; this is "the most painful reality" of the Antioch School, as one of the parents wrote recently in a fundraising appeal. It is a vexing problem that over the years the school has tried and failed to solve.

The school's enrollment is full almost every year. There are no formal admission criteria; the school accepts students on a first-come, first-serve basis, as long as there is room for them. In some years, the racial and ethnic diversity of the student body approaches that of the Yellow Springs community; in most years, it does not.

Yet there always seems to be a varied assortment of cultural identities embodied by the school's families. Their native lands currently include China, Japan, Thailand, Vietnam, Russia, Germany, and the Miami Nation, as well as the United States. There are Muslims, Buddhists, Jews, Catholics, Unitarians, Quakers, Baptists, Methodists, and Presbyterians, along with, probably, some pagans and atheists.

And the parents work at a variety of interesting occupations: massage therapist, professor, police chief, architect, bookseller, social worker, doctor, landscaper, psychologist, homemaker, lawyer, conflict mediator, teacher, business executive, environmental activist, government administrator, politician (candidate for Congress), scientist, electrician, professional storyteller, professional magician . . .

The Children

In a group discussion about the children of the Antioch School are their teachers:

Ann Guthrie, Nursery
Jeanie Felker, Kindergarten
Brian Brogan, Art/Science
Kit Crawford, Younger Group
Chris Powell, Older Group
Facilitating is Don Wallis

Don: Let's talk about the children—what they're like, how they act, their qualities, their characteristics. What sort of people are they? Just say what comes to mind.

Jeanie: They question everything. *Everything* is open to question. When you ask about the children, that's what first comes to my mind—their wonderful ability to question.

Brian: Yes, totally, I agree.

Jeanie: Their kindness—that's the next thing that comes to my mind. They are all really kind.

Kit: They help each other.

Chris: They love to play.

Kit: They respect each other.

Chris: They are really in their bodies. They're just kind of comfortable being who they are, living their child life.

Brian: They are very social kids. They keep joining together in groups, and the groups keep changing, which seems very pleasureable for the kids. I like that.

Kit: They keep finding things that belong to them to refine and actualize.

Jeanie: Yes! They have real integrity.

Kit: They trust each other.

Jeanie: They have an uncanny awareness of each other.

Brian: They get *busy* in their free time.

Jeanie: They're self-directed. They don't wait for someone to provide direction.

Don: They go out in all kinds of weather to play. They get all muddy and wet.

Brian: They invent games.

Jeanie: They are creative in their play.

Kit: They are creative in their thinking.

Jeanie: They do love to play outside. They are really close to the outdoors. They notice when the trees bud, and what's coming up out of the ground, and—

Chris: Interesting *bugs*—

Jeanie: — all those things, yes! They love *all* those things that happen outside.

Ann: They're good-humored.

Kit: They have *great* sense of humor!

Jeanie: They love music. They love art. They love stories. They love poetry.

Don: And animals. They *love* animals! Why *do* they love animals so much?

Chris: It's part of their closeness to nature.

Ann: They are nurturing their natural kindness.

Don: They're little animals themselves . . .

Brian: Another trait: they are outspoken.

Chris: They are challenging.

Ann: They question authority.

[Pause.]

Don: Are there things they do that bug you?

Kit: Oh, yes. I'll confess. They *correct* me all the time. It bugs me.

Ann: They correct me, too. [*She shrugs, smiles.*] So I call a glove a mitten, so what?

Chris: They *love* to correct me. Especially when I say, "Wash your hands with hot soap and water."

But, you know what? We all *want* them to be outspoken and challenging, and we *want* them to question authority, and then — Oh no, they *do* it!

And we all want them to be independent, and we want them to be self-determining, and then — oh no, they're *stubborn*!

[Laughter all around the group.]

Ann: It's all part of their strength.

Don: They are strong.

Jeanie: Another trait: they are honest.

Kit: At our morning meeting today, a younger child wasn't sure if she should say what she felt. And Lucy said to her, "It's all right—it's all right for you to say that." Meaning: bring it out, air it out, tell your truth. Whatever it is, we can talk about it here.

Chris: And they sure do *talk*.

Kit: Oh yes, they talk all the time!

Brian: All over the school, they are talking!

Kit: A torrent of words comes flowing from the mouths of these children!

[Laughter all around.]

Brian: Seriously, though—they are *good* talkers. *Very* good. They are really articulate.

Don: They ask interesting questions.

Chris: They do. They really do. They are free to ask what they want to ask. They're free to disagree with the answer. They're free to make mistakes. They're free to *learn*.

Brian: They're very confident. They are self-contained, self-possessed.

Chris: Yes, yes, I agree with all this. But there are some people who think our kids are rude. That they're not respectful. Not polite. Not civilized. They think they act like wild children! Because they're not used to children interrupting an adult to ask a question—asking, like, "What does that mean?" Or responding to some pronouncement by saying, like, "No, that's not right!" — the way our kids are wont to do.

[Appreciative laughter.]

Don: I admire them. They are good learners. They express their interest. They participate in their learning.

Ann: They are good teachers.

Kit: They *are!* They pass on to each other their ideas, their culture, their skills. They share their gifts with each other.

Chris: They teach each other. And the younger children teach the older children, as well as the older ones teaching the young ones. They learn from each other.

Jeanie: And we all learn from them. Everybody ends up being enriched. I know I do.

Brian: Me, too. It's true.

Kit: It's wonderful.

Ann: Here is what I am thinking about, sitting here, listening: It's an amazing thing, to be with these children.

Each year they come together, all these different children, all their different temperaments, so divergent in their ways. And yet they all do come *together*. Every year they make a group.

And I think it's because they need each other. They *do*. Each one of them is necessary to everyone else. Whenever one of them is gone, there's a little empty spot that everyone feels.

This is what these children teach me.

Our School

The Older Group children, all twenty-three of them, sitting together in a circle, talking about their school with a couple of inquisitve visitors:

How would you describe your school?

It's nice.

It's small.

The whole school is like a community.

Everybody helps you out.

We mix different grades, so you can have friends that are in different age groups. Like, I'm in fifth grade and I can have a fourth-grade friend. Most of my friends are older, but I can be the younger kids' friend, too.

It's like everybody is the principal. It's like there are seventy principals.

You learn different stuff. Like, riding the unicycle. You ride in parades. Unicycling is something no other school has. When you go out in public and ride the unicycle, everyone says, "Wow! You're good at that. How'd you learn to do that?" And you tell them, "I taught myself at the Antioch School."

How do kids learn here?

You do things at your own pace, instead of all together at the same time.

The older kids help you. It's easier when you learn with your friends.

We have more free time, so you can do stuff with people.

If we didn't get as much free time, we'd probably want to talk more when we're supposed to be working.

The teachers help you. If they give you a homework assignment, and you can't do it, you don't get graded for it. You don't feel bad.

What if people have problems?

If there are problems, you talk about it, and you figure something out.

You ask your friends, what would they do? And everyone contributes their ideas. And if you don't like somebody's ideas, you don't go, "Oh, I don't want to do that." You think about how it might fit. Maybe they don't like your idea — you can work to make it so they do like it.

If you make a mistake with a friend, and you realize you made a mistake, you go and apologize. If you make a mistake in school, and you can fix it, you just fix it. If you can't, someone helps you.

Sometimes it takes a while to figure things out.

What have you learned about yourself here?

Just be yourself. Don't try to make some kind of fake image.

If someone is not being themselves—like, they're trying to impress you—you can say, 'You don't have to impress me."

I've learned that I'll fit in, just being myself.

I've learned two things. The negative thing is that I don't like unicycles.

[Laughter all around the group.]

The positive thing is that even though you throw together a kind of run-down building, a bunch of kids who are different, and a big field for soccer or whatever—you get chaos at first, but eventually it clears up. People go to the place where they're needed.

Brian Brogan   Jeanie Felker   Kit Crawford   Chris Powell
Dianne Collinson   Ren Smith   Ann Guthrie

Teachers at Work

Ann Guthrie, Jeanie Felker, Kit Crawford, and Chris Powell have been teaching together at the Antioch School for the better part of two decades. Kit came in 1984, Jeanie in 1987, Ann and Chris in 1988. They are a team. They are close to one another, strongly bonded as friends and colleagues.

They have a lot in common. They are in their mid- or late fifties. Growing up, each of them rebelled against various forms of educational repression they encountered. They have been drawn strongly to alternative education, as students and teachers. And as parents: each of them sent their children to the Antioch School.

Each is softspoken, gentle, perceptive, sensitive to the subtle nuances of children's feelings. They each feel a close affinity with nature, and with animals. They are avid gardeners. They like to laugh.

And they are honest, genuine, authentic—these traits perhaps the most important of all, for at the Antioch School it is imperative to be *real.* This defining truth finds spontaneous expression in the teachers' meetings from time to time, as in this discussion about a learning project that failed to interest the children:

> **Jeanie:** It wasn't direct, it wasn't concrete, it just wasn't real to them.
>
> **Kit:** It's got to be authentic. You know these children—with them, if it's not *real,* it's not going to work.
>
> **Brian, Ann, Chris,** *in unison:* That's for sure!

Brian Brogan, the Art/Science teacher, began teaching at the Antioch School in 2001. He is a decade or so younger than the other teachers. His working relationship with the children differs from theirs: they each have one group of their own to teach all day; Brian teaches children from all the groups at different times of the day. Brian shares many of his fellow teachers' characteristics: he's thoughtful, gentle, soft spoken, genuine; he's a dedicated gardener; he is an observant, perceptive teacher of children. And his daughters, Ursula and Saskia, attend the Antioch School.

Like his fellow teachers, Brian loves to share thoughts and observations about the children of the school. During "free time" when the children are outside playing, the teachers are either out there with them or standing at the windows observing them, and Brian often joins the other teachers at the window wall, to join in their talk about the children:

"Did you hear what Ben G and Hue did at Morning Meeting?"

"Did you see Emily riding the unicycle at free time?"

"Have you seen Henry's drawing of the nucleus of a cell?"

This is an important part of the teachers' day. They are watching the children fully engaged in active moments of their learning and growing; moment by moment, the teachers can see it happening. They *enjoy* doing this. They talk about the children and the work they're doing, the things they say, the changes they are undergoing, the movements they make in the progress of their lives . . .

As they talk the teachers laugh with delight sometimes; at other times they smile and shake their heads in wonder. A casual observer would not guess they are hard at work.

The Antioch School teachers work smoothly together, as indeed they must, for it's the teachers who run the school, day by day. There is a board of parents and teachers elected to oversee money matters and set institutional policy. The teachers and Didi, the school manager, run the rest of it. They are the school's administration. There is no principal or headmaster, no superintendent, no executive director.

None seems to be needed. The teachers work so well together they make the notoriously burdensome labor of school administration seem pleasant, most of the time, and sometimes even creative.

Here's how they do it. This is a scene from an emergency meeting the teachers called to deal with a crisis. In jeopardy is the all-school holiday play, a traditional celebration of the Antioch School community that is always held at Christmas time in the Antioch College theater. Suddenly—it's just three weeks until the play's scheduled performance—a decision by the college has rendered the theater unavailable.

The teachers are gathered in the Art/Science Room, waiting for Didi. She's on the phone appealing the college's decision . . .

Finally she comes into the meeting:

Didi: Well, it's bad news I bring you. That was the college. They're adamant. There's no way we can use the theater.

Chris: Even though we've used it every Christmas season for umpteen years?

Kit: Even though it's a school tradition?

Jeanie: And a community tradition.

Kit: Even though we've planned for this, and scheduled it, and the kids —

Chris: Ryan and Anna are writing a script for the play they want to do. And Ryder's working on a one-act about Hannukah. And—

Brian: This is really a bummer.

Kit: It's a loss of tradition.

[Pause.]

Chris: Or, maybe a change in tradition.

Jeanie: Yes . . . I was just thinking—

Ann: A different kind of celebration?

Chris: An alternative celebration?

Kit: I love it—I feel something's moving—

Jeanie: Light! Everybody celebrates light in some way . . .

[Pause. Jeanie thinks her thought.]

Jeanie: A festival of light!

[Everyone smiles.]

Didi: A procession of folks holding candles, bearing light—

Brian: The children could make lanterns—

Ann: A bonfire—

Didi: Hot chocolate, marshmallows—

Kit: Just keep it simple . . . The kids can put on their plays here at school. There doesn't need to be a big audience in a theater, there doesn't need to be a big Christmas play. All the kids can join in this festival.

Ann: Everyone can gather around the bonfire . . .

Jeanie: Singing around the fire . . .

Chris: Lovely lights . . .

Kit: It would give me a whole lot more time with my kids.

Chris: Yes! Putting on a play is always so time consuming.

Jeanie: We need that time. The kids need it.

Ann: It would be like a gift. A gift of time for us all.

[Pause. A few moments of silence.]

Didi: So—we've made the change, then?

[Everyone exchanges looks.]

Chris: Yep, we've made the change.

Ann: A festival of light!

Didi: Okay. I'll send out a notice in the morning, to let everybody know.

[The meeting ends.]

That's how the teachers run the school.

Freedom in the Air

The modern era of the Antioch School's history began when Bill Mullins and Beverly Price came to teach at the school in 1963. They came as a team, Bill as teacher of the Older Group and Bev to teach the Younger Group. Until they joined the faculty, the teachers of the school's Younger Group and Older Group typically were recent Antioch College graduates who stayed for only a year or two. Bill and Bev were experienced, well-trained teachers who stayed at the Antioch School for the rest of their careers. Bev taught the Younger Group for thirty-one years, retiring in 1994. Bill is still active; though he "retired" in 1989, he serves part-time as the Older Group's assistant teacher.

Bev Price was an extraordinary teacher, as Bill discovered when she enrolled in a course he taught at the University of Minnesota. It was a course in methods of education and the students were teachers. One day Bill went to Bev's school to observe her teaching methods:

"I was enormously impressed! Here was this room full of thirty fifth-graders, and she had them doing all kinds of stuff. It was wonderful how she had groups of kids in different parts of the room doing different learning activities, working on different projects. They were all working very hard, and with very little direction from Bev. Each group had picked out what they wanted and needed to do and were working on it.

"That was the way the whole day went. It impressed me so much that I spent all of the next class talking about what I had seen in Bev's classroom."

After that, Bill and Bev often engaged in long discussions about schools and children. Bill had taught in several schools, and he had earned a masters degree in education and a Ph. D., yet always he found himself rebelling against conventional education: "I was constantly thinking, 'There's got to be a better way to do this.'" He recognized that Bev had found a better way. In their discussions they focused on reforming education through new methods of teaching. "We didn't approve of anything that was going on in the schools," Bill recalled.

But when they came to the Antioch School they approved of much of what they found there. They liked the school's multi-age classrooms, and they loved its freedom from tests and grades. They were impressed with the Nursery teacher, Pat Dell, a masterful teacher with a gift for perceiving the meaning of play in the life of each child. And they were impressed with the school's art teacher, Margaret Landes, "a wonderful person," Bill said, who had been for many years a warm and guiding presence at the school. Bill and Bev shared the these teachers' beliefs in learning as a natural process and their emphasis on free choice and self-direction for the children.

Bev brought to the Younger Group the teaching style that had made her Minnesota classroom so special. She composed an individual learning plan for each child every day, handed to the child along with a personal note, first thing each morning. There was in her classroom a sense of dedication to the shared experience of learning that bonded the children closely to Bev; often their teacher-child relationship lasted long after the children graduated from the Younger Group.

In the Older Group, Bill set about making changes aimed at enhancing the children's already considerable freedom. He threw out all the desks and chairs and replaced them with sofas; he put a ping-pong table in the middle of the classroom; he built a free-standing "balcony" where kids could go to read or write or talk with a friend, or just to be alone, to think and dream and imagine . . .

"We were placing great value on the children having the freedom to find their own way," Bill says. "We wanted them to be able to choose their own path, to direct their own learning . . .

"This was the Sixties, and there was a lot of freedom in the air," Bill said. "A tremendous amount of educational experimentation was going on. Alternative schools—we called them 'free schools'—were starting up all around the country. It was an exciting time. People were questioning everything, trying new ways. At the Antioch School we were all reading Holt and Dennison and Neill. *Summerhill* was a big inspiration. I liked a lot of Neill's ideas. I even encouraged the kids to read *Summerhill*."

The kids liked what they read. "A child is innately wise and realistic," A. S. Neill wrote in *Summerhill*. He urged educators to "allow children freedom to be themselves." They should "make the school fit the child, instead of making the child fit the school."

John Holt, in *How Children Learn,* praised "the natural learning style of children." They are "open, receptive, and perceptive," Holt wrote.

> Therefore, we do not need to "motivate" children into learning, by wheedling, bribing, or bullying. We do not need to keep picking away at their minds to make sure they are learning. What we need to do, and all we need to do, is bring as much of the world as we can into the school and the classroom; give children as much help and guidance as they need and ask for; listen respectfully when they feel

like talking; and then get out of the way. We can trust them to do the rest.

George Dennison, in *The Lives of Children*, wrote a classic celebration of children's play. The finest learning and personal growth that children experience, Dennison wrote, occurs when they are freely at play: "Children are capable of positively curative effects on one another when their relationships are allowed to evolve naturally."

Imagine a troubled child, Dennison wrote, and imagine the "qualities of the environment that we might wish for him":

> We would say, Let it be an environment that is accepting and forgiving; and let it be one that takes him out of himself and involves him in group activities; and let the inducements to sociability be attractive and vivid, yet let them be measured accurately to his own capacities; and let there be real pressure in the environment, let it make definite and clear-cut demands, yet let the demands be flexible; and let there be no formal punishment or long-lasting ostracism; and let there be a hope of friendship and hope of praise; and let there be abundant physical contact and physical exertion; and let the environment offer him a sense of the varieties of skills and behaviors that lead to greater rewards, greater security; and let the rewards for this kind of growth be immediate and intrinsic in the activities themselves.
>
> These attributes of a healing environment are almost self-evident. Surely it is self-evident, too, that this environment is precisely the ordinary one of children at play among themselves.

The child-affirming beliefs that inspired the Antioch School teachers in the Sixties have had a great and lasting influence upon the school. Over the years, these beliefs have evolved into an educational philosophy, based on trust in the child, that is the essential way of being of the Antioch School today.

A Child-Centered School

As important to the children as the development of academic skills is their emotional, social and physical growth. Children are encouraged to realize their capabilities in the whole spectrum of living. Love, respect, encouragement, letting the children be—these are the most important parts of the curriculum. The children learn self-discipline, they learn to use self-initiative, they learn to make choices. They learn to help others. They learn to try, not to be afraid to do. And mostly, they experience the joy of being children.—Antioch School Parent-Teacher Curriculum Committee, 1979

It was their experience as Antioch School parents in the 1970s and '80s that inspired Ann, Jeanie, Kit, and Chris to become Antioch School teachers. As they observed their children's response to the ways of the school, and as they worked closely with the teachers of their children, their felt their minds opening to what education could be, what a school and a teacher could mean to a child.

That these realizations came to them in terms of their own children made them all the more profound. Jeanie Felker remembers a poignant moment:

I have had many Antioch School parents say to me, 'I wish I had gone to school here, or a school like this. I wish I could have had this, somehow When they say this, it comes from the heart.

I was one such Antioch School parent, long before I became a teacher here. I said this very thing myself.

The first time I had a conference here with my child's teacher—Neysa was in the Younger Group, with Bev Price—afterwards I went out and sat in my car and wept. I *wept*. Because I realized I had never had a teacher know me in the way Bev knew Neysa. It is something so precious!

In moments like this one, a new generation of Antioch School teachers was created. As the teachers of the older generation retired, Ann, Jeanie, Kit, and Chris succeeded them. They brought their own skills to their work with the children; and they brought the understandings they had absorbed, as parents, from the teachers of their children. In this way, an Antioch School tradition was strengthened and passed on.

Ann, in the Nursery, is the kind of perceptive, insightful observer of children that Pat Dell was. Jeanie has the kind of deeply knowing relationship with her Kindergarten children that Bev Price had with Jeanie's child. Kit's Younger Group is a learning community, a model of individual and group self-responsibility and self-direction, as Bev Price's classroom was. And with Chris as its teacher the Older Group is grounded, as it was with Bill Mullins, in an energetic pace and diversity of activities, free-flowing outdoor play, and the healing wisdom of the group.

Here is Ann, observing her Nursery children becoming aware of one another, initiating the process of connection, beginning the work of relationship:

At the same time that the children acknowledged the exceptional qualities in themselves, they also recognized additional qualities in one another, whether it was novel ideas, innovation in block building, having the ability to comfort a friend or solve a problem, being skilled at engineering, having a passion for collecting or sounding out words, being fast at running, having an organized mind, or the ability to tell a story or to make someone laugh with a joke . . .

They could see the other person.

They knew, for example, that Amelia could sense someone's distress or need from across the room, and that she could quietly appear by that person's side to help soften or solve the problem.

They were aware that Alaina, genuinely interested in others, would walk up to another child she had not met, introduce herself, and within minutes incorporate that person into conversation or play . . .

Here is Kit, describing her Younger Group children helping one another, teaching each other and learning from each other, forming the foundations of their *group*:

Every fall, the new kids are shepherded around by buddies, helpers. These buddies answer their questions, sit by them, become their first reading partners, and generally keep close, so being new isn't too scary. The older kids relish being helpers. They help teach everything: vowels, rhymes, songs, math games, where to go, what to do . . .

I have seen the most wonderful forms of teaching happen when children teach children. There is a respect for the learner that is uncanny. There is close tracing of where the learner is, and a communicated message: "I know where you are on this, because I was there too, not too long ago, and I learned it and so will you, see?"

And the children teach the teachers. This is a scene from my notebook:

It's free time in the Older Group, and Shardasha is doing computer art. "Hey Chris, look at *this*!" She has created a pattern of trees in a forest, finding ways to color it in with intricate background shadings of green, subtly turning to bright red and yellow-orange. The colors are glowing in a weave-like pattern, like a mystic web.

Chris stares intently at Shardasha's creation, impressed and curious. "How do you *make* that?"

Shardasha says, "Here, I'll show you how." And she does, the student teaching the teacher.

The children's teachings can be deeply meaningful. Jeanie describes what they mean to her:

"I think the children actually free me, in some ways, to learn things that I never would approach myself. Or that I have stopped myself from approaching, because of my own childhood. And suddenly they will open me up to this whole other way of seeing—and being—and doing . . . They free me to move into that in ways that I *never* would have done without them!"

Ultimately, Jeanie says, the children teach their families:

I watch children learn and grow here, and I watch their parents grow along with them. They grow in trust of their children. They grow in trust of themselves. It comes through what they see here, what it feels like to them. It comes through at a deep level. They see their children just naturally growing in such good and strong ways, and they see it, day after day . . .

And then one day they realize they can trust their children to do this. Because it is *natural* to do this, because this is what human beings *do,* when they are allowed to, when they are supported and believed in. When they are trusted.

First, the parents see this in their children — then they realize that it's true for themselves, too. They look deep within and they see it in themselves. They begin to trust themselves. They gain a new sense of trusting life.

Trust

In group discussion, the teachers of the Antioch School:

Ann Guthrie, Nursery

Jeanie Felker, Kindergarten

Kit Crawford, Younger Group

Chris Powell, Older Group

Brian Brogan, Art/Science

Facilitating the discussion is Don Wallis

Kit: Trust is essential to all that we do here.

Jeanie: Everything revolves around trust.

Don: Trust in the child—

Chris: And the children's trust in themselves.

Ann: And their trust in each other. The group.

Don: Essentially, what is it you trust?

Jeanie: In the child's ability to learn and to change and to grow. Their perpetual forward movement as human beings. I really have trust in that.

Chris: We all have trust in that. We see it and we respect it.

Don: You see it?

Jeanie: In my experience year after year after year, child after child after child, I see it. That's how I can trust it. I *see* it. I see that it's real, over and over and

over again. Different child after different child, different group after different group—

Ann: All those individuals within the group, all the different places where each child is. And where they *all* are, together.

Chris: And we trust that children are on their own time frame, their own developmental schedule. That each child has an individual clock for learning and growing.

Kit: They proceed *when they are ready*. That's so important!

Chris: And there might be a pause in a child's understanding of some things, or desire to understand some things—a pause in the progress of their development. But in the grand scheme of things—as

19

we know from seeing it, over and over—there will be that development. So when there's a pause, there's not a panic, like "Oh this child will never learn." We trust that the child will. And they do.

Jeanie: The pauses are important in their own right.

Chris: Some major progress, some growth may be going on there.

Ann: The children will pause, and internalize, and ruminate and digest—and then come up with the next question they're going to ask. Then they go on with their learning. Each child has her own way of doing this. We know that here, and we trust in it. We allow it to happen.

Kit: The children expect each other to treat each other well. And they do. If a child does something out there that's risky, like really working hard on the unicycle, for example, the other children will manage to tell that child who is taking a risk, "Good job!"

Chris: I see this happen all the time.

Brian: It happened today, in the Art/Science Room. Henry was grousing about his art work, saying he was going to give up art, he didn't want to be an artist anymore. And Jade said, "Henry, what are you saying? You're one of the best artists I've ever seen!" And Henry heard that, you know. He said, "Yeah, I'm just having a bad day." I'm pretty sure he'll back at it tomorrow.

Kit: Henry thrives on that kind of support, he really does.

Brian: I think the children are inspired by each other's successes, as opposed to being jealous of each other's successes. And that's a product of trust, I think. Trusting yourself, trusting that you are okay enough to appreciate someone else's triumph.

Don: So, trust is intentional here. It's part of the curriculum, so to speak. It's part of what you teach.

Jeanie: Yes. It begins with Ann. I watch Ann work-

ing hard on those concepts in the Nursery, and in the Kindergarten we work very hard on those concepts, too. And I'm sure Kit and Chris and Brian are working on those concepts—

Don: You mean, the concepts of appreciating each other, and mutual respect, and giving support, and—

Jeanie: And it being all right to be who you are, it's all right to be different from the person next to you. And supporting those differences—having those differences be wonderful things, as opposed to frightening things, or things that keep us separate. All these things speak directly to trust.

Chris: I think trust builds on itself, it just builds and builds, like it has a kind of snowball effect. And I think that is what the Antioch School tradition is about, and the culture of the school. It's about trust, starting in the Nursery and building up through the Kindergarten and the Younger Group and the Older Group—and then beyond the school, out into the

world. With children who have experienced that, trust just surrounds them. It embraces them. And then when a new child comes into the school, it embraces that child, too. That's the nature of trust: it just builds and builds . . .

Ann: You know, I'm sitting here hearing us all talk, and I realize all over again how very clear and definite we are about all these things that revolve around trust. And one of the reasons the children go in the direction they go—being supportive and caring, showing one another respect, helping each other—is because that's what we have framed for them here, very carefully and consciously. We really pay attention to it.

Jeanie: We work at it. And so do the children.

Don: And they learn it.

Jeanie: They *do*. They really do. Each in their own way.

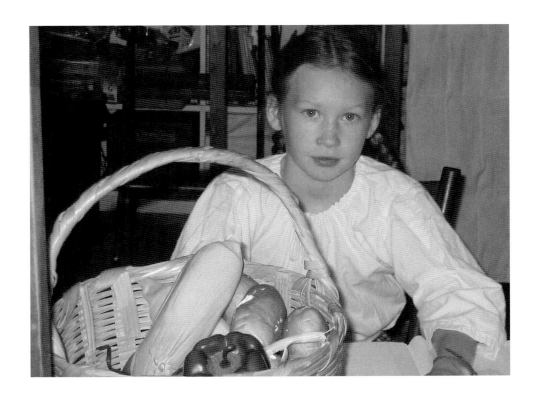

Jade Rides the Unicycle

She carries the unicycle outside to the porch, and begins to ride it.

She rides it down the length of the porch, close to the wall, so she can grab the rail if she starts to fall. She turns around and starts riding back along the rail, but she falters, lurches forward, veers away from the wall, and she falls. She falls down hard on the concrete pavement of the porch.

She gets up, her face taut and closed in. One arm is wrapped around her back, to reach the place where it hurts most. She stands there for a long moment, not moving, staring in through the window, seeing nothing. The unicycle lies in a heap at her feet. Then she gathers it up and gets back on it and rides it down the rail.

A minute later she comes into the hallway and sets the unicycle down by the door. She has fallen again—I can see it in her face, and the way she moves as she walks. She walks straight ahead, standing straight up, looking at nothing. Perhaps she is whispering something to herself.

She walks into the Younger Group room. No one else is in there—Kit's on the playground, and so are all the children. Jade stays in there, resting, crying a little, maybe. She just needs to be by herself for a while.

She comes out again, and picks the unicycle up from where she set it down, and wheels it out the door. She gets back on it and begins to ride.

She rides the unicycle down the length of the porch, staying close to the wall, her shoulder almost touching the rail. When she gets to the end of the porch she veers away from the wall, making a sharp turn out into the yard. She thrusts her arms up into the air, seeking balance—waving her arms now, high above her head—riding the unicycle, her child's body dancing above the turning wheel.

Deep Down Inside

Ryan, out on the porch by himself, riding the unicycle—falling, getting up, getting back on, riding, falling, getting up . . .

He rides close to the rail, holds on to it, then shoves off from it and away. He pedals forward, veers off balance, falls, goes down—goes down hard.

Gets back up. Rides. Falls. Gets back up . . .

He stays out there for a long time, doing this again and again.

He rides off around the corner of the school, and comes walking back without the unicycle. He's stored it away in the shed, out of sight.

He is walking in a slow stride, no hurry, head down, thinking about something. He is dark-haired, dark-eyed, broad-shouldered, solid. From this distance he looks like a man, walking along; it seems like a man's thoughts—worries—are on his mind. He is mulling them over. You can see the man he is going to be . . . Now he is only—what age? How young? Nine years old.

Inside the school he walks to the water fountain, leans down to get a drink. Then he's standing up stretching out his arm, flexing it, peering at a skinned-up place on his elbow.

Brian, passing by in the hallway, stops and looks at it too.

"Better go wash that out, Ryan."

"I don't—"

"Yes, you do. Go on now."

He does.

This is Ryan, the boy who wrote:

I will tell you
what a poem does.
It makes you feel
deep down
inside
yourself

 ## Keep Your Strength Up

1• My Dad's Toomer
By Hana

It all storid
when I was a baby
He was driving the car
he seckrych to a halt
and had his frst seshr
and my Dad had srgry
and he was balld
and 8 yer's later
all the pepl in the clas
rote a card to my dad
becas he was going to
have a srgry
My mom is driving
my dad there
and i went to
Philus and Ron's hous

Hana illustrates her story with a series of drawings:

First there is a simple drawing of Hana as a little girl, her hair blowing in a breeze. Then come drawings of her father driving his car, having the seizure, and lying in his hospital bed, a spidery web of tubes and wires connected to his head and body.

With "8 yer's later" Hana is shown, a big girl now, in a long dress. A happy clown, perhaps a smiling child, illuminates the passage about Hana's schoolmates writing get-well cards to her dad.

When her mother takes her father to the hospital for the surgery, Hana draws them driving off; the car is seen from behind, leaving their house.

The last drawing is of Hana, walking along a path. She has carefully drawn her feet: they are large, nicely formed, strong, solid; they carry her walking along the path to the home of her friends.

2 • Keep Your Strength Up

This is the day of her father's surgery. Hana is quiet, pensive. So are the other children in the Younger Group. They know—they feel—what Hana is going through. They know this is another surgery in what has been a long series of surgeries for Hana's dad.

At their Morning Meeting, the children talk about it.

"I bet it's hard for you," Chloe says to Hana, and around the circle the other children begin to murmur similar thoughts. Kit stops them, and nods toward Hana, inviting her to speak for herself.

She says she is scared. After the surgery, she says, her dad will be "all bald and weak." Hana is wearing blue—blue sweater, blue pants, blue socks. She stands up so everybody can see them. "Blue," she says, "is the healing color."

After the Morning Meeting ends, Ben G comes up to Hana and says in a hushed, solemn voice: "I am sorry your dad has to go through this, Hana." He holds her gaze for a long moment.

Tasha is standing beside her, waiting to speak, her hands clasped in front of her in a gesture of prayer. Tasha says, "Hana, I hope your dad will be okay."

The Younger Group sets to work making get-well cards. Kit calls them together for a meeting so they can share their ideas about what to say to Hana's dad. As the children come up with their messages, Kit writes them on the chalkboard:

Get well

We love you

Take care of yourself

Hana's message to her father is:

Keep your strength up

Through the morning Hana spends time on the sofa with Kit, going over some worksheets, listening as Kit reads a story from a book. They talk in low tones about the characters in the story. They are being together, in a quiet way.

Kit's soft voice.

Hana's eyes are pure brown. You can see deep down into the well of her eyes.

In the early afternoon, an e-mail message from Hana's mother arrives. Didi takes the message to Kit, and Kit gives it to Hana. They read it together, standing in the doorway of the Younger Group room. It says her father's surgery was successful; he is resting now in his hospital bed

Hana reads the message again, by herself, slowly sounding out each word. Then she puts her arms around Kit and embraces her. They hold each other close for a long moment of time.

Quickly the good news spreads through the school . . .

Later in the day, Hana comes to Kit and tells her she wants to write a Card of Thanks. On a sheet of blue posterboard she has drawn a big red heart. Now she begins to write a message inside the heart.

She asks Kit, "How do you spell 'support'?"

Before Kit can answer, Hana raises another pressing issue. "My family," she says, "would want to sign this card."

Kit nods.

"But they're not here," Hana says.

Kit waits.

"Can I sign their names?" Hana says.

Kit: "You mean, acting on behalf of your family?"

Hana: "Yes."

Kit: "Yes."

Hana completes the message:

Thanks for your sueport, Y.G.

From The Katz-Steins

Dan, Abi, Zac & Hana

She posts it on the window wall for all to see.

3 • Trust in the Child

Hana's father continued to struggle with the illness, diagnosed as incurable. A year after the surgery, Hana, now a member of the Older Group, was the focus of a discussion by her teachers:

Kit: Hana has been spending a whole lot of her time coming back to visit in the Younger Group room. I think that's what she needs to be doing right now, because of who she is and what she needs.

Chris: I think it's really important for her to be able to do that.

Kit: When she comes in the room, we don't ever talk about why she comes back. I don't ever say much. I just snatch her up in a hug.

Jeanie: Remember, Kit, she did the same thing moving from Kindergarten to the Younger Group?

Kit: That's exactly right. That's her pattern.

Jeanie: I think it has a lot to do with the life issues she's been working on. It's so comforting to be able to lose something, and then be able to go back to it. I think she is looking at loss in her life and trying to understand that, trying to think what it might be like if and when it happens. So I just think this is really important for her to do, and very insightful of her to do it.

Don: How that is insightful of Hana?

Jeanie: Children often do things that are intuitive. I don't think it's a rational, logical process at all—I think they're just intuitively doing what they need to do. They are looking at what they need to look at, and then looking at what they need to look at again and again, and again and again. I think that's what Hana is doing now. I have watched her go through so many hard things in her young life! Her father has been so very, very ill almost all her life. From the time she was in the Nursery, she's just had one hard thing after another. She has just sort of lived at the edge. And she has really lived it well, I think. I really do. She knows how to care for herself.

Kit: Yes. She's doing very, very well, really.

Jeanie: When she comes into my room, she paints at the easel. She just paints.

Jeanie makes the motion of Hana painting.

She leaves little messages on the easel. She's keeping in touch, you see. Given that her life is sort of at crisis level, she's found a way to keep a real continuity. She can come back to the Kindergarten and for her it's like, "This is still the same, I can count on this, it's here for me anytime I need it. This is a foundation I have, where my feet can always touch the ground."

Don: She'll leave messages on your easel?

Jeanie: Sometimes she'll write "I love you," or "I miss you"—whatever little message she needs to put there. She's touching base, plugging back in.

Brian: Hana has her moments of anger, too. She gets irritated by things. And yet she is also kind of amazingly self-contained.

Chris: She does seem to know where she needs to set her boundaries, and where she needs to give herself space and time.

Kit: I think that although she is holding on within, she is also on the precipice, vibrating. It's really hard, because it's really right there in her every moment, all the time.

Don: Something happened with Hana in the Writers Group yesterday. We were writing letters to President Bush, and our conversation was about the war in Iraq, and how horrible it was, and how everybody loses in war, nobody gains. And I said it's the children who lose the most of all. Hana looked kind of startled when I said that. She asked, "Why?" I said, "Well, they lose everything they have. They lose their parents, their families, their homes. Their loss is greater because they're so young—they lose almost all they've ever known all their lives."

Hana took this all in. Her eyes were beaded right on me as we talked. Then she wrote her letter. She really worked on it. She was writing long after the other kids had moved on. She wrote:

"Dear President Bush—I hope you will stop the war. You are killing children. They are losing everything. My father has a brain tumor. I am afraid I will be like those children. *Stop this war!* Sincerely yours, Hana."

Chris: Oh, that's wonderful.

Jeanie: You see, that's what I mean—for her to be able to write those words, that's just so incredible! That is real self-knowledge. It is true awareness, of where she is and what she needs to do. That is incredible, that she could say that.

Ann: And not back away from putting those pieces together.

Jeanie: She hasn't ever backed away!

[Pause.]

Ann: You know, I am just thinking about something. The other morning, Hana came down to the Nursery with an origami star in her hand, and she just very quietly handed it to me. And, I just—I don't save many things, you know, because I have so many to save. But I saved this little star. It just has a lot of meaning for me.

[Pause.]

Ann: She just very quietly kind of gave it to me.

Play Is the Foundation

The Antioch School Nursery School is a place where play is seen to be the finest natural way of learning. Play is the center from which young children learn how to get along with one another, to know themselves, and learn about the world around them. Learning through play is seen as an essential part of being human. It is an ability to be nurtured for its own sake, and as the foundation upon which a child's continued learning will be built.

—Ann Guthrie

Ann Guthrie, the Nursery teacher at the Antioch School, is a quiet, softspoken person, watchful, attentive, reflective, precise. When Ann was a young child her mother, a poet, wrote poems about her, and Ann remembers how much she loved to hear her mother read them to her. When she was nine her mother went back to school to earn a Ph.D. "I became a kind of a latch-key child," Ann says, "and I loved it." She relished the "nice little chunk of time I had to myself, at home alone after school." She learned to be independent, self-responsible, introspective, strong.

She is an observer. She has spent many important moments of her life, from childhood to the present, carefully observing animal behavior. When she was growing up, in Kansas City, the zoo was just a block away. At home she enjoyed a succession of interesting pets—a white rat, a monkey—that she could observe close-up. Best of all, Ann says, there was a pony farm next door. She was always out in the back yard watching the ponies across the fence. "Even though we lived in the city, there was this pony farm right there, and that made all the difference."

Ann went to Antioch College to study biology—she switched to education—and at one point she devoted herself to making an extensive study of a colony of cats living in a barn. She would go into the barn at ten o'clock at night and stay until two in the morning, carefully watching the cats, making notes on their activity, charting their behavior as individuals and as members of their group. Ann says she loved doing this; she found it deeply interesting, rewarding, enlightening.

When her daughter, Caitlin, was born, Ann trained her observer's eye on her child, keeping a journal of moments of growth in Caitlin's life, from infancy to childhood. It is an extraordinary exploration—intimately detailed, sensitive, insightful, moving—of the beginnings of a life, and of the foundations of childhood, and of the intricacies of the bonding of mother and child. Here is a passage from Ann's journal:

And so she is one day old, a sweet package, who wants to be in my arms always, a nipple in her mouth, lazily nursing. She will fall asleep, but if I put her down she will wake immediately. I doze and walk about with her in my arms, but I didn't realize the muscular endurance I would need. I find that after an hour or two of this my back is strung with hot wires and my arms are falling out of their sockets. Finally this morning. I discovered she can asleep snuggled on my stomach while I doze on my back.

But last night was very difficult. By two a.m. she was wide awake and wanting to be held, while I was utterly overwhelmed, stupid with exhaustion. Richard held her and I held her in tandem—rocking, nursing and hoping for the necessary magic to fathom her.

Interestingly, as much as I wanted Richard's help, as much as I didn't want to interfere with him or impose myself, I found that when she cried, *I had to have her back.* And in a very physical way. My body ached for her, breasts, bones, brain and skin. . . .

I lay all night last night with my back pressed against Richard, curled around Caitlin. My dreams are all of her. For me it was a twilight sleep, keeping a connection, monitoring her breathing while we slept.

When Caitlin grew old enough to go to school, Ann enrolled her in the Antioch School. Eventually Ann followed her there, becoming the school's Nursery teacher in 1988. Over the years since then, Ann has developed her own deeply held personal philosophy of early childhood education:

I believe that children belong to an innately curious species and that if you provide a rich environment, in an atmosphere that supports self-direction and encourages a sense of wonder, that children will *want* to do the rest.

I believe that childhood belongs to the children, that young children learn how to get along with one another, to know themselves and learn about the world around them through play and playfulness.

I believe a primary role of a teacher is to find and feed each individual child's innate direction rather than *creating* that direction in an invasive way.

In some very basic way, I trust in others' abilities to find their own direction, to be self-directed.

I also trust in myself: in my own powers of observation and intuition, and in my ability to sense or feel what is "good" for a child and to step in, to direct the child, if that is appropriate.

Teaching is a subtle art. . . . I believe that good teaching comes out of good observing, knowledge of child development, intuition, an ability to read the individual, and from a good sense of timing. A good teacher knows when to step in and when *not* to step in. . . .

I believe that teaching is much more art than science.

I believe that teaching is also learning.

In the Nursery, Ann's relating to the children is gentle and understated ("teaching is a subtle art"), and she speaks to the children always in the same quiet, low-key tone of voice. She is consistent in all ways: in her adherence to the daily schedule of activities, in the methodical way she moves about the room, in her calm, soothing manner. Her way of being with the children encourages them to sustain their own energy and initiative, their own momentum of learning and growth.

Here is a moment I preserved in my notebook:

Ann is watching Lena, Anna, Meranda and Annie as they gather around the tadpole tank. Each child is using a magnifying glass to study the tadpoles.

"They've changed," Lena says.

Ann leans forward just a bit, and says: "Did they change, Lena?"

—Such a subtle response! So sincerely does Ann ask the question, and so simply and gently— not challenging, not leading Lena on, not expecting her to answer in any certain way. Ann's words serve to affirm the energy of discovery as belonging fully to Lena. The child made the discovery, and she announced it, and now, by her response to Ann's question—however she chooses to respond—the child will confirm it.

"*Yes,*" Lena says, in a hushed voice.

She keeps her eyes on the tadpoles. So do Anna and Meranda and Annie. "This is *cool*," Anna says.

Meranda now is using two little magnifying glasses, one in each hand, one for each eye, to study the miracle of the tadpoles.

Silently Ann watches over this scene.

"I'm a translator," Ann says of her role in the life of the Nursery. To facilitate communication among the children, Ann must translate the intention of a child into an expression another child can recognize. To do this, she must know—by "my own powers of observation and intuition"—what the child's intention is, and how to clarify it for the other child's understanding.

Here is Ann translating an interaction between Gabriel and Mia:

Gabriel has a beautiful jeweled ring he has brought from home, and he comes over to Mia,

wanting to show it to her. Awkwardly he thrusts it close to her face.

Mia: "Gabriel, that's rude."

Gabriel is surprised, taken aback, puzzled.

Ann approaches them: "Gabriel, do you know what rude means?"

Gabriel: "No."

Ann: "Can you explain what rude means, Mia?"

Mia thinks for a moment, then says: "Not nice."

Ann: "Gabriel, do you want to show her your ring?"

Gabriel holds up the ring for Mia to see. This time he stands a step or two back from Mia, holding the ring at a proper distance.

Mia admires it: "Oh Gabriel, that's a very nice ring."

Gabriel: "Mia, would you like a ring like that?"

Mia, politely: "No, I don't think so."

"And that was perfectly acceptable to Gabriel," Ann said later, when I asked her about it. "He got what he wanted, which was to interact with Mia. That was his intention. The thing about the ring was just a vehicle for that. Gabriel really wants to be able to interact with people. He wants that so much! He knows people are fun. So I translated Gabriel's intention for Mia, and she did the rest. Gabriel took it all in. He's learning. He saw what he needed to do to get what he wants."

What he wants is what Ann wants for all the children: "I want them to see themselves as capable and to *feel* themselves as capable," she said. "My goal is for the children to feel confident that they have the tools to express to one another what they need and what they want.

"Some children have that when they first come into the Nursery. Those who don't can usually achieve it, with help and lots of practice.

"Sometimes—not often—when a child isn't making progress, I don't translate, I just tell a child what the task is. I say, 'You have to figure out how to talk and behave so that everyone is comfortable.' The child might say, 'Is this a time-out?' I say, 'No, it's not a time-out. You've just got to think about this and learn to do it.'

"It's so important! This school is about learning and enjoying and being in *groups,* as well as respecting the individual."

Ann paused, and smiled. "I have to confess. Personally, I'm not one of those people who's naturally drawn to being in a group. Here in the Nursery is where I've learned how it works."

Here is another scene from the Nursery, this one reflecting the effects of Ann's relationship to the children, her personality, her comforting presence:

Sam has bumped his head and it hurts. He's lying down on the rug, in pain. Ann is applying an ice pack to his head, and holding it on the back of his neck. She is kneeling down beside him, stroking his back. Sam lies still, resting, not uncomfortably, it seems. But he's got a big bump.

At the table Tommy, Alex, Asa, Douglas, and Saskia are having a snacktime discussion involving the bark of trees and the bark of dogs.

Asa: "Trees can't bark."

Saskia: "Dogs can't grow on trees."

Asa: "I know. . ."

Douglas: "If you don't see them climb the tree you might say they growed in the tree, right?"

(Sophisticated thought!)

Sam stirs, tries to get up—he doesn't want to miss this wonderful conversation. He comes to the table, moving slow, looking fragile. He's still hurting from bumping his head. He starts to drink from his cup of juice, can't do it—he begins to cry.

Ann: "Would you like me to help you with your juice?"

Sam, crying: "It's not *in* there . . ." He means the straw he drinks his juice with.

Ann: "Oh, gosh. Let me look over by your cubby. Maybe it fell."

Ann finds a straw for Sam's juice. He sips.

Alex says, "Sam? Sam?"

Alex wants to comfort him, but Sam doesn't respond. Ann sits down in the chair beside him.

Sam folds himself into Ann's lap.

Ann puts her arms around him: "Are you feeling tired, Sam?"

Sam burrows in.

Ann: "Still hurts from that bump?"

Sam burrows in deeper.

Ann wraps herself around him, enfolds him. She holds him, and is still.

It is a moment of stillness, and rest, and healing.

Welcome to the Nursery, begins the visitors guide Ann has written, for parents and others who come to visit and observe.

You will be seeing a group of inquisitive four-year-olds (older 'threes' and younger 'fives,' too) as they go from a joyful hustle-bustle to the quiet concentration of their morning or afternoon. . . . As you look around the room and outside, you'll see the children move from the silly to the serious and back again, from the tension of exploration, discovery and mastery, to the comfort of familiar routines. Listen to their conversations and you'll hear them working hard throughout their play, learning to express themselves as capable social beings.

As you observe, you'll begin to take in the room, their room. It's child sized, arranged to be accessible to them and encourage many areas of growth. You will see:

A book corner for the love of good literature, for the poetry and magic and music in language. . . .

The block area in the sun room, which invites cooperative and dramatic play, development of math concepts, and promotes problem solving skills, from practical engineering to social interaction. . . .

Accessible art supplies for open-ended exploration: clay, paper, crayons, markers, scissors, glue, tape, an easel for tempera painting . . . raw materials with which children can experience the joy of their own doing and making, creation and expression without the limitations and pressures of an end product . . .

The water table for tactile exploration, scientific investigation, and the therapeutic value of water play . . .

The loft, a comfortable place from which to observe, meet with a friend, to see the room from another perspective, to experience the thrill of height, and to always be taller than any adult . . . The puppet stage. The doll corner. The piano . . . Cubbies, individual and inviolate, each child's very own space . . . And, in the play yard outside, there are climbers, swings, trikes, a sand pile to dig in, space and equipment for the joy of moving and the learning of "I can."

The Nursery room is a place of accessibility and possibilities. . . . Blocks and packing boxes are vehicles for their learning. Some others are open-ended art supplies, puzzles, puppets, dress-ups, equipment and spaces that lend themselves to fantasy and imaginative play, and books and songs and music, plus the ideas and experience of their friends. . . .

They make countless snacks to feed themselves and their friends, making lists, walking down the hall on their own or with a friend to Didi's office for supplies, opening juice bottles, pouring pitchers, figuring out how many cups and how many napkins they will need to set the table. They clean up their room and put away their things countless times.

They write and illustrate their stories, write and perform their plays, write and leave messages for one another, and continue to experience and learn the real power of the written and spoken word.

They understand that how they feel and how other people feel is important.

And along the way they build a group, and begin to feel themselves a part of the larger community of the school.

"What it is that I want for the children in the Nursery, in a nutshell," Ann says, is "for them to feel that the Nursery and the school belong to them; for them to have the tools to verbalize plans internally to themselves, and then articulate them to others; for them to have the confidence and ability to find and gather the people and things they need to make their plans happen; and for them to see themselves as capable of solving the problems, whatever they might be, that emerge along the way."

 Buddies

In the hallway by the Nursery, Hasan and Douglas have made a tractor out of two wooden blocks. They are sitting on the tractor looking out the wall of windows. It's a gray day.

Douglas: "We're on the tractor."

Hasan: "On the tractor! I got the keys to the tractor in my hand. Put 'em in my pocket."

Douglas makes the noise of the tractor running: *putt-putt, putt-putt, putt-putt.*

Douglas's voice is thin, high-pitched. Hasan's voice is a deep, rich baritone.

Hasan: "Noise. Fire-balls. Fresh! Frogs jump high, so very high."

Douglas drives the tractor faster: *putt-putt-putt, putt-putt-putt.*

Hasan: "Turn your tractor." The tractor makes a sputtering sound: *sputta-sputta-sputta.*

Hasan: "Shoots out into space!"

They get another wooden block from the pile nearby.

Hasan: "Don't close the tractor."

Douglas: "It's pretty late, buddy."

They lie down, curl up, pretend to go to sleep.

Meranda comes out of the Nursery and tip-toes over to the sleeping boys.

"Wake up!" Meranda says, cheerfully. "Wake up, sweetie pie."

Douglas and Hasan rouse themselves, waking up groggy from their good night's sleep.

"Good boys!" says Meranda.

They look with sleepy eyes out the window at the play-yard, squinting as if in bright sunlight; but it's a drab, gray day.

Douglas: "I want to go everywhere at once."

Hasan is silent. Suddenly the sun shines, filling the window with bright light.

"It's really sunny!" Douglas says.

Hasan looks out, wide-eyed now. He sees a bird in the sky, and smiles.

"Fly all the way to Africa," he says, softly.

Nursery School Morning

The Nursery Schoolers and the Kindergartners are playing together, Ann and Jeanie watching them from near the doorways to their rooms. Ann is paying close attention to Asa and Mia, who are experiencing a bit of conflict over something they've said to each other. Right now, Asa is trying to end the conversation. He has put his hands over his ears and, frowning, he is walking around in a circle. All the while Mia is talking to him—or trying to:

Mia: "Come on, Asa!"

Asa: "Mia, I don't—"

Mia: "Hey, you can talk!"

Asa: "Mia, I don't like it when—"

Mia: "Asa—"

Asa: "—someone's doing a lot of talking. If I do it, I don't like it when I do it."

Ann says, "Mia, should you stop when he asks to you to stop?"

Mia: "Well, actually—"

The buzzer sounds, and everyone goes inside. It's time to clean up before game time, and then snack time. Asa and Mia work together, busily cleaning up the room.

Ann says to them: "You took so long to figure that out and you're still friends."

Mia: "We're still friends."

But Asa is still feeling some agitation. He walks up to Tommy, puts his face in Tommy's face, and through gritted teeth Asa hisses, "IT'S TIME TO CLEAN UP!!"

Tommy is unruffled. He does his part of the cleaning up at his own leisurely, laid-back pace. Douglas, working nearby, says to Tommy, "The more faster you can clean up, the more faster you can eat."

Tommy grins at Douglas and says, "The more faster you can clean up, the more faster you can eat boogers!"

Asa comes over to them and says, sternly: "Whoever is playing this game has to put it away!"

Tommy puts the game away in its box and places it on one of the shelves.

The children clean up the room. They pick up everything off the tables, they sweep the floor, they sponge the tabletops clean . . .

Mia has gotten a game of checkers off the shelves. She sits down at one of the little tables and announces to Asa, "I'm going to play this game."

Asa says, "You know what? It's a two-person game. Are you sure you know how to play that game?"

Mia: "Oh, I think people have played it by themselves."

Asa stands next to the table, watching her closely as Mia begins to play the game. He doesn't try to join in. Mia plays it by herself, as was her intention.

Hasan stands by the table watching her, saying nothing. He's studying what she's doing. After a while he walks over to the shelves full of animals and books and toys. He picks out an earth mover, and then he assembles a train of wooden cars. He hooks up the train to the earth mover and begins pulling his load across the floor.

Douglas says, "What are you doing?"

Hasan: "Look what I'm doing."

Douglas: "Cool!"

Douglas is playing on the floor with Tommy and Amelia. Tommy is saying, "Shut off your head. Like this." He puts his hands over his eyes. "I shut off my head. I can't see."

He can see, though. Peeking between his fingers, Tommy crawls over to Amelia. He leans down close to her.

Amelia says, evenly, firmly: "Don't do that."

Tommy quickly veers away, and crawls back to his place on the floor.

Tommy begins making a loud, wet, sputtering noise with his lips: "*B-b-b-b-b-b.*" Amelia starts doing it: "*B-b-b-b-b-b.*" Tommy gets up close to

Douglas and starts doing it in his face. Douglas tells him, "Don't do that to me, do it to yourself."

Ann walks up and says, softly: "Could you three be just a little quieter?"

Across the room, Asa now is sitting at the table with Mia as she plays her game of checkers. He's being careful to keep a certain distance . . .

"Nursery schoolers," Ann says, "it's snack time."

The snack table is laid with orange slices, grape juice, pretzels, peanut butter and crackers . . .

Snack time is underway, eight kids and Ann sitting around the table. It's very pleasant and calm and orderly.

Hasan says, in his sleepy voice: "Please pass me over the juice."

Alex passes it to him.

Ann: "Who's not here today?"

Everyone starts naming the absent members of the group: "Annie, Gabriel, Sam. . ."

Douglas starts naming those who are here at the table: "Mia, Alex, Asa, Tommy, Amelia, Henry, Douglas, Lena . . ."

Ann laughs, and they all smile together at Douglas's joke.

Hasan is pouring himself more juice, singing softly to himself:

" . . . Pour it all the way to the ceiling . . ."

Ann: "What would that do?"

Hasan continues singing:

" . . . Draw it all the way down from the top of the sky . . ."

Ann: "From the Big Dipper?"

Mia says, "From the top of the sky! Actually, we *are* from the sky. That's science."

Ann is enjoying this snacktime conversation.

Alex gets up from the table and wanders off across the room to get a stuffed animal—he selects a soft, fuzzy lamb—and a pillow and a book. He goes to the storytime area and lies down on the rug, lets out a burp, sighs, settles himself down. Hugging the lamb, he begins to read his book.

Asa rises from his chair, takes his cup and nap-

kin to the trash can, and neatly throws them away. He comes over to Alex and starts talking to him:

"I am your best friend," Asa says, "and you are my best friend. I am Mia's best friend, and she is my best friend. I am Tommy's best friend, and he is my best friend . . ."

Asa works his way through the whole group of the Nursery children, proclaiming their mutual best-friendship. Then he goes to the shelves and gets a book—it's *Willy the Dreamer*—and an animal—a lion, with a long tail—and sits down on the floor beside Alex.

"Mia wants the lion," Alex says.

"Too bad," Asa says. "I'm not going to give it to her. It's my favorite animal."

Hasan comes over, gets a pillow and a book, settles down on the rug, and starts to read. Douglas, carrying a bear but no book, sits down next to Hasan. Hasan's book is about astronauts in outer space. When he sees that Douglas doesn't have a book, Hasan begins reading aloud to him: "Good zap . . . Little grog . . . Zook . . ."

Amelia picks out a Carl Sandburg book, *From Daybreak to Good Night,* gets a pillow and an animal, and curls up on the rug. Mia settles near Amelia with the book she has chosen, *No Roses for Harry.* They read their books together, showing the pictures to each other.

Amelia is chanting in a sing-song voice, "Baa-baa black sheep. . ."

Henry joins the group. He snuggles in beside Mia, making a row of three of them sitting together. Henry begins reading his book, *A New Coat for Anna,* with his arm around his animal, a sleek striped tiger.

Asa says, "I know what. We can all sit together!"

He crawls over close to Henry, so now there is a line of four—Mia, Henry, Amelia, Asa—and a cluster of two, Hasan and Douglas. Tommy is sitting next to Alex, making another cluster of two. They're all together now.

Ann takes her seat in the rocking chair, a signal that it's story time. In her lap is a big, thick book full of *George and Martha* stories.

"Shall we do 'lights off'?" Ann says. "We haven't done that for a while . . . Everyone has to agree before we turn off all the lights."

Alex says, "I want the lights on."

Ann: "Sounds like some of us don't want the lights off."

Asa: "Turn them off!"

Ann: "We all have to agree."

Alex: "I don't want them off."

The lights stay on.

Ann begins story time in the way she and the children always begin it. She holds out her hand so the children can see it, and she begins to sing:

"Where is Thumbkin . . . Where is Thumbkin?"

She extends her thumb, holds it up for the children to see:

"Here I am . . . Here I am."

Amelia begins to sing along.

Alex begins to sing along, too.

Mia is doing thumbplay, holding her hands together behind her back.

Ann sings: *"Where is Pinky—Where is Pinky?"*

She holds up her little finger.

"Here I am—Here I am."

Now all the children are singing and doing thumbplay and fingerplay.

They all sing together:

"Where is Everyone?—Where is Everyone?"

Loud chorus now:

"Here I am!—Here I am!"

They sing:

"How are you today, friends?"

"Very well, I thank you."

Then, softly:

"Run away . . . Run away . . ."

And again, one last time:

"Run away . . . Run away . . ."

Are You Ready?

Overheard in the Nursery:

Mia: "Alex, do you know where we live?"

Alex: "No."

"Yellow Springs, Ohio!"

"Oh."

"Alex, do you live in America?"

"No."

"We live in America!"

"Oh."

"Alex? You know what?"

"Ummm . . ."

"We're Americans!"

"Oh. "

"Yes! We are Americans, Alex!

Long pause.

Alex: "I'm going to go to the bathroom."

Mia: "Okay."

Alex goes into the bathroom.

Mia waits by the door.

Short pause.

Mia: "Are you through yet?"

Alex: "No."

Mia: "Okay."

Long pause.

Alex: "Now I'm ready."

Mia: "Don't forget to wash your hands!"

Hard Work

Wooden blocks, old-fashioned, well scuffed from years and years of service, are kept in a collection in the "sun room" corner at the Nursery end of the hallway, stacked there along with an assortment of wooden toys, cars and busses and tractors and cranes.

Working with the blocks now—it's early morning, shortly before nine o'clock—are Douglas, a Nursery schooler, and Reed, a Younger Grouper. They've pulled a couple of blocks out of the stack onto the carpet in front of the Nursery room door.

The buzzer sounds and Reed, seeing it's time for him to be in the Younger Group room, says "Make a good road, Douglas," and walks away. Douglas says, "Bye."

Douglas now is working alone. Henry's father, accompanying Henry into the Nursery, says to Douglas, "I'll bet there's someone in the Nursery to help you, Douglas."

"I don't need help," Douglas says.

Gabriel comes out, and Ann comes out. She leans down to Douglas and they talk, quietly.

"Going to be a road," Douglas says. He says it *roe-duh.*

Gabriel starts adding blocks and boards to the construction. "No!" Douglas says. "Can't put that there."

Ann says, "Douglas, can you explain to Gabriel?"

Gabriel asks, "Why can't I put it there?"

Douglas: " 'Cause the bus needs to go through."

Ann says, "Did you hear that, Gabriel? Can you hear what Douglas is saying?"

Sam comes out of the Nursery, joins them. "I can make a road," he says.

Douglas says, "I know! We're all three making a road!"

Douglas's voice is even-toned, calm, serious. He's intent on his work. He is willing to respond to the others, willing to have a conversation, but it's something he does while he's doing the main thing, which is build the road. He is working furiously, constantly in purposeful motion. He has a plan. When he gets a block from the stack and lugs it back to his construction site, he knows exactly where he wants it to go, and he puts it there. Then he goes and gets another block.

Ann says, "Douglas, can you tell Sam where the highway is?"

"Here. Right here," Douglas says. He points to where the highway is. Sam watches closely, taking it all in. Then he goes to the stack and wrestles a block back to the site.

"Look. Look," Sam says. "It goes *here.*"

Douglas says, "Put a block *there.*" He points to the place where a block needs to go.

The blocks now cover the entire floor of the hallway at the Nursery end, wall to wall.

Henry's father comes out of the Nursery and Henry follows him, calls to him, and his father stops and turns and kneels down. Henry leans his body into him, holding onto him, and his father lets himself be held for a while.

Then gently he says, "Now go ahead and play. . "

He slowly pulls himself away from his son and begins walking down the hall.

Henry gets a block from the stack and tries to play, but his heart is not in it; his eyes are cast down, his motions are tentative. He has something on his mind.

Douglas goes to the stack and brings out a wooden bus and runs it over the highway, making turns here and there, following a route he has mapped in his mind.

Ann is watching closely.

Sam, trying to get a block from the stack, says "Help me!" in a shrill, anxious voice. Gabriel goes to him and helps him.

Douglas, running the bus on the highway, is triumphant. He is smiling and he cries out, *"Woo-hoo!"*

Gabriel announces: "We're building a sidewalk to that road." He asks Sam: "Would you like to help build a sidewalk to that road?"

Sam doesn't seem to hear. He says to himself: "I can do this." He tries to pull a big block out of the stack, but it won't move. He selects a smaller piece, a long, thin board.

Douglas asks him: "Did you do this, Sam?"

Sam says, "Yeah."

Ann leans down between them: "Douglas, are you telling Sam what you want him to do?"

Douglas: "Well, this bus has got to go through." A block Sam placed on the highway is blocking the path of the bus.

Ann: "Douglas, are you saying to Sam the highway is blocked?"

Douglas: "The bus has to go through there and it's blocked."

Ann: "What can you do to unblock the highway?"

Douglas: "Take the block out. Unblock it."

Ann: "Sam, are you hearing Douglas?"

Sam starts to say Yes, then hesitates. His whole body language changes, and when he speaks his voice is tense and loud: "I don't *want* this to be the highway!"

Sam takes the long, thin board and lays it down on the site, and starts walking on it, balancing himself as if he's walking a tightrope.

"This is my bridge!" Sam says.

Then he puts another board down, making a two-board bridge. Douglas picks up one of the boards, removes it.

Sam says, "Hey, that's my bridge!"

Douglas says, "That's too little for a bridge."

Sam puts another board down; it's a two-board bridge again. "This is a *big* bridge," Sam says.

Ann leans down close to the bridge and inspects it. One of the boards is precariously balanced on the edge of a block. "That doesn't look real stable," she says. "That board could fall off."

Sam fixes it. "It's stable now," he says.

Sam kneels down, head to the floor, looking under the bridge.

"This is a tunnel," he says.

Douglas tries to run the bus through the tunnel. It won't fit. "I'm not using this anymore," he says.

He goes to the stack of toys and gets a truck. It's smaller than a bus, but when he tries to run it under the bridge, he sees that it won't fit, either. "We need a car," Douglas says.

He goes and looks among the toys for a car, finds one, brings it back to the site and gives it to Sam.

Sam runs the car through the tunnel under the bridge. Then Gabriel takes a turn at running the car.

Suddenly Sam knocks the bridge down, and pushes the blocks over on their sides.

"Sam wrecked the highway," Gabriel says.

Douglas says, "I don't mind. He can fix it."

Sam looks dolefully at what he has done.

After a moment, Douglas announces: "The carpet is the highway!" He begins running the car on the carpet.

Sam says, brightly: "We don't need to fix it, right?"

Soon the three boys are each running a car on the carpet, the new highway. Henry, who has been inside the Nursery most of this time, comes out. Douglas says to him, "Want to help us?" Henry says nothing, wanders slowly back into the Nursery.

Douglas gets a board and builds a new bridge.

"Oops! It's not stable," he says to himself, and builds it again.

"This is a bridge," Douglas says. "Cars can go under the bridge. They can get protected from the rain."

Gabriel picks up one of the boards of the bridge. Sam grabs it from him and says, "This is mine!" He makes a motion as if to hit Gabriel with the board, but does not.

Sam glares fiercely at Gabriel, who looks at him and says: "I'm not bad!"

Ann, appearing in the doorway, leans out and says, "Gabriel and Sam, let's talk, so we can figure out what to do . . ."

The three of them gather inside the Nursery doorway and have a brief meeting.

Now Douglas has built a tower, stacking up big blocks on top of one another. He's stacked up six of them—it's a very tall tower, almost as tall as Douglas.

It's not stable. The tower wobbles and falls, its pieces clattering on top the blocks of the construction site.

Ann says, "Douglas, is there a way to keep you safe, and keep everyone else safe, while you build those towers? Is there a way to do that?"

Douglas begins retrieving the fallen blocks. Then he begins building a new tower. Henry re-

emerges from the Nursery and now, rather magically—it seems to happen in an instant—he and Douglas have built two new towers, each of them three blocks high. They are stable.

There are four boys playing now, Douglas, Sam, Gabriel, and Henry, running their cars over the carpet and the blocks.

Suddenly their play gets very loud and shrill, with Douglas, Sam and Gabriel making automobile noise by screeching together in a raucous chorus. Henry's car makes no sound at all.

Ann comes out and says, "Nursery schoolers, how can you make your cars quiet? Will you figure it out?"

Douglas nods, firmly. Immediately the boys are quiet again.

Douglas and Henry are playing with a car that has two wooden people riding it. Douglas says, in a serious tone, looking intently at Henry: "One of them can be the Dad." He points to one of them: "He can be the Dad."

Sam has a toy tractor and he's running it over the blocks, chanting in a sing-song voice, "Tractor-trailer, tractor-trailer, tractor-trailer . . ."

From the Nursery come two new boys, Alex and Tommy. They get cars from the stacks of toys and begin running them over the blocks. "I need a man," Tommy says. He goes into the Nursery to find a man to ride in his car.

Douglas now slumps down on top of the blocks at the edge of the platform near the Nursery door. He lies down flat on his back, and is motionless, staring up at the ceiling, his arms and legs splayed out from his sides. He closes his eyes.

Ann comes out, sees Douglas, and leans down over him, smiling. "Is it comfortable?" she says.

Douglas makes no response. He stays there for several moments, not moving.

Then he gets up, wobbles a bit, and walks unsteadily into the Nursery. He's tired, and needs to rest. He's done a lot of work.

Girls Being By Our Selfs

Amelia and Meranda, the tiniest of the Nursery children, are playing with a family of tiny animals. The girls are lying side by side on the rug, the animals lined up beside them neatly in a row .

Tommy and Asa are on the floor nearby, playing with blocks.

"Asa, do you know what?," Tommy is saying. "I hate to hear the word *lam-bee-no*." He is smiling but it's a serious, confessional revelation. Asa receives the news stoically.

Tommy picks up a couple of blocks and comes over to the girls. He makes an attempt to introduce one of his blocks to them: "This is my friend, Nocky . . ."

Meranda glowers fiercely at Tommy.

He smiles, genially. "I was just *kidding,*" he says.

Meranda and Amelia gather up their animals and bring them across the room to the little round table.

"They can't get us here," Amelia says. "We can be by our selfs."

They begin playing with their animals on the tabletop. They are taking care of one of the animals, who is ill and in pain.

Meranda: "She needs a shot to get her blood out of her."

Amelia: "You can't make her do that."

They change the subject. "You know what, Meranda?" Amelia says. "I changed my whole bedroom . . ."

They have about a dozen animals, carefully arranged on the tabletop. Amelia's are lined up standing in a row. Meranda's are gathered in a circle, lying on their sides. They are sleeping.

"Morning time!" Amelia announces to Meranda's animals, calling them to wake up and play.

"They're still tired," Meranda says.

Amelia persists. "You guys," she says to the animals, "stand up for a second. I want to tell you something."

But Meranda's animals remain asleep.

To her own animals, who are wide awake, Amelia says: "You know what? I want to tell you guys something." She begins telling them something about a tornado siren.

Gabriel comes over to the table. "Is there a problem?" he asks.

Meranda just glares at him.

Gabriel has an airplane he's made from legos and he begins flying it around in the air above the table.

"Stop doing that, Gabriel!" Meranda says. "Stop!"

She takes up her animals and holds them close to her chest, protecting them. She frowns mightily.

Ann comes over. She says, "Is everything all right?"

"No," Meranda says. She continues frowning.

"Yes," says Gabriel. He keeps on flying his plane.

Meranda says to him, "Don't break our animals. Because we don't want them breaking."

Ann says, "Is there a way you can fly your plane, Gabriel, so you don't hurt the animals?"

Gabriel flies his plane higher in the air, far above the animals. He starts flying it around in circles up there.

Ann: "Will that work, Meranda?"

"Yes," Meranda says.

She lays her animals back down, and they go to sleep.

Gabriel wanders off, flying his airplane.

Ann wanders off, too.

Meranda and Amelia resume their play.

"You guys," Amelia calls out in a sing-song voice. "Wake up, it's morning!"

The animals rise to meet it.

Ceremony

The Nursery children are outside, playing around the tire swing, when Douglas discovers the bird. Amelia pokes her head in the doorway and announces it: "Dead sparrow, Ann."

Ann hurries out to join the children. They are grouped in a circle, their heads bowed down toward the ground, staring at the small brown body of the bird. They are silent, and Ann does not disturb the silence.

Finally Douglas speaks. "What can we do?" he says. He wants to do something.

Ann glances around the group. "Well, let's see. . . ."

She waits for a child to respond.

Gabriel does. "We're going to dig a hole and bury it," he says.

Asa says, mournfully: "Sparrow is my favorite bird." He says it again, in a whisper: "Sparrow is my favorite bird. . . ."

Everyone is looking at the sparrow.

"I know where we can bury it," Henry says. He points toward the stone wall. "Back there."

"Where?" Alex says.

"I'll show you," Henry says. "Follow me!"

"Follow Henry!" Mia says.

Henry breaks away from the circle, and the other children follow after him.

"Get the bird, someone," Henry calls back.

"I'll get a box," Ann says. "And we'll need a scoop."

Mia says, "I'll find a scoop to do the job."

Ann and Mia go into the school to get a box and a scoop. In a moment they are back. With them is Morgan, from the Kindergarten.

Ann places the bird in the scoop and carries it as they rejoin the group, now gathered around the burial site Henry has led them to. It is a small round space hidden inside a fringe of bushes at the edge of the stone wall. It's a nice spot.

Ann says, "Morgan has a good idea. He thinks if we have a sharper tool, we can dig a better hole."

"That's right," Tommy says. "We can get something from Brian."

"I can go get a sharper tool," Ann says. "Let's leave the bird in the scoop while I walk down to Brian's room."

While she is gone, the children begin preparing the gravesite. Alex and Morgan clear a place on the ground, sweeping the leaves away with their hands.

Tommy gathers a few little wildflowers. He carefully arranges them in a little group, and brings them to me.

"Would you like these?" he says.

They are purple flowers, soft and lovely in my hands.

"Thank you, Tommy," I say to him. "These are very nice."

"Whose alligator is this?" Morgan asks. He's found it on the ground.

"It's Tommy's," Alex says.

Morgan hands the alligator to Tommy.

Alex is leaning down close to the bird. He says in a whisper, "Oh, it smells like something I know."

"Its beak was moving!" Henry says. He is hoping the bird might be alive.

"Somebody moved it," Mia says, matter-of-factly.

Ann is back with a shovel. Morgan and Henry show her where to dig the hole, and she begins digging it with the shovel.

We are all grouped in a circle around Ann, watching as she digs the hole.

Liam comes out from the Kindergarten. He stands with us, looking intently at the body of the bird. We are all silent, until Mia says, "I think that's deep enough."

"Let's put some leaves in," Gabriel says.

"Yeah, put some leaves in," Douglas says.

"It will be like a little bed for him," Asa says.

The children gather some leaves, and carefully they place them into the hole Ann has dug.

"We'll save some of these leaves for covers, okay?" Asa says.

Silence.

"Is that okay?"

"Okay," someone says.

Ann puts her hand on the handle of the scoop and pauses for a long moment.

The children are silent.

Ann places the bird onto the bed of leaves.

"Birds eat worms," Douglas says. "All birds eat worms."

"Are we ready to cover him?" Ann asks.

"Yes," someone says.

Ann fills the hole.

"In case he comes to life—" It is Asa who says this.

"We should mark it," Mia says.

"Here's a stick," Sam says. He places a small twig atop the grave.

"A special stone," Gabriel says, placing a stone on the grave.

Morgan, too, has a stone. Carefully he puts it on the grave.

Henry says, "When we finish this, let's head back."

A few of the children began to drift away . . .

Gabriel says, "If someone steps on the stones they'll trip, if they're not looking."

"Gabriel, that's a good idea," Ann says. "If we could move the stones over just a bit—"

Gabriel moves the stones.

The group has dispersed now. Ann goes off to be with the children. Gabriel goes with her. The only ones left are Morgan and Henry, and me.

Morgan has found a special leaf—it is big and round and very green – and he lays it down gently on top of the grave. He looks at it, unsatisfied.

"Maybe if we had some pretty leaves . . ."

I am standing next to Morgan, holding the wild-flowers Tommy gave me. I offer them to Morgan. "Maybe you can use these. . . ."

"Hey, thanks!" Morgan says, surprised and pleased. He kneels on the ground and spreads the purple flowers over the big green leaf.

It looks very nice.

Morgan and I turn away, and start walking to-gether back to the Nursery.

But Henry stays at the gravesite. He is on his knees with a stick in his hand, hard at work, trying to pin the big leaf to the ground, so it won't blow away in the wind.

He is the last to tend the grave.

Peace

Oh, Hasan! Hasan is so bright. He is so wonderful.
He has real integrity. He's got to understand it all.

—Ann

In the Nursery, Hasan and Saskia are playing together at the small round table.

Hasan says to her, gently: "Saskia, when you grow up, don't you go out on the streets."

Saskia says, with her sweet smile: "O but I have to, Hasan."

Hasan, quietly pleading: "Don't go out on the streets, Saskia. Let me do that for you."

Saskia, still smiling: "But Hasan, I have to."

The next day, early the next morning, Hasan comes to Ann. He says, "I might as well be sick and just stay at home."

Ann asks him why.

"Nobody listens to me," Hasan says.

Ann asks him what he means by that, and what does he want to say that he wants to people to hear?

"I am Muslim," Hasan says, "and I want people to believe what I believe."

"Oh, Hasan," Ann says, "there are so many beliefs."

Hasan says, "Muslims, what we do is, we teach our beliefs."

Ann nods, listening.

"Ann," Hasan says. "A woman shouldn't be working. A woman shouldn't go out on the streets."

"Hasan," Ann says, "if that were true, I couldn't be your teacher."

Hasan looks at Ann for a long moment.

He says, "Your beliefs fight my beliefs."

Ann says, "Hasan, my beliefs do not fight any beliefs."

Hasan pauses. He is silent for a long moment.

Then he says, speaking carefully, slowly: "Muslims believe that your beliefs fight our beliefs."

"Hasan," Ann says, gently. "My beliefs are that no beliefs fight other beliefs."

Hasan is silent again.

The rest of the Nursery morning proceeds . . .

When it is time for lunch, the children wash their hands and gather around the table. They all sit down, except for Hasan. He remains standing by his place at the table.

He has something to say.

"Ann," Hasan says.

Ann says, "Yes, Hasan?"

"Ann, your beliefs don't fight my beliefs."

"That is right, Hasan," Ann says. "That is right."

Then Hasan goes around the table, child by child, looking at each one as he speaks to them:

"Amelia, your beliefs don't fight my beliefs . . .

"Saskia, your beliefs don't fight my beliefs . . .

"Henry, your beliefs don't fight my beliefs . . .

"Grace, your beliefs don't fight my beliefs . . .

"Julie, your beliefs don't fight my beliefs . .

"Sam, your beliefs don't fight my beliefs. . .

"Mia, your beliefs don't fight my beliefs . . .

"Alex, your beliefs don't fight my beliefs . . .

"Asa, your beliefs don't fight my beliefs . . .

"Lena, your beliefs don't fight my beliefs . . .

"Douglas, your beliefs don't fight my beliefs . . ."

Learning Is Natural

Once I climbed a tree.
It was fun.
It was verry, verrry fun.
I liked it.
My mom said stop.
I did not stop.

—Liana, Younger Group

The teachers, in group discussion:

Don: You speak of *expectation*—you all use that term—as being essential to what happens here

Jeanie: Yes. From trust comes expectation. It's really a key to the energy the kids bring to learning, to self-direction, to making choices and taking responsibility, to problem solving and bringing the group together—to all of it.

Kit: I think we all expect the children to be competent, reasoning, capable, thinking beings. I don't think any of us ever answer any questions the children can answer for themselves, or do anything for the children that they can do for themselves. And I think that changes how they see themselves It helps them to see themselves as being capable. It helps them to feel comfortable being who they are.

Jeanie: It really is an *expectation*. We expect that if they have a problem, they'll be able to solve it; if there's something they need to do, they'll be able to do it. They don't really need my intervention—my support, yes, but not my intervention, most of the time. They *are* capable! They can *do* things. They can do things for themselves.

Brian: They *want* to learn.

Jeanie: Oh, they do, they *do*. They want to *learn*. They want to know. They want to find their own answers. They are always quite thrilled when they ask you a question and you turn it around and ask it of them—"What do *you* think?" They always have a thought. Or when they ask you to do something for them and you say, "Do you think *you* can do that?" And they know just what to do, and they go ahead and do it. It's almost like they're asking you to affirm their ability to do things, and once you do, they're thrilled about it.

Kit: Yes, because it's *their* expectation too. *Expectation.* There are some truths we all work with and that's a big one. And then, to put it into practical use—you have twenty-three children, and so you have twenty-three different ways that their expectation is going to interact with your expectation, on their own terms and in their own specific ways. Responding to all that, every day, moment by moment—that's what we do, that's our work. That's how we teach.

Jeanie: You often use the word *minimalist,* Kit, when you're talking about your teaching.

Kit: Yes.

Jeanie: That's something I've heard you say many times. And I think that's part of expectation, that the expectation of the child maximizes when you minimize.

Kit: Right. You can't walk up to a child and say, "I expect you to—"

Jeanie: No, no.

Kit: You have to say that in other ways. And communicate it in other ways. Just—communicate your trust in them, by the way you are with them. I think we all do that here all the time, in a hundred little ways every day. We do it each time we interact with a child. It's in the way we regard them. Because because it's what we *believe.* We believe in them.

Don: Kit said you can't just walk up to a child and say, "I expect you to—" That you can't expect the child to do or be a certain way. Could we talk about that for a moment? Because that's what so many people in the world do with their children.

Jeanie: That's probably what most of us experienced growing up.

Kit: Well, on occasion I do say versions of those things to the children. On occasions when I really want to be clear, and when I feel that I need to communicate something to a child pretty directly, I say things like, "In this school, we are kind to other people." Or, "In this school, we make certain that everyone is included." But most of the time I don't just come out and say these things. Most of the time I don't need to.

Chris: Right, because the children will state those expectations all by themselves. In the Older Group at the beginning of each year the children discuss their expectations. I know you all do that with your groups, too. We have a meeting with everybody there and we say, "Well, what should the Older Group rules be?" And the children set up the rules, based on their expectations. They are expectations about what kind of environment they want to live in, what kind of person they want to be, how they want to be respected. That's always what the children's rules are about.

Now, down through the course of the year, I'm in the position of sometimes having to remind them what their expectations are. Because they'll go off course sometimes, and forget that they had those expectations of themselves. But it always does originate from the children. The expectations come from them. That's where a big difference is, about this school. It's opposite to most schools, where the discipline is from the principal down. Here, it's coming from the children up.

Don: The expectation is the children will learn. How is that communicated to them? I'm thinking of being with the Younger Group and every child in the room is working very hard, and nobody's making them do it, it's all very clearly self-directed, and they're all busy and happy—it's *very* impressive. It's wonderful to see, really. So I make a point of paying attention to what Kit says to the children, to try and see what she does that creates this great learning environment. And Kit, all you say to them is something like, "Well, you all know what to do now." And all the children in the room are doing their work, and their work is great, I've seen it and it's excellent, day after day . . . And so my question is, What energizes these children?

Jeanie: You ask the question as if it's something external, and I don't think it is. It's internal. Learning is natural. It's right in *here*.

[*She places her hand over her heart.*]

Chris: Yes! The excitement of learning is *inside* us. It's intrinsic. Children *love* to learn!

Jeanie: *Everybody* wants to learn. Learning is so exciting and rewarding and self-enhancing and empowering, and on and on and on. I mean, I don't think I've ever known a child who didn't want to learn. I just can't imagine that.

Don: Well, can we explore this a little bit? Because I can take you to a lot of schools where you will not see the children wanting to learn.

Jeanie: That's because it gets—

Ann and Chris: It gets taken away!

Jeanie:—taken away from them, yes.

Brian: I think children always want to learn—it's just that they are often blocked from learning.

Chris: Yes, they get blocked by people taking over for them, and doing things for them that they could do for themselves. And blocked by people putting unrealistic expectations on them, so they start fearing failure. There are just *so* many things that can block learning!

Ann: What I think the teachers here do is to remove blocks—

Jeanie: Yes, I agree.

Chris: And not put them in the way in the first place.

Kit: All this is ringing a bell with me. In my teaching now I'm struggling with what to hold onto and what to let go. I struggle with how much I'm willing to give up to the "gods of learning." And what informs me now is this:

My part of the control thing is to say to the children, "We are going to learn something about trees." That's my expectation. I simplify it. I just say "something about trees." That's what I hold on to. I'm ready to let go of the rest of it, and let them figure out *what* they want to learn about trees. They'll find something. They will find *great* things to learn. They'll find all you'd ever want to teach them, and

more. But I have to let go of what *I* wanted them to learn, and where *I* wanted them to go, and where *I* wanted to take them. I have to throw that out and say, "The only thing is, you've got to learn something about this." They take it from there. And it's a wonderful ride—if only I can have faith!

[*Pause.*]

And I do have faith.

But when children come up and say, "What do I do now? What do you want me to do?" I think that's sad. I don't know what to tell them. I *don't* tell them. I don't want to confuse them. I want it to be crystal clear to them that, "Hey, I don't do your work." Because's it's got to be up to them. *They* must find out what their work is. If they don't know that about themselves, then it's time they find it out. Because they are out of touch in some ways—out of touch with their better expectations of themselves.

Brian: In the Younger Group right now the kids are excited about taking a spelling test. Ursi said, "Hey, we're having this test!" All smiles. She was *playing* with those spelling words. Regina and Erin were, too. They were really excited about it—it seemed like fun to them that they were taking a test.

Kit: It's kind of a treat for them—it's the only test they get to take. And you know, the children take control of the spelling word list. I have no control over the list—they're making up their own lists of words to spell.

Jeanie: I remember them coming down to the Kindergarten, saying "Guess what word I gave myself today!" They'd have this enormously long and complicated word they were learning to spell.

Kit: That's what these children *do*. They just kind of take it over. That is the tradition here, for everything that we do at this school, be it reading, writing, putting on a play, making puppets—whatever it is, the children take it over and make it their own.

Brian: And as for reward—sometimes the learning itself is the reward.

Kit: Yep. All kinds of good feelings go along with that.

 ## Love and Work

Zakiyyah is upset, in tears, a sad expression on her face.

"Why is she crying?" Izzy asks Kit.

"It's her feelings," Kit says. "It's okay. Everyone has them."

Chloe is talking earnestly to Zakiyyah, explaining something important. Zakiyyah listens, her eyes full of tears, gazing over Chloe's shoulder out through the window at the world outside.

Erin has gotten a book from the shelves and she sits down on the sofa next to Zakiyyah and begins reading it to her. Zakiyyah settles into the soft cushions.

They are in the Younger Group library space. Ben G starts to go in there but Kit shoos him away. She tells him, "This is Erin and Zakiyyah's space right now."

On the sofa by the door, Taylor is reading a book he has chosen from the library, *Matilda* by Roald Dahl. He's sprawled out over the end of the sofa, intent on his reading. Indy sits down next to him with a child's picture book, *One Lonely Sea Horse.* In it are sea animals made of fruits and vegetables — "food sculptures," Indy says. Taylor yawns, stretches, looks over at Indy's book. Indy asks him to read a word for him, and Taylor does. It's *oyster.*

At the little round table, Kit is working with Hue. She's finishing putting together a Little Book. Hue is very tan, very strong and healthy looking, her teeth bright white when she smiles. "I can," she is saying, responding to something Kit has said.

At a table by the window, three children are reading with Ren. Ursi and Hypatia are in the loft, reading a book together. Izzy and Christina are sitting side by side at a study table, each reading a book. Chloe and Lucy are in the pioneer kitchen, setting up something on the woodstove. The whole room is quiet, comfortable, busy with work . . .

"Kit, I've been helping Brecon," Ben G says, showing her the book they read together.

"I saw you," Kit says. She raises her voice a little, so everyone can hear her: "I've been seeing a lot of helping today."

Now it's time to shift to new work. Kit calls out the new learning tasks — working in folders, making Little Books, doing special work with reading. The children know what to do. Quickly they move around the room, from one workplace to another. It takes about a half-minute; then the room once again is quiet, busy with work . . .

Kit sits down on the sofa with Max, to do some special work on reading. They're sitting side by side, close to each other, comfortable on the sofa.

"Tell me your vowel sounds," Kit begins. "Let me hear *a*."

Max makes *a* sounds.

"Now," Kit says, "What word can you think of that's got an *a* sound?"

Max thinks for a moment. He smiles at Kit.

"Max!" he says.

Kit is delighted. She laughs out loud.

"*Max*," she says. "Yes! What a good one to choose!"

They begin to read a story that has a lot of *a* words in it. Kit holds the book open so Max can see it.

Max's task is to focus on the words, read them, know what they mean. He struggles at first.

"Are you seeing this?" Kit says, pointing to something in the first set of sentences.

Max reads, haltingly.

Granny had a nap. The cat had a nap. The rat sat.

"Good," Kit says.

The rat past the cat. The cat ran. The cat ran and ran. The rat and cat ran.

Max hesitates, struggles, stops in confusion. Kit

says, gently, "Pay attention to the space right there in between."

Max reads, "The rat ran," then corrects himself: "No, the *cat* ran."

"Good," Kit says.

Max is working hard; this is difficult for him, and he is exerting great effort, focusing his attention on the details of his task. And yet he is relaxed, and seems confident. He smiles from time to time. He is a sweet child.

Granny had a trap. Can Granny trap the rat? The rat ran past the trap.

Kit says, "When do you see the question mark?"

Max: "I didn't really see it—I saw it coming."

Kit: "Good thinking! You saw it coming."

The sad cat sat.

Max misreads the sentence. Kit says, "Are you

kind of jumping ahead, like this?" She points to something on the page. "Try it again."

Max tries, stops, shakes his head. He stares at the words but cannot read them.

Kit says, "Try it one more time."

The sad cat sat. The rat had a nap. The cat sat and sat.

"Good job," Kit says. "Let's take a break Go get a drink of water now. Then come back and we'll read some more."

Max runs off to the water fountain in the hall.

Christina, sitting at the round table nearby, has been closely watching Kit's work with Max. She might be a teacher someday.

Ursi begins telling Christina about the story she's writing for her Little Book: "There's this *family,* and they're crossing the *Mississippi,* right? And there's no *bridge . . .*"

Ursi's excited, her green eyes flashing as she talks. "Think that will be a good story?"

Christina nods. She's steady at her work.

Miri, Morgan's mother, is helping out in the Younger Group today. She sits down at the table with Ursi and Christina.

"Oh look at how many words you've written, Christina!" Miri says.

Ursi tells Miri about her story: "It's about a *family,* they've got to get across the Mississippi, and there's this *flood . . .*"

"Cool," Miri says. "They cross the Mississippi River? That's awesome . . ."

Kit and Max complete their work. Kit stands up and says, so all can hear: "Okay, YG, you can stop working now. Have some free time."

Someone starts chanting in a rhythmic sing-song, "Free time, free time, free time," and other children pick it up, and it's floating around the room as the children put their work away . . .

"Isn't it computer time, too?" Morgan says to Kit.

"It's free time," Kit says.

"I know," Morgan says, "but don't some people have computer time now?"

"Well, I dunno," says Kit, gazing out the wall of windows. "It's a pretty nice day out there . . ."

Soon everyone has gone outside, and the room is empty — except for Zakiyyah, who is lying on the rug in the center of the room. She is resting. Kit kneels and whispers something to her. Liana comes in with a blanket she has gotten from Didi. Carefully Liana covers Zakiyyah with the blanket, and then lightly touches her hand.

Liana goes outside to play. The room is very quiet now. Kit is sitting in her rocking chair, relaxing for a moment, and watching over Zakiyyah, who has fallen gently asleep.

A Real Word

Jeanie shares a learning adventure:

The Kindergarten children are a group of strong individuals. Their interests are diverse and their learning styles varied. There are master builders of marble tracks, geologists who can spot a good rock from incredible distances, experts on the tire swing, conversational wizards, gifted dancers and painters. And yet one love unites them all. They are lovers of words, tellers of tales, students of stories. So it is no wonder that I have a room full of children looking hard at letters and contemplating reading.

We have a Helper Chart in our room. It tells the children what their job is each day and who their working partner will be. And so they began their reading with their names.

Some names were easy.

"Olivia. That's the one that begins with O."

"Miles. That begins like Mom."

"Gracie. She's the only one that begins with G."

"Remember? Jesse's got a J," they reminded each other as they worked to read the Helper Chart.

Reading by initial letter was an easy challenge for these children. They had discovered reading strategy number one.

But then they found Lena and Landon. Two L's. Their first strategy no longer worked; they needed another. After contemplating the two names for some time, one child said, "Oh, I see. Landon is long and Lena is short."

A second strategy discovered: Sometimes you can recognize a word by its size and shape.

Next were the words Sam and Samantha. Sam helped us right away.

"I've got the shortest name in the whole class," he said. "S-A-M. That's all. Just three. And Samantha is real long because she's got Sam and antha." Their logic held.

Then they were faced with Sophie and Saskia. They counted the letters in each name.

"One, two, three, four, five, six. They are the same," they said, puzzled.

"They both have the same numbers of letters," I said. "Is there any way they are different?"

The children looked hard.

Finally one said, "There's an 'e' at the end of one. That must be Sophi-e."

"Hey! The other one has an 'a' at the end. They are different."

"But they both have 'i'," added another child.

"Yeah," countered another, "but all the other letters are different."

A new truth emerged. You can't always tell what a word is by the first letter; you can't always tell by its size. You have to look at all of the letters in a word.

For several days I found clusters of children sitting by the helper chart practicing writing names. They practiced over and over until they could read each name and their knowledge was complete.

A few days later a group of children sat at the table writing. Testing a new theory, one child began to string letters together and asked me, "What word is this, Jeanie?"

I looked at the long line of random consonants. I said, "When you put letters together they don't always make a word, but you can always read them."

Then I phonetically read the collection of letters. Laughter rang out around the table.

"What does that mean?" they asked.

"I've never heard that word before," I admitted. "What do you think it means?"

"It's something to eat," said one child.

"And it doesn't taste very good," said another.

"I think it's Russian," giggled another.

The game continued until one child wrote B-O-B.

"What's that?" she asked.

"Bob," I said.

She worked hard and put her book on the rocking chair to be read to the group at story time. When I picked up her book to read it, she said, "I can read it, too. The title of this book is *Bob Snores*."

And indeed every page was filled with the word Bob and a long series of zzzzzzzzzz snores. We all laughed.

The next day a friend also wrote a *Bob Snores* book and read it. The book turned into a series of books, and we read them for days . . . until someone asked, "Isn't he ever going to wake up?"

The original author pondered the question. The next day, she could hardly contain herself until we read her book. The next to the last page said just "BOB."

"My goodness, " I said. "I think Bob woke up. What do you think he is going to do?"

"Turn the page! Turn the page!" cried the author, hopping excitedly from one foot to another.

Slowly I turned the page. It said "BOB zzzzzzzzzzzzzz." The children burst into giggles at her joke.

And the *Bob Snores* series ended.

There was a hush around the table. Everyone leaned in to see.

"You wrote a real word," they said. They studied the letters and how the word was written.

For weeks the children had been drawing stories in blank books, and I had written their words for them. The next day the same child who had written "Bob" announced, "I can write my own book. You don't have to help me."

On "F" day, we drew and graphed our Favorite Foods. Pictures on the graph seemed incomplete, and the children began writing the names of their favorite foods as well. They worked together to spell the words they needed and said, "There! Now that looks right."

At quiet time now, instead of choosing toys on the rug, children are always in the library looking at books, discussing what they see, telling stories from the pictures . . .

Philosophers

Older Groupers, in conversation:

Stefan: You know what? The universe just goes on and on, you can't really know what it is or why it is. It drives you crazy just to be thinking about it

Jesse: I think about it . . .

Stefan: Like, why did we come to this planet? Why do we exist?

Jesse: What I really think about is—when I die, what will happen?"

Crystal: Another life!

Jesse: What I know, or think I know, is—it doesn't end.

Don *(facilitating)*: Some people who have been near death say they experienced a wonderful sense of well-being, of peace and love and harmony with all things in the universe.

Stefan: Wow!

Marlee: I wonder if bad people have that, after they die? I think they do.

Ryder: Yes. Definitely.

Claire: I agree.

Stefan: Bad people, you can't really blame them. Like, a bad person, maybe his grandfather, and his grandfather before him and all, going back eight hundred years—maybe one of his ancestors hated life, and he inherited all that. So it's not his fault.

Jesse: Can we really do things we hate?

Stefan: People do things they hate for money. Like, they work so hard to get it.

Ryder: Taxes! I *hate* taxes.

Don: What else do you guys hate?

[Pause.]

Claire: I hate it when people ignore me.

Jesse: I hate it when people agree, but really they don't agree, they just pretend they do.

Crystal: Like us?

Jesse: No. No, this group is different.

Stefan: Money's just not worth it. I mean, what *is* money? Why do people want it so bad? It's like, we go to school so we can get a job, so we can work to get money, so we can buy food and stuff. It's crazy. Why don't we just *share* the food? Why don't we—

Marlee: Because people are *afraid.*

Stefan: —just share *everything*? We could all just *help* each other. Just make sure everyone has *enough.* Then people wouldn't have to work, so they wouldn't need a job, and so they wouldn't need money. People would just *live.*

Claire: How would anybody learn? How would they know how to write and read? You need a teacher. That's a job.

Jesse: Not everybody uses money. Half of Africa doesn't use money.

Don: I once knew a man who didn't use money. He built his own house, raised his own food. Never went to the store.

Ryder: Oh, that's awesome!

Jesse: Cool.

Stefan: Tight.

Don: What are people afraid of, Marlee?

Marlee: They're afraid of everything 'cause they think it's something, but it's nothing.

Stefan: What if you had everything you wanted— would you be happy?

Ryder: Oh, sure! Good luck.

Jesse: No.

Crystal: Why not?

Jesse: Because you'd have no companions. You'd be above everyone else.

Stefan: If you could have everything you wanted, you could have all the friends you wanted.

Jesse: Yeah, but they'd be fake friends.

Don: I wonder, do we have enough of what we *really* want?

Marlee: The trouble is, we don't have enough of what we *don't* want.

Stefan: If you could make one law for everyone,

what would it be?

Ryder: Everything is free.

Crystal: Get rid of TV.

Jesse: Yeah, I watch too much TV.

Marlee: Me too, I watch it too much.

Stefan: I don't have TV.

Jesse: Whenever I watch too much TV, I feel bad. I feel guilty. I wish I hadn't done it.

Ryder: I watch the news every morning.

Crystal: I watch *Animal Planet.*

Ryder: *Animal Planet*—*yes.*

Don: One law?

Stefan: No cars.

Claire: No way! You've *got* to have cars. How could people get anyplace?

Jesse: They could walk, Claire.

Claire: I mean, to faraway places.

Jesse: Like—?

Claire: Like California.

Jesse: People rode horses to California before there were cars.

Ryder: Well, that's gross abuse of the horse!

Crystal: Yeah, how'd you like to carry someone on your back all the way to California?

Marlee: She's right. It wouldn't be fair to the horse.

Claire: You've got to have *cars.* People aren't going to give up their *cars.*

Jesse: They're going to have to, or they won't be able to breathe.

Stefan: There are cars that can run on water.

Claire: There are hyrdogen cars.

Stefan: There's a car in town that runs on french fry oil or something.

Ryder: The veggie car! Let's hear it for the veggie car!

Crystal: You know what? We're going to do all this junk to save the planet, and then the world's going to blow up.

Ryder: Save the planet? Listen, the planet is already *screwed.* Like, it's going to be *destroyed.* There's nothing can be done about it.

Jesse: We are all of us destroying the world.

Crystal: After we destroy the world, *then* the new cars will come out. Too late!

Stefan: It's like, you guys have no hope. Remember that time I came home and I couldn't see anybody, anywhere? And I was sure everybody was dead, that everything was destroyed. And then I saw my friend Luke was there, and I knew it wasn't true.

Don: Are you saying the planet will survive, life will go on, it'll all work out?

Stefan: Yeah, I think it'll all work out. I do, yes. I mean, I've never known it not to.

Affirmation

The child must know it's all right

to be who you are.

—Jeanie Felker

Jeanie Felker, the Kindergarten teacher of the Antioch School, is small, trim, graceful; she is perceptive, insightful, poetic, determined. As she goes about her day at the school Jeanie smiles and laughs a lot, her voice is soft and melodious, and her manner is unfailingly pleasant, yet there is about her a sense of being engaged in a deeply serious, purposeful task. To serve the cause of children is her calling, her life's work. You sense that when the occasion demands she is a fierce defender of the rights of a child.

Jeanie brings her own childhood experience to her work as a teacher. She can be very much like a child herself, given to spontaneous flights of joy and laughter, pure delight in simple play. She knows what it's like to be a child. And she knows what's at stake for children growing up, how important the nature of their childhood is. She knows this as one who had a full, rich childhood; then lost it.

We lived in a small town in Illinois. There were two of us children in the family, my sister and me. We had a kind of Fifties ideal childhood—we lived in a real neighborhood, we played with kids of all different ages, we knew all the families along the street. We played with tin cans in the alley, we made mud pies, we played cowboys. We tried to see if we could fly by jumping off the roof of the woodshed. A real childhood! I was fortunate to have it.

But it ended when I was ten. We moved to Chicago. For me, it was like going from paradise to hell. We moved to a suburb, a planned community, an "ideal utopia"—but there were no trees. The place was called Park Forest and there were *no trees*. I felt like I had lost my whole environment, all that I had known and cared about . . . It felt like I had lost my childhood.

Jeanie remembers herself as a child:

I would spend hours outside by myself, lolling in the grass, looking at bugs, sitting in the trees . . . I had a best friend. She was an extrovert. I was introverted. We were inseparable. She had allergies so bad sometimes she couldn't hear. When her ears would get stopped up, I would be her ears for her.

I thought there was a witch under my bed. I was terribly afraid of it, you know. At night I'd run into the room and jump in the bed real fast—I was afraid if I just walked, the witch would grab my foot and pull me under the bed . . .

Sometimes in the Kindergarten, I tell the children about the witch. They know! They recognize it. I tell them about the time I got my courage up to reach down and put my hand over the edge of the bed. *What happened?* they say. I look at them for a moment, and I say, *Nothing!* And they laugh and laugh and laugh!

Jeanie laughs too as she tells this. She rolls her head back and laughs wholeheartedly. "They laugh because they *know*," she says of the children. "They know all about it!"

In her work as a teacher, Jeanie focuses her energy on *seeing the child*—perceiving each child's distinctive, defining qualities of character and personality; understanding, respecting and accepting the child. "There is something about being seen, being truly known by others, that has always seemed to me to be a very basic human need," Jeanie says. "To me, it is the source of trust in others, of self-acceptance, of growth. It is the very place where learning—learn-

ing of all kinds—can take root and flourish."

Seeing the child, the teacher can build with the child a relationship based in *trust*. The child learns to trust the teacher to know her, to see her as she is; then the child can begin to see herself—to learn who she is, and to accept herself for who she is. She learns to trust herself.

"The child must know it's all right to be who you are," Jeanie says. Only then can a child accept others for who they are, and trust them, and feel trusted and accepted.

As an environment of trust is being created in the Kindergarten, the children themselves put it into practice, in their own ways. They do this moment to moment, day by day in the life of the Kindergarten. Here is one such moment, recalled by Jeanie:

It was during playtime one day. Zakiyah, a wonderful child with great social skills, who sometimes self-dramatizes, withdrew from the group. She began crying sadly, saying "No one will play with me."

Morgan came up to her and said, "You can play with me." Zakiyah brightened. "Okay," she said, and they began to play. Just like that.

Morgan said, "You know, you're like my little brother. He cries until he gets his way. Then he stops crying.'"

Zakiyah kind of chuckled, and smiled to herself. They went on playing together.

They both knew it was true. Morgan said it kindly and gently. It was like saying, "I know you"—just an observation. So Zakiyah could just take it in. She could accept it. She could appreciate it—she had been truly seen, and it was all right.

Jeanie models trust for the children by her practice of affirmation. "You really know how to draw an elephant, Cecelia," she says, softly, as she moves quietly around the Kindergarten room. "You're knowing just what to do with that puzzle, Danny."

She bestows these affirmations many times throughout the day. They make up something like an ongoing conversation she has with the children, renewed and continuing day after day. She rarely tells the children what to do, or how to do something—she sees them as quite capable of making these determinations for themselves.

One day I asked her about what I thought I had seen, four Kindergarten boys expertly playing a game of chess. "What was that game they were playing?" I said. "It looked like chess."

"It *was* chess," Jeanie said. "*Their* chess. They play it their way. They make up their own rules. That's how it is with all the games we have. It's up to the children to figure out how they want to play them. When we have a new game and I open the box, I throw away the directions. They ask, 'How do we play this game?' I say to them, 'Well, what do you think? What do you suppose all those pieces are for?' And the children take it from there."

"Part of trusting a child," Jeanie said, "is to see the child as capable, to have confidence in the child, to trust them to be able to do what they need to do."

Jeanie's work with Liam, a new child in the Kindergarten, illuminates the workings of trust.

Liam was very inside himself at first, when school began. For Liam, it was a matter of learning to trust himself. That's why when I'd see him doing something I'd be sure to say to him, "Liam, you know just what to do."

One day at lunch Liam came up to me and said, "Could you open this cheese?" I said to him, "Can you think of something you could use for opening it?" Liam thought for a moment, and said, "Scissors." I said to him, "I'll bet that will work." Then I said, "I was pretty sure you'd know how to do it."

Jeanie enacts this process again and again each day with each of the children in the Kindergarten. "It's like a dance," she said. "You want to be careful that you don't fill in for the children what the children can fill in for themselves. You trust them to have the capability to fill it in. They understand that

you see them as competent, capable, problem-solving. Trust comes from this. Strength comes from this."

Liam gained strength enough to take a risk, Jeanie said. "Liam needed to be able to trust that he could be himself. To just be himself. That he could be angry, and it would be all right. That he could be wrong—that he could break a rule—and it would be all right."

One day he did break a rule. Everyone is supposed to come in from the play-yard for storytime. On this day Liam didn't come.

"And that was all right," Jeanie said. "I didn't go get him. I trusted Liam to decide what was best for him in that moment. Liam *loves* nature; he was outside, and I am sure he made good use of the time he was out there. So I affirmed that, by my reaction. I wanted him to know that it was all right."

Later, Jeanie said to Liam, "You missed the story. I missed you being there. I like reading to you."

Jeanie explained: "Now if Liam started missing a lot of storytimes, I might go get him, because learning to be a member of the group is important. I might say to him: 'It's hard for me if I have to come get you. Everybody's together and waiting for the story. I need your help. Come join us, so we can all be together.' "

So we can all be together. The goal in Jeanie's Kindergarten—and the goal throughout the school—is that each child, and all the children together as members of the group, will be truly seen, and will truly see each other, creating a whole-group relationship grounded in trust. "Once that's in place," Jeanie said, "learning explodes."

It happens gradually, day by day, child by child. Along with Jeanie's affirmations of each child, the children are alert witnesses to Jeanie's affirmation of *all* the children in the group. When Jeanie affirms Cecelia's ability to draw, all the other children hear this; and when Danny's puzzle-solving prowess is affirmed, everyone in the group is aware of it. So the children come to know each of the other children in their group as capable people, worthy of respect—worthy of trust. As their trust in each other deepens and grows, so does their trust in themselves. In this powerful, all-connecting way, the children's sense of trust flows freely within each child and within them all together. This is the *group*.

In the best sense, it is the children themselves who make this happen. Jeanie encourages it, supports it, guides it; but it is the children who *do* it. And for that, they must have the freedom—free choice, free play, free time—to discover and explore their own ways of doing it.

That's why Jeanie throws away the instructions on how to play chess. Or when choosing a plastic model skeleton for the children to use in their study of the human body, Jeanie chose a disassembled skeleton, so the children could take the hundred-plus pieces and figure out for themselves how to put the body together.

The Kindergarten room itself serves the children in this same free spirit. Jeanie made this delightfully clear one day when she took me on a tour of the room.

She showed me the loft: "This is where the children act their first plays, write their first stories . . . They feel free to make mistakes up here."

She showed me the little room under the loft. "This is our library," she said. "A lot of writing and reading goes on in here. And a lot of dramatic play, too. The children put on skits and plays using the library and the loft. They'll have families living in both places, one family upstairs in the loft and the other family downstairs in the library, and everybody's going up the stairs and coming down the stairs, moving around from family to family . . .

"And," Jeanie said, "sometimes this room is a body of water. Quite often it turns into the ocean, for some reason. Maybe it's because of the windows. You can jump through the windows into the ocean and swim."

We stepped inside the little room.

"You see children swimming in here," Jeanie said. "They're on their bellies on the floor and they're just swimming away."

Jeanie started doing crab strokes, standing there in the little room.

"They're swimming and they're coming up to breathe, raising their heads up out of the water, gulping for air."

Jeanie raised her head up and gulped for air.

"So," she said, "this little room under the loft"—big smile—"is a library, it's a theater, and it's a body of water."

Her big smile signified the pleasure Jeanie takes in knowing the children use their space so well.

"And," she said, "it's a quiet place, too. The children come in here when they want to be quiet."

"They want to be quiet sometimes?"

Jeanie's expression changed. She looked at me curiously, as if wondering if I were a visitor from Mars.

"Don," she said, "what do you think? These kids are in here with thirteen other people, six hours every day. That's an *intense* amount of people to be interacting with. How would you feel? Wouldn't you want some quiet time?"

"I'd *need* quiet time," I said.

"That's right," Jeanie said, turning abruptly, leading me out of the little room. "We *all* need quiet time."

In the Antioch School parents' handbook, Jeanie describes some of the ways the children learn—naturally, by experience—the essential principles of mathematics, as they go about their days in the Kindergarten room. Climbing the stairs into the loft, she says, the children "change perspectives on the world." Entering the tiny library space, the children are in a place where "two people fill up the whole world."

Many of the ways we use math come from the children's questions. "How high is our ceiling?" We try to estimate. Our answers run from "fifteen feet one inch" to "about as high as a kite when you first start to fly it." We measure it then.

Sometimes math grows out of the children's play. Sometimes when they run across the play-yard I ask, "How big did I look when you were over there?"

"About as big as an ant standing on its hind legs."

"Can you make me look smaller?"

They take off across the play-yard again and run back yelling: "We did it! You were just the dot above an I."

We also use our bodies, hands and feet to measure. "Jeanie, how far can a jackrabbit jump?" We research the question. Measuring carefully, we see how far we can jump. Then we see how many times we would have to jump before we could go as far as the jackrabbit does in one hop.

One spring day we sat in a circle on the rug to plan our Easter Egg hunt. The kids decided to count to see if everyone was there. Counting in a circle was just too funny—soon we had 109 Kindergartners sitting on the rug. "We couldn't stop," one child said. "Numbers are really fun!"

The learning goals Jeanie has for her Kindergarten children suggest the special nature of her teaching:

To support a sense of connectedness to the Earth.

To teach caregiving as an important part of everyone's life.

To provide the children with opportunities to conquer their physical fears (heights, water, small spaces), always at their own speed.

To help children "listen to their bodies." To provide children with opportunities to use their bodies expressively through creative movement and pantomime so they can see that bodies have a language, too.

To reinforce what children seem to instinctively know, that bodies are more than a container for our minds, that bodies can help us acquire knowledge and bring us joy.

To help children realize that they are part of a world shared by other living creatures of equal importance.

To help children learn caring, and that there are creatures smaller than they whose existence depends on their benevolence.

To help children learn that all of life is a cycle, and to give them opportunities to see that over and over again.

 Kindergarten Rules

1. Don't hit. Just use words.
2. Don't kick. Just say what you want.
3. Don't push. Take turns.
4. Be kind to spiders.
5. Don't grab the juice pitcher.
   Say, "Please pass the juice."
6. Don't call people names.
   Just use their real name.
7. If you want seconds at snack,
   don't take all the crackers.
8. Don't yell at the guinea pig.
   Zippity likes gentle voices.
9. Don't hit the guinea pig cage.
   Animals get scared too.
10. Listen to your friends.
11. Don't make too much rules.

Quiet Time

In the Kindergarten, it is Quiet Time.

Danny is talking with Oona in the little room under the loft.

Lying sprawled out on the carpet in the middle of the room are Morgan and Hypatia, putting together a jigsaw puzzle. Hypatia is talking earnestly about something that is worrying her. "Really," she says, "I just don't know what to *do*."

She makes an exaggerated gesture signifying dilemma, shrugging her shoulders and holding her hands out, palms up. As she talks she moves the puzzle's pieces around, looking for ones that fit.

"Why don't you have a meeting with her?" Morgan says.

Hypatia says, "She's my best friend and she's my neighbor." A silent pause. Then: "She would be extra mad."

Francesca is lying down by herself on the little mattress in the space under the stairs to the loft. This is a place to be by yourself, for moments when you want to be alone. It's like a tiny room, and seems very private, but there is nothing separating it from the main part of the Kindergarten room. Francesca, lying on her side with a blanket, can see everyone and everyone can see her; and yet she is alone, too, in her own space. She is catnapping, drifting in and out of shallow sleep.

She's resting.

Emma Liz wanders down the stairs from the loft and stands at the bottom, crying softly. "Oh, Emma, you sound so sad," Jeanie says from her chair at the little table near the window.

Silence from Emma.

"Come here, talk to me," Jeanie says to her. "What makes you feel so sad?"

"They're playing pickup sticks and they won't let me play," Emma says.

"Oh, and you wanted to play pickup sticks, too."

Azsa says, "She wants to go pee-pee, too."

Jeanie sits with Emma Liz at the little table, in silence . . .

Zakiyah is playing quietly with a family of small rubber animals, by herself. Emma Rose and Oona are in the little room under the stairs, playing together. Anna is on the floor near the door with Cece and Azsa. They have a jigsaw puzzle's pieces spread out around them.

Emma Liz now has gone into the little room. Sounds of her crying are heard.

Azsa says, "Not again! What's happening now?" She strides purposefully into the little room.

Emma Liz: "I can't *play*."

Azsa: "Why?"

Emma Liz: "I can't play with *anybody*." She cries.

Azsa turns on the light in the little room. She takes some jigsaw puzzle pieces and shows Emma how they fit together.

Emma Liz stops crying.

Azsa: "See? It's not so hard. Stop crying now." She turns off the light, and leaves the little room . . .

Brecon comes up to Jeanie, his body language a complaint. He says, "Nobody's helping me."

Jeanie says, matter-of-factly: "You told people you didn't need any help. That's why they aren't helping you."

Brecon takes this in. He stands there, thinking it over.

Azsa walks up.

"Azsa's here," Jeanie says. "Azsa will help you."

And Azsa does; she helps Brecon sweep up some cracker crumbs from under the snack table.

Soon they are finished, and Azsa goes back to the other side of the room. Brecon is alone again.

Danny, who has been watching all of what's been happening, comes over to Brecon. "I'll play with you," Danny says.

Oona, in the little room under the loft playing

"Everybody can play!" Oona says.

But Anna remains with the jigsaw puzzle, working on it intently by herself.

Zakiyah and Francesca emerge from the corner of the room where they have been playing together. They've been reading a book by looking at the pictures and creating words to fit them. Now they stand side by side in the middle of the room, looking around and blinking their eyes in what appears to be wonder, as if they are seeing the room for the very first time . . .

The four boys are playing chess now, lying on the floor in a circle around the chessboard: Danny, Liam, Morgan, Brecon. They look like little old men sitting around a poker table, settled calmly into the game, waiting patiently for each other to make a move. They seem to have been doing this all their lives. Their conversation—idle chatter between moves—is about watching videos, going shopping at Kroger's, reading a Harry Potter book.

Suddenly, Liam turns to Danny and says, "Danny, some day you're going to have to leave. You're too loud."

Danny doesn't look at him. His eyes stay on the chess board. He says, speaking slowly, clearly and a little bit loudly: "I'm not loud." He says this as a statement of fact. He's not debating the matter; he's not even discussing it. He's just stating a fact.

And the chess game goes on. The four boys are oblivious to all the activity going on around them—the dynamic, constant, purposeful movement, the forming and re-forming of personal relationships, the play and the work and the resting from work . . .

In the midst of it all, the boys remain engrossed in their game. All eyes are on the chessboard.

They make their moves slowly, carefully, saying little. Old men!

with Emma Rose, calls out to Emma Liz, who is sitting alone in the space under the stairs: "Emma Liz, you can play."

Emma Liz says, "Okay!" Her face brightens and she goes quickly, happily into the little room to play with Oona and Emma Rose.

A few moments later, Azsa announces: "I'm going to play with Oona," and she goes into the little room, leaving Cece and Anna behind on the floor, still playing with their jigsaw puzzle.

Cece calls out, "Oona, can I play with you?"

"Yes," Oona says, and Cece goes into the little room.

To Make a Better World

The Kindergartners in action, described by Jeanie:

Thoughtful, gentle Emma Rose told us at our Morning Meeting that her mother had read her an article from the newspaper about the Boy Scouts collecting food for people in need.

"I wanted to collect food from my family," she said, "but there's not much of us. So I thought maybe we could collect food here at school."

Part of the group was supportive, part of the group was skeptical.

"Is it true, Jeanie, that not everybody has food?"

I asked the group: "What do you know?"

Several children said they were sure it was true that some people were poor and couldn't buy food.

One child added, "I know that in Africa some children don't have enough food or water, and that is really sad."

Another child said, "I think everybody has food, because you can't be alive without food."

"But not everybody has *enough* food," someone said. "Some people are hungry. And that doesn't feel good."

Everybody agreed that being hungry wasn't a comfortable feeling.

"There aren't very many of us," said a child.

"Yes there are," said Emma Rose.

"No there aren't," countered the other child.

"Let's count," suggested a neutral party.

The children counted themselves, slowly and methodically.

"Thirteen of us. That's not enough to feed a lot of people."

The conversation lagged. I suggested they think about it and see if they could find a way to solve the problem.

We went on with our day, and no one mentioned the proposed project again.

The next day Emma Rose said, in her gently insistent way: "I was just wondering when we were going to start on my idea about collecting food."

"We can't," someone said. "There's not enough of us."

"Unless," one child mused, "unless we ask the kids in the Nursery."

"And the Younger Group," added another child.

"And our swimming partners," suggested another.

"Let's ask the whole school! *That* will be enough," crowed another child.

And so it began.

The children wrote the following letter to the whole school:

Dear People,

We want to give people food that don't have some because they are hungry. It doesn't feel good to be hungry. Please bring food in boxes, cans or bottles to the Kindergarten room and we'll take it to hungry people.

Love,

The Kindergarten

Each of the children signed the letter.

Then they made a plan for distributing the letter. Some children thought we should send a letter to each group's room. Others thought we should put a letter in each family's mailbox. They decided to do both.

"How many letters will we need?" I asked. One group counted classrooms, another counted mailboxes. We needed 75 letters. One child took our letter to Didi's office and made 75 copies.

Three children went to deliver the letters to the classrooms.

Another child started stuffing the mailboxes; she successfully reached the lowest row of mailboxes and then said, "I can't reach any higher. I need Oona. She is tall."

She scampered down the hall and returned with her friend. Oona could reach all of the mailboxes in

fully labeled. Some children read labels and found the word they needed. Their bags read *pasta, vegetables, soup.*

Other children worked together sounding out words. Their bags read *frut, bens, dzrts.*

The rest of the afternoon was spent sorting the food and deciding into which bags the food should go.

Days passed, and the bags grew fuller. As the children tried to lift the bags, someone said, "These bags are getting heavy. I wonder how much they weigh?"

The next day I brought my bathroom scale to school. We weighed the food and wrote the weight on each bag.

The children would have liked to send the food to the hungry people of Africa, but I had to confess I didn't know how to do that. I told them that Anna's mother knew of a place in Xenia where we could take the food. They would let us put the food we brought on the shelves ourselves.

On our scheduled day, we took our food to the Food Pantry in Xenia. We were greeted by a wonderful woman who said, "First, we need to sort the food that you brought."

"We've already done that—see?" the Kindergartners proudly pointed to the bags.

Then they worked diligently, putting the food on tables and carrying it to the proper shelves.

A week later, we received a letter from the Food Pantry thanking us. The letter said:

Dear Children of the Antioch School,

Your donation of food was greatly appreciated. We would also like to thank the students for helping stock the shelves at the pantry. It is always heartwarming for us to find this kind of spirit and caring in the youth of today. It is our hope that these feelings, taught when young, will carry on into adulthood. Then, perhaps, the world will become a much better place for all. May God bless you!

As I read the letter to the children, they gently reached out and hugged each other.

the second row, but the top row was too high even for her.

"A chair!" her shorter friend exclaimed. "That will work."

And it did.

Soon all of the mailboxes were filled . . .

Bags of food, generously donated by our school families, began to arrive. At first, the children were satisfied just letting the bags of food accumulate. But then they became curious about what was inside each bag.

"We should sort the food," one child suggested. "That way, when we take it in, they'll know just what we are giving them."

Out came the paper bags. Each bag was care-

The Decision

On the Kindergarten floor the children have created a big yellow square. It covers the corner of the room where they meet for story time. From sheets of bright yellow construction paper they cut out many little squares—there must be a hundred of them—and carefully arranged them, jigsaw puzzle style, to make the one big square. It's a nice piece of work, and the children are pleased with it.

But when Brian comes to take them outside to build fairy houses, the children are so excited—Hypatia is singing, "Oh I *love love love* to build fairy houses!"—they walk on the square, messing it up. Now the little squares are tattered and scattered about; the big square is not square anymore.

"We have got to clean it up," Asa announces to the group. They have assembled in a circle around Brian and Jeanie.

"Just leave it," says Annie. She's eager to go outside.

"Yeah, just leave it," says Anna W.

Gabriel feels it should be cleaned up, and so does Anna M.

"I can clean it up when we get back," Asa says. "I will do that."

"I think we all should do it," Anna M says.

Around the circle the children murmur agreement; everyone should clean it up, not just Asa. But some of the children say that no one needs to clean it up—just leave it like it is.

"Well," Jeanie says, "it looks like we have a problem to solve."

The children solemnly nod in agreement.

"How are we going to decide?" Jeanie says.

One of the children says, "Let's take a vote."

They do, raising their hands to vote for either cleaning it up or leaving it.

The vote is indecisive. Some of the children voted for both options, some voted for neither. And after the vote some who voted one way say they think they've changed their minds.

They take another vote, and the same thing happens.

The children are bewildered, confused. There's an unhappy hubbub around the circle.

"Actually," Francesca says, raising her voice—the group grows quiet—"I don't care."

Why don't they just make a random choice, she says. They could write "clean it up" on one piece of paper, write "leave it" on another piece of paper, put the two pieces of paper in a sack, and have someone reach in the sack and pick one of them out. They'll all read it together. Whatever it says, that's what they'll do.

The children mull this over.

Asa says, "To be *fair*, we need two people picking—one who wants to clean it up, and one who wants to leave it."

"We need *three* people picking," Gabriel says. "One who wants to clean it up, one who wants to leave it, and one who doesn't care. *That* would be fair."

"Yes!" some of the children say. But Anna M, speaking softly, says, "That's too many people picking," and everyone realizes she's right.

Francesca speaks again. "Here's a way we can do it. Everyone writes their name on a piece of paper. We put all the names in the sack. Then we pick one out. If it's the name of somebody who wants to clean it up, we clean it up. If it's the name of somebody who wants to leave it, we leave it."

There are low murmurs of uncertainty. Asa's face is cloudy.

Francesca clarifies. "Like, if it's Danny's name that's picked out of the sack, we clean it up, because Danny wants to clean it up. If it's Annie's name, we leave it, because Annie wants to leave it. And whoever picks has to be someone who doesn't care. They just close their eyes and pick one out."

"Francesca," Jeanie says from just outside the circle, "you're saying that everyone's name goes into the sack?"

Francesca affirms this. "Everyone writes their name—"

"That's a good idea!" someone says.

"—except the people who don't care."

Asa still is trying to speak.

"And," says Francesca, "the person who picks out the name is someone who doesn't care."

Now Asa is satisfied. "That's fair," he says.

Asa leads the procession to the table, where the children gather to write down their names . . .

The children put their names in a sack. Henry is the last to write his name. It's on a big piece of paper that Henry wads up so it will fit in the sack. He drops it in.

Francesca says, "Can I pick, since it was my idea?"

Everyone agrees. Francesca closes the sack, shakes it up, opens it, and picks out a name. It is Henry's.

All eyes go to him. This is a suspenseful moment. No one knows whether Henry wants to clean it up or leave it. The children are waiting anxiously for Henry to reveal where he stands. He takes his time. His eyes dart all around the circle before he answers.

"Leave it," Henry says.

"*No!*" Gabriel cries out, and he puts his head in his hands, and sinks to the floor.

Everyone else is somber, solemn, silent.

Asa sits staring into space. He says, slowly, in a quavering voice: "That makes me very angry!"

Jeanie is beside him. "Yes," she says, "it's hard not to get your way, isn't it?" She says this to him gently, and as a matter of fact.

 # Red, Red

The Kindergarten is having Color Days. Today is Red Day. The children wear red shirts and red socks, red pants and red ribbons, and they read red books, speak red words, think red thoughts . . .

And they paint red pictures. Their paintings are really *red*, richly red, the reds vivid and strong. Some of them are transcendently red, as red as the red rose in Georgia O'Keeffe's painting on the wall.

The children's paintings are on display in the hallway, so people passing by can see them. Each painting is carefully signed by the artist. Oona signs hers with the Os big and round:

OOna

Jeanie is dressed in red, surrounded by red-clad children.

"Isn't it *beautiful?*" Jeanie says. "We have so many *artists* in our group!."

Poets, too. In honor of Red Week, the children wrote a poem:

RED
Red, red
We see red!
Red as a watermelon, a flower and cherries
Red as juicy as strawberries
Red as a fish, a cardinal, our wagon
Red like our candles, cups and napkins
Red as sticky as masking tape
Red as hot as a fire flame
Red as red as a sore throat feels
Red as a monster and apple peels
Red, red
We see red!

Three Boys

Sitting together on the floor in the Kindergarten, playing a board game—it is "Green Eggs and Ham"—are Danny, Gabriel, and Alex. Gabriel is wearing an orange monkey around his neck.

Danny is taking several turns in a row, moving his token all around the board.

Gabriel: "Why do you keep taking turns?"

Danny doesn't answer. He keeps taking turns.

Alex to Danny: "That's not the way you play."

This has been going on for some time now.

Gabriel to Danny: "I want to play a game with-*out* you."

Danny: "Well, I'm going to play."

They tussle. Gabriel leans into Danny, Danny leans into Gabriel. They're pushing and pulling each other, trying to get control of the board.

Jeanie comes over, joins the group, speaks to the boys, listens.

Danny: "Well, I wanted to play."

Gabriel: "Well, I—" Upset and flustered, he cannot articulate his position.

Jeanie speaks softly to them. They restart their game. She stays and watches.

Danny again takes several turns in a row, moving his token in quick jumps forward.

Gabriel objects. "That's not the way you play, Danny!"

"Did you hear him, Danny?" Jeanie says. Her voice is just above a whisper.

Alex starts explaining the rules, reviewing the way to take turns. "It's my turn now, Danny," Alex says.

But Danny takes the turn. Gabriel grabs Danny's token, Danny grabs it back.

"Don't do that!" Danny says.

Jeanie leans in between the boys. She says, "Danny. Gabriel."

Alex resumes his review of the rules, explaining them again to Danny and Gabriel, as if this is a brand new game they've never played before. "That's how the game goes," Alex says, brightly. "Now it's my turn, Danny."

Alex takes his turn, demonstrating how to do it properly: he spins the arrow, announces the number the arrow points to—"Three"—and moves his token three squares forward.

"How do you win?" Danny says.

Alex tells him.

Danny says, shaking his head firmly: "No."

Alex: "That's what the rules say."

Danny: "No."

Danny begins to take a turn. When he moves his token, Gabriel objects.

Gabriel: "You were on 6."

Danny: "No."

Gabriel: "You were on 6, Danny!"

Danny: "No. No."

Danny's voice is quiet, flat, definite. Mostly he keeps his eyes on the board. He seems calm. Gabriel is frustrated, stressed, tense. Alex is alert, on task, intent on keeping the game going.

Alex says, pointing to a place on the board: "You go there, Danny."

Danny: "No. No, I don't, because—"

Alex: "Actually—"

Gabriel: "I guess you're out of the game, Danny."

Danny: "No."

Alex: "Whatever. Let's just keep playing."

Danny moves his token. "I win."

Alex: "When you win, I still want to play the game."

Gabriel: "But that's not the way—"

Alex: "Actually, I think you go here."

Danny: "No."

Alex: "I think you do."

Gabriel: "Yes! You do."

Danny: "No."

Gabriel: "Last night we played soccer. We had fun."

Danny: "Playing soccer?"

Alex: "I got new soccer shoes."

Danny's voice rises: "You did? I should have been there. Damn!"

Alex's voice rises, too: "That's a bad word!"

Danny: "No. It's not."

Alex: "Yes, it is. My sister said so!"

Danny: "No."

Alex: "My sister said so."

Danny: "It's not true."

Alex: "Uh-*huh*. Yes it is. "

Danny: "No it isn't."

Alex: "Let's keep playing."

Gabriel: "My turn?"

Alex: "It is."

Danny takes the turn.

Danny: "I win."

Gabriel: "No you don't."

Danny: "Yes I do. I win."

Gabriel: "You're wrong!"

Danny: "No I'm not. I win."

Gabriel: "You're wrong. I am *sure*."

Danny: "No."

Gabriel: "You're definitely, definitely wrong."

Danny: "No, I'm not."

Gabriel: "You can't win the game. Only if you get *here* can you win the game." He points to a place on the board.

Gabriel takes his turn.

Alex takes his turn.

Danny takes his turn. "I win!"

Alex: "I still want to play the game."

Danny: "Yeah, me too."

Alex: "So let's keep on playing."

They do.

Gabriel, pointing to Alex: "I believe *him*."

A pause. The boys relax for a moment, and are quiet. They seem to be taking a time-out. They look around the room, shift their positions on the floor. They don't say anything . . .

They start to play again.

Alex, nodding toward Gabriel: "It's his turn."

Danny: "No."

Alex: "Actually—"

The Beautiful House

Jeanie and the children are at the little house on the play-yard. It has four walls and two windows and a peaked roof, about five or six feet high. Inside the little house there's room for maybe two tiny-sized kids. Today the Kindergartners are painting the little house, inside and out. They're just getting started.

Brian is working with them. He shows me the plan, created by the children in concert with Jeanie, who wrote it down on a big sheet of wallpaper:

Outside
1 wall brown with red hearts
1 wall brown with a green person
1 wall red, purple and orange blocks of color, yellow too
1 wall red

Inside
1 wall green with rainbows and clouds
1 wall rainbow stripes
1 wall purple
1 wall pink

Zakiyah is saying, "This is going to be the prettiest house in the world!"

But Oona is unhappy: "I don't want this brown brush. I want the red brush. I don't want—I want—" Jeanie goes off with Oona into the Art/Science Room.

Francesca daintily scrapes her brush clean.

Zakiyah has smeared some red paint on her *birkah*. "Excuse me," she says politely to Cecelia as she slides past her into the house. She's going to paint the inside.

Cecelia has spilled some paint on herself. "I'm painted red!"

Zakiyah calls out, "Brian, the house is turning green!"

"You mean red?"

"It's *green* in here."

Brian takes a look. "Wow, somebody's painted green in here," Brian says.

Zakiyah: "Somebody's going to *live* in this house!"

Hypatia: "It's so pretty!"

Brecon is saying, "How are you doing with the green, Liam?"

Brian: "How about here, somebody. We need to put some brown right here."

Brecon: "I want to do orange."

Jeanie and Oona come back to the little house. Jeanie says, "Oh the wall is almost brown!"

Zakiyah: "Yes, that wall is turning brown!"

Emma Rose announces: "Anna is very messy with that red." Emma is observing carefully everything that's going on, painting very little herself.

Brecon says, *"I'm* pretty messy."

Francesca: "I know."

Brecon: *"You're* not messy."

Francesca nods: "I used to paint"—she thinks for a moment, searching for the phrase—"very often."

Brecon gives her a quizzical look.

"I'm used to it," Francesca explains.

Cecelia says: "Look how beautiful this house is!"

Francesca: "When it's finished, then it will be beautiful."

Zakiyah says to Francesca: "Want to come inside?"

Francesca: "No."

She stays at the same spot, painting carefully, skillfully. Her work is smooth and neat.

Hypatia, laughing gaily, is saying in a sing-song voice: "I got paint on my dress, I got paint on my skin, I got paint in my *hair!* I'm messier than anyone here."

Emma Rose says, "That's because you've got

paint in your hair."

Jeanie says, "This is going to be a *beautiful* house. Oh yes! A *beautiful* house!" She really means it; Jeanie's *very* excited.

Hypatia: "I'm going to paint *brown.*" She says it *brow-unn.* "I don't want to get any more *red* on me."

Francesca: "Want to trade brushes, Hypatia?"

"Okay," Hypatia says, handing Francesca her brush. "But it's pretty messy."

Ren comes over to watch the proceedings.

Hypatia is happy to see him. "Ren, look! I've got red all over me. I've got red *here,* and *here,* and *here* . . ."

Ren takes a picture of Hypatia, then begins taking pictures of the house with the children all around it, painting.

Zakiyah, inside the house, exclaims: "It looks so *pretty* in here!"

She says it to herself, or perhaps to everyone— she says it to the world. And suddenly a chorus of children's voices fills the air with praise:

"It's a beautiful house!"

"It's so pretty!"

"It's the prettiest house in the world!"

Brecon spills some blue paint onto the ground. "I know what to do," he says. He kneels down and begins scooping cedar chips from the ground onto the puddle of spilled paint, covering it up. "This will take care of it."

Jeanie says, "You're knowing just what to do, Brecon."

Zakiyah emerges from inside the house. Her eyes are round and glowing as she gazes upon the little house. "It looks *so* beautiful!"

She says it *bee-you-ta-full!*

"Look, Jeanie, look how beautiful it is!"

Zakiyah's beautiful face, so full of light, softly framed by her blue *birkah,* speckled now with flecks of red.

Jeanie exclaims, "Oh yes, you are right, Zakiyah! It is so *beautiful.* It *is!*"

Jeanie seems thrilled. Her face lights up in genuine wonder as she looks at the children and the beautiful house.

She says, smiling at all the children: "When you people put all of your ideas together, you make a beautiful house!"

Zakiyah begins dancing a celebration dance, flailing her arms and wriggling around, singing, "Oh yes, oh yes, it is good to live in a beautiful house, oh yes it is . . ."

Hypatia and Cecelia and Anna go off from the house to play nearby in the sandpile, called Dirt Mountain by the kids. They discover a big bee buzzing around. "Bumblebee Mountain!" Hypatia calls out, christening the sandpile with its new name, at least for today.

Zakiyah, back inside the house, calls out to Jeanie: "If you come in this house, Jeanie, you will be proud of us! "

"Oh, I *am* proud of you!" Jeanie calls. "Are you feeling proud, Zakiyah?"

"*Yes!*" Zakiyahh sings out.

Brian has been running back and forth from the house to the school. He's been in constant motion since the painting began. Now he stops for a long moment. He's observing the scene, taking it all in. He says, softly: "Kindergarten is where it's at."

Oona now is painting with her hands, she's finger-painting the house, smooshing paint onto the wall in round sweeping swirls. It makes for a nice effect, a free-flowing pattern that lends the house an air of enchantment.

"Oh, Oona!" Jeanie says. "It's lovely . . ."

Brecon, too, begins to paint with his hands and his fingers. He says, "I'm going to make a purple sunset."

Emma Rose says, "I have a great idea for a rainbow . . ."

Francesca: "We're going to get this house *done.*"

Emma Rose: "Wow, that's good, Brecon!"

Oona kicks over a can of blue paint, and it spills out onto the ground. "My fault," she murmurs, gazing sadly at the thick blue puddle on the ground.

Brian says to Oona, "What will you do about that?"

Oona does what Brecon did, scoops cedar chips onto the puddle of paint, covering it up.

Suddenly, Danny says: "I'm *finished!*" He says it definitely—there can be no doubting that he's *finished!*—and he marches off to Bumblebee Mountain.

Emma Rose is smiling with wonder at Brecon's hands and arms, fully covered now with bright blue paint. She says, "Brecon, the blue monster!"

Brecon: "I'm an artist."

Emma Rose: "Yes, I know you're an artist."

Brecon: "A messy one!"

Francesca: "I'm not messy." And indeed she is not. She has been painting steadily all this time, and yet there seems to be not a trace of a wayward streak of color anywhere on her.

Emma Rose: "That is a beautiful sunset, Brecon."

Brecon: "I know it is. But I messed up my hands, for God's sake."

Emma Rose's eyes flutter. She whispers to Francesca: "Did you hear what Brecon did say?"

Francesca: "What did he say?"

Emma Rose, quoting him exactly, and imitating his voice exactly, too: " 'I messed up my hands, for God's sake.' "

Francesca giggles.

Brecon goes off to join Danny on the sandpile, where Hypatia is dancing around and calling out, "Worm! Worm!"

Anna M, who has been playing on the sandpile with Hypatia, walks up to Brian, holding her hand out toward him.

"Brian," she says, "do you know why Hypatia is screaming 'worm'?"

Brian: "No. Why?"

" 'Cause there's a worm," Anna says. She shows it to Brian—she's got a worm in her hand, wrapped around her finger.

"I'll go put him in the garden," Anna says, and she trots off to the garden a few yards away.

Emma Rose says, "How about we paint our names in brown?"

Zakiyah says, "We're working really hard, aren't we?"

Hypatia: "Maybe somebody could paint a bumblebee!"

Zakiyahh is talking to the little house, fondly: "Beautiful house . . ."

Francesca: "Who's going to live in it, I wonder?"

Zakiyah: "Me."

Francesa: "Me."

Emma Rose: "Maybe all of us can live in it."

Zakiyah: "Yes!"

Francesca: "Let's sign up!"

Emma Rose: "We'll see how many . . ."

Zakiyah: "We're going to make this house for sale."

Francesca: "It's going to be for one dollar."

Zakiyah: "And all of us in the Kindergarten can buy it."

Emma Rose: "We're going to have to get some money . . ."

Zakiyah: "Brian, do you want to be the one to sell this house?"

"Not me," Brian says. "I'm not a very good salesperson. Maybe Emma Rose can sell it."

Emma Rose ponders this for a moment. "I could make a price tag . . ."

Clean-up begins. All the children pitch in and do it. Brian helps them; he wants to make sure they get all the paint off their skin.

Jeanie walks up to Brian and says, "Did you see what Brecon did? He got his *hands in* it!"

Jeanie makes a whirling, swirling, freestyle motion with her hands, just the way Brecon did when he was painting his purple sunset on the beautiful house.

Hush . . .

Jeanie loves to tell this story:

Every Tuesday afternoon this year, we have gone down the hall to the Art/Science room. We needed to go down the hall just as the Younger Group was beginning their reading time. To help the children focus on moving quietly, so as not to disturb the Younger Group, we would play a game. We would all sit in a circle on the rug and I would whisper each child's name, asking:

"How quietly will you go down the hall?"

And they would whisper back:

"As quietly as a . . ."

For weeks, all fifteen Kindergartners would respond:

". . . as quietly as a mouse."

This game wasn't going where I hoped it would go.

Then in June, I said to the children: "This is the last time this year we'll be going down the hall. How quietly will you go?"

And their answers came floating back to me as gifts:

". . . as quiet as a cloud in the sky when there's no wind."

". . . as quiet as the rabbit that sits in my yard in the morning."

". . . as quiet as a shark moving through water."

". . . as quiet as a flower before it blooms."

". . . as quiet as a shoe sitting on the floor waiting for someone to put it on."

Thirteen poets went tiptoeing down the hall.

Free Time

The sun is shining.
It is very warm outside.
I love the world.
—Regina, Younger Group

The teachers, in discussion:

Don: The old saying is, "Play is children's work."—

Ann: The old saying is true.

Don: By children's work, do you mean children exploring, questioning, discovering—learning, growing, changing—becoming themselves? Is that what children's work is?

Jeanie: Yes. And it's done through play. Play is how children learn. For children, play and work, play and learning, play and growing up—they're inseparable, really.

Don: Well, let's talk about that, the role of play at this school. I think that's something a lot of people don't understand. Free time is maybe the best example, because that's when the kids are just purely and freely at play. But it's not just play, is it?

Jeanie: Not at all! Because children's play is never "just play"—

Ann: It's serious work.

Jeanie:—and that's why free time is so essential. It's at the heart of all we want these children to have. That sense of choice, that sense of themselves, that sense of their place in the world. Feeling their sense of responsibility to each other, and their responsibility to the community. All of that is so important! It's essential for every child. And there's no way you can give that to them without free time.

Chris: Developing the capability for self-direction, for working with others, making choices, taking responsibility for the choices you make. That's what the children are *doing* in their free time. That's what free time *is*. In some ways, everything else—all that we do here—flows from that.

Kit: Like everything else, it starts with Ann in the Nursery.

Ann: It starts when I see the children are ready to go outside by themselves. When they are ready to take that risk—to trust in themselves, and trust each other, to make that journey out into the world—I am there to help them know that they can do it. And I have to give them the time to do it in. Their own time. *Free* time. So they can to do it *themselves*.

That's why I stay inside when they go out. I'm looking through the window, I'm keeping an eye on them—but I'm inside, and they're outside. They know I'm saying to them, "You can do it. Go out and do it." Then they know they can. If I went out with them, there's no way they could feel that stepping off into their own sense of themselves . . .

Jeanie: A big part of what I'm trying to do in the Kindergarten is help them learn to make their own choices, discipline themselves, direct their own learning. So that's what they do for most of the time we're together. Not structuring the time is a real intentional thing that I do. I don't call it free time. It's the majority of the time, actually. Most everything I do is based on the children's choice. I really don't have a word for it. It's the child's selecting their own activity—their own play, their own learning—and going ahead with that.

In the early morning and the early afternoon is when the children decide what they're going to do. We have rest time together and talk and decide. We talk about everybody's ideas and plans. It's a very active time. They make their own decisions, they make their own plans.

Kit: This year's Younger Group is pretty amazing. These children are really good free time users. As soon as it's free time, there's no casting about for something to do—immediately they're skipping off happily to do whatever it is they've chosen to do with their free time. And when this happens, I realize that they were learning to make choices all along, as they were coming up through the Nursery and

the Kindergarten with the two of you. They were learning about making choices, because choices were there for them to make. You two saw to that.

Now that they're in the Younger Group, they have a lot of choice all the time. They can choose what to write and draw and how they want to do it. There's lots of choice always there for them now. But free time is special. When it's free time, they just light up. Energy rises—it's like a flowing river, it just moves and expands from one thing to another.

The ballet dancing happened that way. It started out as just some music playing in the background. Then Ben G started doing his ballet steps to the music. Some of the other children saw him and they started to move and sway and jump around. Pretty soon the room was filled with dancers. They got a ballet troupe together. They choreographed their own dances and they had rehearsals and everything. Now they're putting on shows for the whole school. They're performing for everyone—it's like a gift they're giving to us. All of that came out of the dynamics of free time.

Now they've started something new. All of a sudden, they've started writing stories in their free time. They couldn't wait! Got their Little Books out and started writing.

Chris: What I love about free time is that all ages of the children play together. The choice of who to play with is open to everyone in the school. It's not confined to Older Group, Younger Group, Kindergarten, Nursery. The children can go everywhere and do things with everybody. They're playing outside, they're playing inside. They're playing games, they're dancing, they're writing stories. Whatever they're doing, there's a freedom of movement between all the age levels, and so there are relationships that develop between the youngest and the oldest and everybody in between.

Jeanie: I love seeing the tag games that go on between the Kindergarten children and the older children. The way that the Younger Groupers and the Older Groupers get together and play basketball or wall-ball. Or even better, invent a game.

Brian: "Over the Bar," that's a terrific game they invented themselves.

Ann: Free time is also an opportunity to rest and think and reflect and imagine. To pull back a little bit from everything that's going on, and maybe just look around, and observe, and think about things. Just take time to do that.

Brian: I noticed Liana doing that today. It was during free time in the afternoon. The kids were running those little cars up and down the ramp and it got quite noisy and everything, and Liana was there but she wasn't involved in it at all. She was just very

quietly observing what was happening. In the midst of all that she was claiming some time for herself, to just be there, sitting there watching but not engaged, you know, in the activity.

Jeanie: She *was* engaged. Observation is an active thing. She was very engaged.

Brian: That's right, she was totally active. She was really *thinking*. She was really contemplating. You could see her wheels turning, you know. You could see that something was happening that was very important for Liana's life. I thought it was neat, what she was doing.

Chris: I think that's what's been going on lately in the Older Group. They've been taking themselves out of the all the busy mix of the day's activities and taking time to do something quiet and thoughtful. Jenna and Luke playing chess, Patrick and Emily knitting together, Anna and Henry on the sofa writing a story. I think they felt that was what they needed to do, and so they started doing those things.

Brian: That's what's so cool about free time. There are so many things you can do, things to get involved in and try out and experiment with.

Chris: You can choose to do what the other kids are doing, and do it with them in a group, a small group or a large group. Or with an adult. Or you can choose to do something different from what anyone else is doing, something new that you come to all by yourself.

Jeanie: All these things are just so critical, I think, to who we are as human beings. All the different people, all the different ages interacting like that— freely, by choice, because they want to and like to. Because it's free time. It helps the children to see that from the youngest child to the grown-up, we're all connected. They see themselves in the big picture. They feel part of the whole.

 Dirt Mountain!

Jeanie: They were children creating a whole world of their own, making rivers, making waterfalls, making castles—how much more powerful and wonderful can you feel?

Ann: They were digging down to the earth's core.

Jeanie: Really heady stuff!

Chris: And they kept making it better all the time. Changing it. Restructuring it. Improving it. There was a lot of pretty sophisticated engineering. And they dug tunnels big enough for some of them to go inside. They made tunnels that *connect*. That's really exciting!

Brian: They all found roles for themselves, jobs to do that needed to be done, to make the whole thing work. And they liked their jobs. They liked being a part of their society, fitting in and doing their part.

Chris: Everybody felt they had a really important part. Like, carrying all that water—if you didn't carry water, there couldn't be a river.

Brian: There was a lot of problem solving. Like, how do you get more water to the river? They tried a hose, they tried wagons, they carried it in buckets . . . They worked out all kinds of ways to haul water.

Kit: One of the limits they had to work within was, there was only one sandpile. And the expectation of the Antioch School is, if there is one thing, we all have access to it. Everyone gets to use it. So they had to work that out.

Chris: Everybody was involved. The whole thing was very fluid. Roles changed as children would come and go.

Jeanie: All ages mingled together. Different people got interested in different parts of the creating. There was a lot of taking responsibility. There was a lot of taking care.

Ann, in a report to the school community:

It began in late April when the Kindergartners came to the Nursery asking us if they could use our water faucet to bucket water out to Dirt Mountain. Well, of course they could, we told them.

What followed was the first of many days of intense water play. Countless more buckets of water were carried. Nursery children joined Kindergartners, and they were joined by Younger Groupers and Older Groupers. Water was poured, holes were dug, channels enlarged, dams made, rivers, pools, and deltas were cooperatively created.

At a sort of height of delayed gratification, some Nursery children learned they could gather several buckets of water from different individuals and then release them all together in a powerful and carefully crafted deluge.

It was great fun; and it was an adventure in learning. Think of it. Every time they carried a bucket of water and released it in the sand, they were discovering and experiencing:

Weight, mass, volume.

Gravity, force, energy.

The heft and liquid properties of water.

How they could work as individuals, and how they could work in a group.

How to wait for one another, and how to forge ahead on their own.

Randomness / predictability.

How subtle shifts create big changes.

Those weeks of play on Dirt Mountain make a good metaphor for learning. As they build and excavate, the children are analyzing, theorizing, making predictions, creating, correcting . . .

They are sometimes surprised by the unexpected; they are wondering, making connections, and starting all over again in a fugue of discovery . . . They are up to their elbows and knees in their work

which is their play which is their work.

On a biochemical level, there are powerful brain chemicals, neurotransmitters, releasing in response to, and as a part of, the children's playfulness and their joy of insight and discovery . . .

This is the chemistry of joy and play in learning.

It is all so complicated. It is all so simple. Through their playfulness these children are building a vast library of experience and discovery and personal understanding of their world, and of themselves as part of it. This happens each time they have the time and space to discover in this playful, joyous way.

Really Hard Work

It's free time for the Nursery schoolers. Annie, Anna and Lena are in the hallway, whispering:

Annie: "Hey, you guys! Do we want to make something?"

Anna: "Yeah!"

Lena: "Yeah!"

They start bringing blocks out of the Nursery, setting them down on the floor near the door.

Lena begins crawling on the blocks.

Annie: "Lena, Lena, wrong way."

Anna: "Wrong way, Lena."

They set up a series of three pairs of triangle-shaped blocks, on their sides back-to-back. They form a series of ramps, slanting up one side, down the other. They're set up in a row, one after the other, so to crawl over them means you go up, down, up, down, up, down. It's fun.

All three of the girls start crawling on the ramps.

Then Annie starts lining up some square blocks alongside the ramps, forming a little wall. The other girls start doing this, too.

Annie says, "It's not finished."

Lena goes into the Nursery. The others follow her. They're getting more blocks and bringing them out to build the walls.

Lena puts another set of ramps down, so now there are four sets of up-and-down.

Annie: "You guys, this one's going to be bigger than the other kids', right?"

Anna: "Right."

Annie is working hard.

Lena: "I'll be right back." She goes into the Nursery.

Annie and Anna crawl on the ramps.

The sun is warm, shining through the windows. There is bright light all around.

Some of the Younger Group kids come walking down the hall: Rylie, Shardé, Max. They walk lightly over the ramps, almost losing their balance. Annie,

watching them, puts her hand over her mouth, laughing to herself.

Annie gets some blocks and begins to put them into place in the wall.

Suddenly she stops. She stands still, staring down at the floor. She says: "I see a rainbow!"

She looks all around her, eyes wide.

Annie, excitedly, calling out: "Ren, Ren, everybody, look! I see a *rainbow*! It's right here!"

She points to a spot on the carpet where the sun's light shining through a stained-glass prism in the window wall has created—yes, a beautiful rainbow.

Meranda comes out of the Nursery to see it. The tiniest of children, she is dwarfed even by Annie, as they stand together looking at the rainbow.

Meranda is barefoot.

Annie says, "Meranda, you need shoes on. You're going to slip."

Meranda corrects her: "I won't slip."

Douglas comes out of the Nursery, blinking his eyes in the light of the sun. He looks around slowly. He sees the rainbow but it's the girls' work-in-progress that catches his eye. He begins inspecting it.

Morgan comes out of the Kindergarten room, looks at the girls' construction, does a double take.

Morgan, incredulously: "Hey! Did the *Nursery* do that?"

Anna nods, uncertainly.

Morgan is impressed: "I *thought* so. Wow!"

Annie and Anna exchange secret smiles.

Meranda starts to pick up a big block. Anna steps forward and cautions her: "Meranda, this is very hard work. And that might be heavy."

More of the Kindergarten children come out, curious and surprised. Cecelia, a serious look on her face, stands with her hands on her hips and studies the Nursery girls' construction.

Then Cecelia makes an announcement:

"Whoever's building this, I need to tell them something." She awaits a response.

Silence.

Cecelia turns to Douglas: "Is it you?"

Douglas: "No."

Cecelia turns to Sam: "Is it you?"

Sam: "No."

Annie steps forward, looking solemnly at Cecelia. Their eyes lock.

Cecelia, speaking slowly, carefully: "I am wondering . . . Can you figure out a way to make a shorter bridge, maybe?"

Annie just looks at her.

Cecelia: "You see, we're trying to make a house, so we need to use some of these blocks."

Silence.

Cecelia: "If we need some, can we have some?"

Annie, evenly: "Not all of them."

Cecelia: "We'll need to take some of them . . ."

Ren has been listening from the Nursery doorway. He's filling in for Ann today; she's home with a cold. He is impressed, he says later, that Cecelia spoke to Annie as Ann would have spoken to her. She said the same words as Ann would say, carefully, gently: "Can you figure out a way—?"

Now Ren, too, does what Ann would have done. He steps out from the doorway and leans down to Annie and says, softly: "Annie, can you show Cecelia which blocks she can use?"

Annie considers this for a moment. She thinks it over, and then points to the blocks in the wall she's built. Cecelia nods—she accepts the offer—and she begins taking some blocks from the wall.

Oona and Azsa come out from the Kindergarten and begin helping Cecelia build the house. They're building it next to the ramps that the Nursery girls built. Annie and Anna and Lena and Meranda are crawling and walking and scooting over the ramps. The two projects are going on side by side—suddenly it seems that everything's happening all at once in this small, sunny space in a little corner of the school. The children are *very* busy.

Ren, exclaims: "Wow, major construction!"

Tommy emerges from the Nursery, takes in the scene, turns to me wide-eyed and says, "Did they do all this? How did they do it so fast?"

"Hard work," I tell him.

Tommy nods his head vigorously.

"Really hard work," he says.

Danny and Brecon come out of the Kindergarten. They start walking on the Nursery girls' ramps.

"Don't, you guys," Oona says.

Annie says, "Don't, you guys!"

Danny and Brecon stop. They walk away.

Oona turns to Annie, and says: "Don't copy me. I don't like it when people copy me. "

Meranda is standing beside Oona, carefully watching her as she picks up blocks and puts them on the house. Oona notices that Meranda is watching her, and stops her work. She stands there gazing at Meranda, a slight smile on her face, inviting her to speak.

Meranda: "I need a little block."

Oona nods. She picks up the smallest block in the pile and holds it out to Meranda: "Is this one okay?"

Meranda nods yes, her brown eyes shining.

Oona: "Good! Here you go . . ."

Now construction fills the hallway wall-to-wall, from the Kindergarten doorway to the Nursery. Azsa, busy with the blocks, is chanting: "Time to work. Time to work. Time to work . . ."

Out of the Kindergarten come Zakiyah, Anna, and Emma Rose. Out of the Nursery come Saskia, Alex, and Hasan. They all stand staring at what's happening.

Oona says, to everybody: "Isn't this a great idea?"

Annie calls out: "We are sharing this!"

From the Nursery comes Sam, announcing: "Story time! Story time! Story time!"

Ren is right behind him: "Nursery schoolers, come in now. I need to ask you something. We're going to figure out what we're going to do . . ."

Rules of the Game

Kit has assembled the Younger Groupers to talk about the new tag game they've been playing in their free time. The children are sitting on the rug, grouped in a circle around Kit in her rocking chair. Kit is solemn. She puts a question to the group: "Who has gotten hurt today, playing this game?"

Around the circle, many hands go up. "Okay," Kit says. "We have to talk about this."

The children begin talking. Lucy says to Henry that he hurt her. Rylie says to Taylor that he hurt her. Taylor says she hurt him first. Ben G says he got "strangled" and knocked to the ground. Henry says, "I saw him on the ground. I saw him crying."

Zachary starts to say something, then stops. His expression is pained; it is painful to him that people were hurt.

"I got kicked," somebody says.

"How many of you got kicked?" Kit asks

Hands shoot up.

"I got pushed," someone says.

"How many of you got pushed?" Kit asks.

Hands go up.

"I don't think I pushed you, Regina," Jacob says. He thinks for a moment. "I may have."

Zachary says, "I have a rule to propose." But the group isn't ready to consider solutions yet; first, they must examine what caused the problem. It is a serious moment. There are solemn expressions all around the circle. What went wrong?

"We made rules but we didn't keep the rules," Liana says.

Jade says that sometimes people break the rules by accident. "I know how that can happen," she says. "People are running so fast they can't stop, and so they crash into somebody."

"Let's make rules," several of the children say all at once. Rapidly a succession of rules are proposed and agreed upon:

"No pushing."

"No kicking."

"No grabbing."

To clarify the "no grabbing" rule, Liana demonstrates on Henry the proper way to tag someone. "Don't grab," she says, "just touch their arm and say 'you're tagged.'" She does this to Henry: "You're tagged, Henry," she says, and Henry looks at her and solemnly nods, acknowledging the tag.

Around the circle, everyone's relieved. Kids start talking, some begin clowning and joking . . . Kit brings them back to their task. "Focus, everybody," she says. "Take a deep breath."

Everyone is quiet again.

"What shall we call Liana's rule?" Kit asks the group.

Liana says, "Don't grab, just touch."

Wade says, "Tag, don't touch."

Taylor objects. "Tag is too easy," he says.

Two or three boys nod their heads vigorously.

Paloma counters: "Grab is too hard."

Zachary raises his hand to speak. "If the rule said that people had to really grab you, that's easy for the boys, but it's too hard for the girls."

"Yeah," Paloma says. "It's okay with you guys," she says, looking at the boys who favor a grab rule, "but—"

"But it's not okay with the rest of us," says Zachary.

Another rule is proposed by Quinn. It calls for people who are tagged to give themselves up peacefully, and go to jail without a struggle. "You have to sacrifice yourself," Quinn says.

Around the circle there are nods and murmurs of agreement.

Kit says: "Let's make sure you all understand the rules you've made. Here's what I've heard you say: 'When catching, don't grab, just touch.' 'When caught, don't struggle, just go.' Does that sound right?"

Quickly Tasha proposes another rule: "No tricking people," she says. "No telling people you're on their side if you're really on the other side."

"Yeah," says Paloma. "Like, no faking it."

Several children begin talking all at once. One of them says: "You know that people are just gonna break the rules . . ."

Zachary says: "That really hurts."

Kit calls for attention. She asks the group: "Did you all hear Zachary?"

"Yes . . . Yes . . . Yes . . ."

Everyone heard him.

Kit says, quietly: "Let's be sure we know what Zachary's saying. Zachary is saying that it hurts our feelings when people act like they don't care about our rules."

Everyone is quiet now.

"Close your eyes," Kit says.

Everyone does. They bow their heads.

"Now, raise your hand if you care about our rules. If our rules are important to you, raise your hand."

Everyone raises a hand.

"Okay," Kit says. The children open their eyes.

"Our rules are important to every one of us," she says. "We know that." Kit pauses. "So. What happens when rules are broken?"

"You have to take a time-out," someone says.

Someone else says, "A ten-minute time-out."

"Five minutes."

"How long a time-out depends on how big a rule you broke."

"What if you forget the rule?" Jade says.

"It's not fair," Quinn says, "to get a time-out when you forget the rule."

"Maybe you could get a warning," Jade says.

"And if you get a warning that you broke a rule," Kit says, "what's your job?"

"Remember the rule!" cries a chorus of voices from all around the circle.

"And," says Tasha sternly, "if you remember the rule, you can't pretend that you forgot it."

"You should be honest." It is Quinn and Jacob and Zachary who say this, all of them at the same time. The three of them say it as if with one voice.

"There it is!" says Kit. "Did you all hear it?"

A chorus answers, "Yes . . . Yes . . . Yes."

"What's the rule?" Kit asks the group.

"Be honest."

"Just be honest."

"Tell the truth."

Kit nods. There is silence around the circle.

"Okay, Younger Group," Kit says. "You've done good work today, all of you."

Kit's ready to stop, but the children aren't. They've got more work to do.

"I think we need a rule for getting out of jail," Zachary says. "Like, you can't just leave. How about—to be let out of jail, you have to ask. Nicely. You have to ask nicely to be let out."

"Yeah," Tasha says. "You could just say, 'Excuse me, somebody tagged me, could you let me out, please?'"

"Good suggestion," Kit says.

Richard says, "I think we need to move the base closer in, because some of the first graders can't run as fast as the third graders, and they get caught. It's not fair."

Hana raises her hand. "I think there should be a rule that says you don't have to play if you don't want to play," she says. "Because sometimes people won't let you quit the game. They say they won't be your friend if you don't keep playing."

Kit says, "What can you say to them when you're pressured?"

Lucy says, thoughtfully: "You could say, 'I want to quit. I still want to be your friend.'"

"Right," Hana says. "It's like, 'You're my friend—don't force me into doing something I don't want to do.'"

Around the circle, all the children agree.

Tasha stands up. "Okay, everybody," she says. "We need to talk to the Older Group about this."

"That's right," Kit says. "We do. We'll talk to the Older Groupers. It sounds like you've got something to tell them."

Community

Sometimes in the Art/Science room the pace can be very slow and nice and comfortable. The children are drawing or painting, and while that's going on, conversations are happening. The children are just very naturally talking with each other. And listening to each other. I think this creates a depth of relationship here that is very special. This is such a small place, and the pace is so comfortable, that you can really develop close relationships here. You can really get to know other people.

—Brian Brogan

In the Art/Science Room, Brian is setting up the pottery kiln. Ella, a Kindergarten child, is busy at the workbench, sawing on a piece of wood. I'm sitting at a table nearby, watching her. She's got the wood held securely in a vise and she's sawing away in long, straight strokes. She is standing with her legs spread wide, feet planted firmly on the floor, balancing her body. She's doing it safely, except for eye protection. She's forgotten to put on goggles.

Brian ambles over, looks at Ella's work, and nods approvingly. He's impressed with her work. There's a pause. Then Brian says, conversationally, "When you're doing that, Ella, you need to put on goggles."

"Okay," Ella says. She nods for emphasis. "I know."

She extracts the saw from the wood and runs her finger over the saw-cut she's made, inspecting it closely.

"That's enough for now," she says.

I ask her, "What are you making?"

"Saw-cut," Ella says. She looks directly into my eyes. She is brown-eyed, blond-haired. There is an air of adventure about her.

"So," Brian says, "what shall we do now, Ella? Any ideas?"

Ella thinks for a moment, knitting her brows and searching the ceiling for the answer.

"How about clay?" she says.

"Okay. What kind of clay?"

"Soft clay," Ella says. "The kind with colors."

Brian gets out the colored clay and brings it to the table where I'm sitting. The clay is in batches of blue, yellow, green, red. Ella comes over and begins rolling and kneading the clay into shapes—a blue kitten, a red tree, a yellow flower. She doesn't hurry yet she's working fast. She's very good at this.

She invites me to join her and I do. Or rather, I try to. I roll and squeeze and knead the yellow clay, trying to make something to show Ella—but nothing takes shape. All I've got is a lump. Ella looks at it; she studies it for a quick moment. Her eyes light up. "Butterfly!" she says, pleased and happy. "You've made a yellow butterfly!"

Across the room, another Kindergarten child, Samantha, is sitting alone at a table near the door. She is crying, softly; little tears are rolling down her round, pretty face. Brian goes to her and sits down beside her at the table, and for a moment or two he just sits there, saying nothing, while Samantha cries a little more, then stops.

Somehow Brian knows what's the matter. "We can go talk to her, Samantha," he says. "Would you like to do that? I'll walk down there with you."

Samantha whispers, "Okay."

"Or, if you'd rather, we can stay here," Brian says. "You can go talk to her, or if you want to stay here, we'll just stay here."

"Go talk to her," Samantha says. Brian takes her hand, and together they go walking down the hallway . . .

In what seems no more than thirty seconds later, Brian is back and Samantha is with him. Her eyes are dry now, and she's smiling her beautiful smile.

"Man, that was quick," I say to Brian. "Good work!"

"Naw, I didn't do anything," Brian says. "It was Samantha's doing. She has a quick turn-around time. She can go from sad to happy in no time at all."

There's a twinkle in Brian's eye: he admires Samantha's lively resilience. He's pleased to see her smiling again . . .

Brian is always asking the kids, as they're working on their projects in the Art/Science Room, "What do you need?" When they name what they need— an instrument, a tool, some materials—usually they follow that up by going and getting it. The help Brian's given them is his focusing of their attention on the task. That he leaves the rest up to them shows his respect for them and his confidence in them, and affirms their work as theirs.

Brian is quiet, modest, low-key, unassuming. Day after day he is just calmly himself, open and accessible, patient, undemanding. This frees the children to be themselves, and feel calm and secure in their relationships with him.

I remember an Art/Science Room scene I observed that impressed me. I wrote it down in my notebook:

Art/Science: The Older Group kids are making puppets, working with clay. It's a busy scene. In the midst of it all, one of the older boys, Luke, says to Brian—they are working together, standing shoulder to shoulder—"Brian, when you were a kid, were you a good baseball player?"

Luke's at that age when a kid begins to realize that his dream of becoming a big league baseball player isn't going to come true.

Brian doesn't look up. He thinks for a moment, then shrugs and says, offhandedly: "I wasn't really good. Not bad—just kind of middle of the road. So-so. But I loved to play."

"Yeah," Luke says. "Yeah, right."

Luke gained a lot from this brief exchange.

Brian grew up in a working-class neighborhood of Queens, New York City. His father was a firefighter, his mother a secretary. He had an "old-fashioned childhood," Brian says. He went to Catholic school. "Every day I'd come home from school, change my clothes, and go out and play. I'd always be playing with five or six kids at a time. Our whole neighborhood of kids would be out playing together. We were Irish, Italian, German . . ."

He is very aware that children play much differently now. His children, Saskia and Ursula, who are in the Kindergarten and the Younger Group at the Antioch School, carefully arrange a "play date" with a friend—one friend at a time—for after school. They have their play date at one of their homes, playing together under a parent's supervision, not roaming freely in the neighborhood. Children's play these days is a tightly controlled experience.

"I liked being a kid, growing up in my neighborhood," Brian said. "I think it's sad that having that kind of childhood isn't possible for kids anymore. It seems to me something's missing from the way kids grow up today."

Brian's childhood changed abruptly when he was thirteen years old. His father died of a sudden illness; he and his mother moved from Queens into an apartment in Greenwich Village, with its freestyle mix of artists and musicians and lively street life.

"Living in the Village was like being in a whole different universe," Brian said. "It was my first encounter with people who were culturally different from me. There were poets and folksingers on the street, hip people, crazy people, brilliant people . . . I used to go hang out in Washington Square Park and I'd see all the hippies there . . . My best friend's dad was a famous toy designer, and his mother was a dancer and an artist. Another friend's father was a microbiologist . . . It was just a whole new world of people like that. It was an education just to be there."

Brian attended a high school for kids talented in art. "I didn't like school," he says. "It felt dull. I felt constrained. The good thing about it was I got to know a lot of really smart kids, hip kids, good musicians, young poets, kids with long hair . . ."

When he was in his twenties Brian left New York and went West, to see some of the world beyond the city. In Oregon he went to college, and for a while he taught social studies in a high school. He worked with a history teacher named Paul Davis, whose teaching style had a big impact on Brian:

"Paul would do these really wonderful things in the classroom. In his world history course, instead of teaching the history of war, Paul taught the history of peace. His students loved it. They really learned from him. I saw what he was doing and it inspired me to realize that teaching could really be meaningful work."

In 1986, Brian and his wife, Susan Bradford, rode their bicycles across the country to Yellow Springs, where they both had taken jobs as naturalists at the Outdoor Education Center in Glen Helen. Two years later Brian was offered a teaching job at the Miami Valley School, a prep school in Dayton. He taught there for thirteen years.

In 2001 Brian came to the Antioch School. He felt drawn to it, he says, by the sense he had of the teachers' strong devotion to the school. During his job interview he learned that Ann and Jeanie and Kit and Chris were the school's administrators, as well as its teachers. "It really impressed me," Brian said, "that the teachers would take on all the work of running the school. I felt it really said something about the nature of the school, that they would be willing to take on all that responsiblity."

That Brian took a substantial cut in pay to come to the Antioch School is a reflection of his sense of what work is: "I think of teaching as service. I like the Buddhist concept of Right Livelihood. I have the hope that the children I work with will learn to care about the world they live in, that they will really care about the planet and the creatures and their fellow human beings. I think of my work as a teacher as being in service to that guiding purpose. For me, that's what gives my work meaning."

About teaching at the Antioch School, Brian says:

This is a very distinctive, one-of-a-kind sort of school. I spent my first year sort of wandering around, really paying attention to what goes on here, letting it all soak in . . .

A lot of it still seems new to me. Like, there's a big difference in the relationships between kids and teachers here and kids and teachers at the school where I used to teach. Here, there's a lot more equality between the children and the teachers. We're more or less on the same level. Here, when I'm speaking to a child, we talk to each other pretty much the way two adults would talk to each other—like we're talking now. There is a sense of a shared relationship, and mutual respect, that is very important.

So I've had to learn all over again how to talk to kids. And how to listen to them. At this school the teachers really listen to the kids. I had to learn to do that. I'm still learning.

Really listening—it's hard work. It can be very intense, very energy-consuming, both mentally and physically. I had to learn to make myself sit down and clear my mind of everything else that's going on, and prepare myself to just listen. I had to learn to focus, to really concentrate on hearing what a child is telling me.

The first year I was here, I remember watching Ann in the Nursery as she was working with kids and thinking, "How does she stay awake?" It just looked so tiring, to get down close to a child and listen for seven hours a day. I asked her how she did it and she said, "Every day after school I go straight home and sleep."

The hardest thing about teaching here is knowing when to say something to a child and when to keep quiet. Or when to enter into a situation with a group of kids and when to stay out of it, let the kids handle it. It's very easy to just step in and give them the resolution. It's easy to think you know the right thing to do. And you want to be helpful. But the help the children really need will come best from themselves, from each other, from the group.

I'm still working on that. I'm watching the teachers and the kids, and listening and learning. That's the main thing I'm practicing now, trying to not resolve problems for the children but to let them learn to solve them on their own.

When I'm able to do that, I really do see a lot of power coming from the kids. Sometimes when I'm with a group of kids and I hear one of them say something offensive to someone else, I'll say to the group, "Wow, that would really hurt my feelings if someone said that to me." And the kids might not respond to me saying that. Often it's like they don't even hear me. But when the same thing happens and one of the children says something about it—like, "That really doesn't feel good," or "I don't feel comfortable with that"—then I see the other kids really respond. I see them really pay attention. I see them really thinking about it. It means a lot more to them hearing it kid-to-kid than it does hearing it from me.

As he studied the Antioch School teachers at work, Brian said he was impressed and deeply moved seeing how Kit helped a troubled child one day. The child suffered from a phobic fear of fire, expressed in his obsession with lighting matches, which the adults in his life had forbidden him to do and punished him when he did it. Brian watched Kit as she took a different approach:

> Kit got a box of kitchen matches, and one day after lunch she sat down with the child here in the Art/Science Room. Kit let him light all the matches, one after another. He'd light a match and watch it flame up, and then he'd put it out and light another match, and then another . . .
>
> Kit sat there with him while he did this. I will never forget it. To this day I can see Kit just as she was that day, sitting there with that child, so strong in her support of him. She was really with him, you know. And the child knew it, and felt it.
>
> That's what made all the difference. He worked his way through his fear. Doing that with Kit was exactly what he needed to do. It was a powerful healing.
>
> Seeing that happen, and thinking about it, has helped me find my own direction. Sometimes I sense that a child is feeling a need to work something out. I may not know what it is, and maybe the child doesn't know what it is, but I will get a strong sense that there's something there. So I'll try to give that child a little gesture of encouragement or understanding. Maybe I'll bring out some clay and just put it down beside the child, you know, without saying much of anything, just a little body language to make it clear that "this is yours to work with as long as you need to.". . .

Now, after three years at the school, Brian says he's still discovering things that enlighten him:

"Neetahnah came into the room today, and she had that little cape she'd crocheted. She'd put it on one of her stuffed animals, a little kitty. Wade and Quinn were in here, and Quinn looked at the cape and said, 'Hey, that's really cool. Can you teach me how to do that?'

"Now you know how hard it would be for most boys Quinn's age to ask a girl to teach them something—especially to teach them how to crochet! So I thought that was kind of neat. It kind of struck my fancy."

I asked Brian to sum it up, his experience so far of the Antioch School. He thought for a long moment. Then:

"This school is like a living organism. It has a life of its own. It is alive, and you must not mistreat it. It's quite amazing, really, all the feelings that people have about this school. People really care about it. I have those feelings myself now. It would really be hard for me to leave this place. Already I feel a real sense of loyalty."

 Rockets!

The Older Group is in the Art/Science room, busily assembling model rockets. Amid much clamor and buzz, the kids are working intently, absorbed in the task. They're talking it over, helping each other, puzzling together over the sheets of instructions laid out on the tables in front of them. Some of the workers are happily ignoring the instructions. There's a lot of trial and error going on . . .

Brian is saying, "Now you take your wings out . . ."

"Brian, could I have some help, please?"

"Does it matter if I do it like as it says to do it?"

"You sure you got that right, Pat?"

"Brian, can you help me, please?"

"Brian, does it go on this side?"

"The glue goes here?"

"Man, this is impossible!"

Brian says, "Try working on the parachute instead of the fins."

One boy to another: "I think that goes in the middle. Like that. Yeah!"

Girl: "Brian, I need your help."

Boy to girl: "He's helping a lot of people right now."

Girl to boy: "Will you help me?"

He helps her . . .

Girl: "Oooh, cool, it works!"

Hands-On Art

The Nursery children come in to paint. A group of seven. Ann is with them. This is their first time in the Art/Science Room, so Brian takes them on a tour.

He shows them the cupboard where the paper is kept, and tells them to come get some whenever they want. He shows them the gerbil, Pocket, and the rabbit, Mulberry.

All eyes are on the rabbit. The children seem to be holding their breath. Then Destini says, "He's funny. And he's really gentle."

When Brian tells them the rabbit's name, the children smile; then they all begin to say it, softly, in a rhythmic, gently murmured chorus: "Mulberry, Mulberry, Mulberry. . ."

The children don art smocks and sit down at the long table in the center of the room. It's covered by a white sheet of paper. The children begin to paint on it . . .

They paint bold circles, intricate mazes, elaborate patterns of many colors.

"Look what I made!"

Ann leans down to admire Sam's painting: "I see how the colors are swirling. That's *beautiful,* Sam, the way it all swirls."

Ann's voice is soft, low, nurturing, pleasant.

One child's painting is all red, another child's is all blue, others are vividly mixed: blue-green, green-brown, yellow-red . . . Deep purple emerges from Sam's swirling mix . . .

Brian says, "What we're doing is, we're sharing the colors."

Brian's voice is even, steady, reassuring.

But to the kids, it's not clear how to share the colors. Jar lids of each color are in the middle of the table, one lid with yellow, one with red, one with blue, one with green. Ann and Brian quietly remind the children to mix their colors on the paper, not in the lids. But colors are getting mixed in the lids, as the children keep dipping, and dripping, their brushes in the lids. New colors are being created—and the children love it, all these bright new colors being born . . .

"I'm making a color," Destini says. "Makin' blue. This is *my* blue. This is *my* color."

Tommy, sitting opposite Destini, begins painting his cheeks purple, stroking the paint brush gently on his skin.

Annie says, proudly: "We're painting!"

Ren walks up. The children all hold up their hands, streaked with bright reddish brown, deep purplish black, shiny yellow-green:

"Look at my hands!" "Look at my hands!" "Look at my hands!" Ren inspects them, and is delighted to see them, each and every one.

Hasan, the smallest of the children, wonders away from the table to the workbench by the wall. He picks up a pair of pliers and rather expertly begins to perform a series of tasks. With the pliers he picks up a small woodscrew lying on the bench, and drops it into a cup—a delicate operation . . .

Destini now is painting by hand. She's dripping paint from her hands down onto the paper, then with her hands she mixes the colors together in a soup. She's chanting, "Messy, messy, messy."

Other children begin to hand-paint. Annie shows off her hands of bright flaming orange. Alex's hands are purple-red. He holds them up for all to see: "Look at my hands!"

Now it's time for the children to clean up. Brian helps them wash their hands at the sink . . . Annie's hands are so clean now! A moment ago, they were drenched with paint.

"Time to head back to the Nursery," Brian says. "Want me to walk you down?"

The children chorus, "Yes, yes, yes."

Mia says, "I want to walk myself down."

Brian says, "Okay." But Mia is with them when they walk together down the hall.

How You Make A Robot

In the Art/Science Room, Liam and Brecon are hard at work. They are making a robot. At the workbench, with a hammer and a saw and a pair of pliers, the boys are deconstructing a thrown-away tape recorder, to salvage some of its parts for their robot.

Brecon is going at it with the saw.

Liam: "Don't saw that, Brecon. That's beyond control."

Brecon sets down the saw and picks up the hammer.

Liam: "Don't hammer, Brecon. We'll smash everything up."

Brecon: "We can saw!"

Liam: "Okay, Brecon. We can saw."

Brecon: "We can do it together."

They try to do it together.

Liam: "Here, let's get a different saw."

Liam gets another saw. He starts to saw a piece of board.

Brecon has gone back to hammering.

Brecon: "I'm going to smack these little suckers! They're bad for the robot."

Liam has a set of pliers: "I'll get these babies!"

Brecon: "They're called suckers. Here, I'll get 'em for you."

Liam: "Don't forget to put your goggles on."

Brian, halfway across the room: "That's right, Liam. Thank you for reminding Brecon."

Brecon puts goggles on.

Liam: "We've got a lot of broken parts."

Brecon says to a visitor, passing by: "Do you mind all this noise? We're trying to make a robot here."

He bangs away, hammering.

Brecon: "Phew! This is hard work."

Brecon takes his goggles off.

Brecon: "I need a another pair of goggles."

Brian: "You need to wear goggles, Brecon."

Brecon, cheerfully: "These keep falling off!"

Brian comes over, says, "Here, these will fit you better," and hands Brecon a pair of goggles. He puts them on, starts hammering again.

Brecon: "I did it! I smashed it! Now, that's what I call a robot!"

Liam: "Okay, I got the wheels ready."

Liam puts a set of little metal wheels in place.

Brecon: "Shall I smash it?"

Liam: "No, no!"

Brecon: "'Cause they're bad. They're not good for the robot."

Suddenly, sunshine beams through the door near where the boys are working. Brecon looks up, startled. Immediately he darts outside, stands there looking all around at the bright world . . .

He comes back in, and rejoins Liam at the workbench. They begin fitting the wheels into place.

Liam: "That's not where the wheel should be."

Brecon hammers away.

Brecon: "See, it's good if you smash it down."

Liam: "Brecon, we have had enough hammering. I told you, hammering is not for metal."

Brecon: "All the dead pieces, don't you want me to get them off here?"

Liam: "They weren't dead until you smashed them."

Brecon: "Now I can—"

Liam: "You broke our robot. All the little pieces, we needed those."

Brecon: "All right."

He hammers away.

Brian, looking at his watch, tells the boys, "It's time to go back to Jeanie now."

Brecon: "Okay."

Liam: "Okay."

They put their tools away and go off together, skipping down the hall, back to the Kindergarten.

Let's Take a Walk

The Nursery children are taking a walk around the grounds of the school. Brian is leading them. Ann is with them, too. It's a bright, warm day.

The children have little magnifying lenses that Brian has given them. They're looking up-close at everything—a praying mantis in the garden, the skeletal cow's head inside the garden gate, tiny cherry tomatoes they pick off the vine and squash and taste . . .

When they leave the garden and walk in the grass, Brian says, "Anybody see any deer poop yet?"

The children ignore his remark.

There is a big, round concrete tunnel lying in the midst of a patch of grown-up weeds and wildflowers. Hasan stops and looks at it, leans down and peers into it, thrusts his head all the way into the darkness inside.

At the edge of the high grass, Brian asks the children to turn around and close their eyes and count to ten, slowly. As they begin to do that, Brian darts into the high grass and kneels down and hides. When the children open their eyes and turn back around—Brian can't be seen.

Two or three of the children are worried about him. "Brian? Brian?" They call out his name, anxious looks on their little faces.

Brian pops up, grinning. "You see? You can hide in here and no one can see you. That's what animals do. Want to try it?"

The children aren't sure, but Brian's enthusiasm is convincing—he's having a lot of fun. "If I were a deer," he says, "I'd like to lie down out here."

He leads them a few steps into the high grass and invites them to hide. "Get down low, so I can't see you . . . See if you can be invisible."

Brian goes back to where the children stood when they counted to ten, and now he counts to ten, slowly and loudly. So does Ann. When they open their eyes, they see the children grouped in a bunch, standing in full view, eager to be seen—all except Saskia, who has hidden herself deep in the weeds. She stays there, invisible, until Brian—her dad—calls her out . . .

Brian leads them on a walk down a path through the high grass.

"We're taking a hike!"

"A long, long hike!"

Suddenly, Alaina calls out for Ann, and Julie calls for her, too. They need help—they have ants crawling on their feet and ankles. Ann comforts them, and after a bit she begins walking them back to the school.

Brian decides to come along with the rest of the children.

"Let's go do some drawing," he says.

"Painting," Julie says.

In the Art/Science Room the children begin painting pictures of what they saw on their walk. Saskia makes bold, slashing strokes in four shades of green, then artfully mixes in blues and reds. Julie, working slowly, builds layer upon layer of bright yellow paint into a portrait of a goddess-like sun.

"This is for my mother," Julie says.

Stored near the sink are some big plastic funnels, and when Grant goes to wash his hands he discovers them. He grabs a funnel and makes a trumpet of it, blowing mightily into the small end, creating a loud, brash, blaring sound that is surprisingly musical.

"Fanfare!" Ann says, amused at Grant's celebration of his personality. Sam begins playing funnel-music too, and so does Alaina and Lena and Miles. They form a procession, marching around the room—a marching band! Lena is laughing merrily as she marches . . .

Julie stays with her artwork. She has painted a circle around the sun, and all around the circle there are handprints—her own handprints, delicately

Just a Baby

traced in yellow and colored in with soft strains of purple and red and light blue. It's beautiful.

"Do you like yellow, Julie?" Brian asks her.

She nods, emphatically: *Yes.*

Soon the marching band's music fades . .

A few of the children—Saskia, Sam, Hasan—gather around the sand table. They are working with clay, and talking while they work.

Sam asks Saskia if she wants to play after school.

"Yes," says Saskia. "I'll be a boy."

"No," Sam says.

Saskia says, "I can't be a boy?"

Sam says, "Well, you can, but if you're going to be a boy, I'm not going to play."

"Okay," Saskia says. "I'll let you know if I'm a girl, or if I'm not."

Julie now has completed her painting, and she joins the others at the sand table. She and Lena begin working together, shaping something big out of clay.

Grant takes up the funnel again, this time to perform some experiments with sand. He pours sand in one end and as it comes out the other end, he studies it, close-up. Miles joins him in this work, bringing a funnel of his own . . .

Alaina, noticing the presence of an observer nearby, gazes at him for a few seconds with her big, round, sky-blue eyes. Then she smiles a welcoming smile. "Sir," she says, "would you like to join us?"

Kids are lounging together on the big sofa by the Art/Science Room door, talking about stuff. There's Hana, Marlee, Gabe, Zachary, and Ryan.

Jenna comes by on her way to see Brian, holding a snake cuddled in her arms—it's her snake that she brought from home, a pretty little coral-colored snake named Coral, one month old.

"She's just a baby," Jenna says.

She places Coral in Zachary's lap, and he holds her gently, petting the snake as he would a kitten.

Gabe is sitting next to Zachary, and when the snake crawls from Zachary's lap onto Gabe's lap, he smiles.

"She won't bite," Jenna says.

"If she did bite," Gabe says, "it wouldn't hurt."

The snake crawls onto Ryan's lap, and Ryan recoils and blurts out, "Get it off me, Jenna!"

Everyone laughs. Gently, Gabe takes Coral back.

Jade comes along; when she sees the snake, she stops and stares, and whispers: "Oooh, cool!"

Gabe hands the snake to her. Jade handles it expertly. She puts her head down close and peers intently at the snake.

"This," she says, "is a nice little snake."

"A baby," Jenna says. She wants her back; she wants to take care of her.

Jade gives the snake to Jenna, and she cradles her in her arms.

"Just a baby," she croons, softly . . .

Children in the Garden

Before they go with Brian into the garden, the Kindergarten children talk it over. In the group are Emma Liz, Emma Rose, Brecon, Azsa, Hypatia, Francesca, Anna, Morgan, Cecelia.

Especially enthusiastic is Emma Rose: "What about the apple tree we're planting?" she says. "I have a trowel, and a shovel—a real shovel . . . I can pick the weeds. Lots of 'em . . ."

On their way to the garden, Jeanie is in conversation with Anna: "That's quite a plan, Anna, to make a salad for your family . . ."

The children follow Brian into the garden.

Right away they find a "bees' nest"—it's really a birds' nest—inside the hollow cow's skull by the gate.

Morgan and Brecon improvise karate chops for weeding, as they walk around the edge of the garden.

Azsa is on her hands and knees, scooping up chunks of soil.

Hypatia: "A centipede! Morgan found a centipede!"

Brecon: "I found a worm! I found a worm! I found a worm!" Four kids group around Brecon.

Hypatia: "I want a pet worm."

Anna is kneeling in the grass looking for worms.

Brian: "There are lots of worms. This is good soil."

Hypatia: "Come on, let's try and find the perfect place."

Azsa: "I want to plant some potatoes . . ."

Brecon: "Look what I found—a golden ant!" He holds it cupped in his hands.

Emma Rose: "Brecon, that's not a golden ant, that's a red ant."

Brecon: "I don't care. That's not important."

Brian: "Here's where we can plant onions . . ."

Azsa: "I want to do the spinach."

Brian: "Hey, guys, here's some huge mountain garlic!"

Cecelia smells it, makes a face: "Brian, I don't like this."

Azsa: "This is garlic. You can't eat garlic, ugh!"

Brian says, gently: "Don't eat it if you don't like it."

Anna and Emma Liz and Emma Rose are happily browsing the spinach, pulling off leaves and nibbling on them.

Azsa: "What are these?"

Emma Rose: "Radishes."

Brian: "They're not ready to eat yet, Azsa."

Suddenly Azsa cries out: "Wasp! Wasp! There's a wasp in here! I saw him. Right *there*. For real!"

She runs off, looking very worried and upset. But she stops at the garden gate.

She says to Emma Rose: "Want to play with me on the sandpile?"

Soon the whole group goes off to the sandpile.

Brian calls to them from the garden: "Anybody want to come plant some peas?"

"Peas! Peas! Peas!" The children go running back to the garden, except for Brecon and Morgan, who stay on the sandpile, hunting red ants.

In the garden, Francesca is chanting: "Red ant! Red ant!"

Azsa: "Red ant and black ant!"

"Okay, you guys. Our time's up," Brian announces. "It's time for you guys to go."

Azsa is the last to leave.

She lingers in the garden, looking all around. Suddenly alarmed, pointing accusingly at the garden gate, she calls to Brian: "The gate's open!"

"That's all right," Brian says. "You don't have to close it, Azsa."

Azsa: "Yes, I do. It's open."

She strides to the gate and latches it, tight.

"It's locked!" Azsa announces to the world.

Satisfied, she runs off to join the others.

Anything for You

Early morning. Already the Art/Science Room is bustling with children at work. There's a big gray sign saying *Work House* hanging high on the wall, overlooking this room full of orphans. Brian's boombox is blaring music from a tape of *Oliver!*— the *Work House* sign is part of the set for the Antioch School's spring musical, and the orphans are the Younger Groupers, busily making costumes and props for the show. It opens tomorrow night.

The children, as they work, are singing along with the *Oliver!* music, their young voices filling the room:

> *Consider yourself—at home*
> *Consider yourself—one of the fam-ily*
> *There musn't be—no fuss*
> *Consider yourself—one of us!*

The children know all the words by heart, and their voices ring with a raw British accent, just the way it sounds on the *Oliver!* tape. As they sing, the children wander about the room swaying and spinning, whirling and twirling around—and all the while they're doing their work, cutting cloth for costumes they will sew together, painting the cardboard scenery for the stage . . .

Two of the Older Groupers are here, too—Stefan and Jesse M. Stefan is rehearsing his song for the show. Jesse has his guitar, and with the *Oliver!* music playing inside, he goes outside and makes his own music. He sits on the grass in the soft morning light, strumming and singing a Beatles tune, "Here Comes the Sun."

Liana is working on the playbill for the show. She's sitting at the workbench composing lists of all the characters, all the acts, all the scenes, all the members of the cast, all the songs they will sing . . .

She asks of anyone who's listening: "Like, what's the 'overture'?"

Stefan responds: "It's like, the beginning."

A moment later, Liana asks: "Like, how do you spell 'orphans'?"

A group quickly forms—Chloe, Lucy, Rylie— and huddles around Liana, conferring. They sound it out: "O-r-f-a-n-s."

Liana writes it down.

Next: "Like, how you spell 'Fagin'?" . . .

Stefan is rehearsing his song, "I'd Do Anything for You," singing along with the *Oliver!* tape in his high, sweet voice. Chloe, Liana, and Lucy begin singing it, too. Spontaneously, and smoothly, as if they'd carefully rehearsed it, the four of them begin to sing and dance and act out the scene and the music together:

> Stefan: *I'd go anywhere*
> *For your smile, everywhere*
> *I'd do anything for you*
> Girls: *Would you climb a hill?*
> Stefan: *Anything!*
> Girls: *Wear a daffodil?*
> Stefan: *Anything!*
> Girls: *Leave me all your will?*
> Stefan: *Anything!*
> *Yes, I'd do anything—*
> Girls: *Anything?*
> Stefan: *Anything!*
> All together: *Anything for you!*

Outside, on the play-yard—you can see him through the open door; it's a beautiful day out there— Jesse is riding a scooter, the new one with shiny red wheels. He's moving slow and easy around the cycle-circle, smiling in the sun.

As he comes around by the door you can see him up close, and you can hear him talking to himself as he scoots by:

"Oh, I wish it was always like this . . ."

Choice and Responsibility

Our job as teachers is to guide the children, to help them build
a foundation of how to act with one another, how to work with conflict
and not let that be something that divides and separates.

—Chris Powell

The teachers, in discussion:

Don: So much depends on the children making their own choices, good and bad, and learning from them. I think this is at the very heart of what goes on at this school. Agreed?

The teachers agree.

So, can we talk about the kinds of choices they make, and how they deal with the consequences? Like, what happens when they make bad choices?

Chris: The children choose what interests them. That's the important thing, I think. I'm not sure you can always say that what interests them is what's best for them. But when they are following what interests them, then there's something they need to learn from that.

Brian: Well, I want to say that that they don't always make the best choices, you know. Sometimes they do make bad choices.

Chris: Right. And that's important, too.

Brian: Yes, it's really essential, I think. Because they can learn so much from their mistakes. And it's really important to know that you can make mistakes and it's not the end of the world.

Ann: I think it's a lot about acceptance—self-acceptance, accepting that you're a human being and you're going to make mistakes, and that's just part of life.

Kit: Mistakes do get made. You know, we have so much going right in this school that maybe it seems like these things don't happen here. But sometimes they do happen. Not often; not very often at all. And when they do happen, they mean *a lot* to everybody. If a child has done something that let people down, it's something that affects everybody here.

So, if someone is found to have taken things from a cubby—every once in a while something is mysteriously missing from a cubby—it's a big deal. It feels real bad. We all come together to look at what happened, and we ask the group for rules for how to deal with that better.

And we do it with the understanding that we're all learning. We're all learning and we haven't got it exactly right yet. And there's a way we can learn to make it better. So that just becomes everybody's lesson.

Chris: Right. Mistakes are how we learn. We learn how to make good choices as a result of making bad choices, and learning from that. We have to deal with all that goes with that, including making amends with the people that maybe we hurt or offended. These are *necessary* learning experiences.

Kit: Sometimes children need to make the same mistake over and over and over again, until finally they go, "Okay, I've got it now!" Having the freedom to do that is very important.

Jeanie: And to feel free to take chances, to risk failure, to go ahead and make mistakes. And to make your *own* mistakes. To know that you don't have to make the same choices as somebody else has made. You know, there can be a lot of good lessons learned from making bad choices.

Don: One way the lessons are learned is through the conflict resolution work the children do—the meetings, as you call them. How important are these meetings? Would you say they are an essential part of the school?

Chris: Oh, absolutely.

Kit: The meetings are *very* important. It's how the children learn to take responsibility for their lives, for the choices they make, for their relationships with other people in the world.

It all starts with Ann, in the Nursery. Ann brings the children's attention to it: "you're feeling certain

things and this person is feeling certain things, so what will you do?" Then she gives the children time to reflect on what's best for them to do. Every moment in the Nursery, this is going on.

Jeanie: I watch her do that every day, bringing them to that reality.

Kit: Then they move on to the Kindergarten and Jeanie, and it's the same process on up through the Younger Group and the Older Group. All of us continue to build on what Ann begins in the Nursery.

Don: How do you do this, Ann?

Ann: A lot of my energy goes into working with the children on the skills of talking to one another. When conflict arises, the children deal with it by talking to each other directly, face to face, and working it out. They have a meeting. That's the expectation. There's an understanding that to be with the other children in the group you have to be able to talk and listen and work things out. When they have a meeting, they'll just talk, away by themselves, for a while. I'm usually with them, or close by, to help them if they need me. Quite often, they do it all themselves.

All the different personalities, different temperaments—it's fascinating to watch them come together and work out their differences. Some are more comfortable than others with doing this work. Some children, they're simply amazing! They just seem to be confident and comfortable and capable of expressing themselves in ways the other children can really hear, and understand, and accept. And for some children, that's something they struggle with all year. For them, it's really a hard thing to accomplish.

And some children just do it so *well!* I think of Amelia, who with just a quiet voice and presence is always listened to and respected. I'm in awe of her sometimes.

Don: Why are these meetings so important?

Ann: Because play is so important. Play is the culture of our school. The children are really creating the school by their play—by the ways they interact with one another, by what they do in their free time, by what they choose to learn. They create the school by all the choices they make. So when they make

bad choices, and conflicts result—that's serious.

You know the meetings that the children have, when they come back in from the sandboxes and someone is saying, "So-and-So just pushed me down and I need to talk." I mean, pushing somebody down—that's serious. When things like that happen, the children are not treating each other right, and they know that. It doesn't feel right to the children. That's why they come in to have a meeting about it. They feel their responsibility.

Don: Their responsibility for what, exactly?

Ann: For making it work. And to seek help when it doesn't work. Most of the time, the children do make it work. They really do wonderful things together. But sometimes they can't make it work, so they come in and we all work together and try to get it right.

Don: And by "making it work" you mean—

Kit: Living by their beliefs. When the children are playing, they are putting their beliefs into practice, in real life. You know, we talk about being respectful, and being inclusive, and being self-

responsible. We *talk* about all that, and rightfully so. But it's in their play that the children take responsibility for actually *doing* it. That's when their responsibility becomes real.

Don: When they can't make it work—?

Ann: They have a meeting.

Don: And what makes the meeting work?

Kit: Talking. Listening. Because words matter here. Every child's words are important. We all have this attitude, that what a child says is important to listen to. So we use talking and listening for all the conflict resolution we do, for all the meetings between the children. That's what the meetings *are,* talking and listening.

Ann: Let me tell you about a meeting we had in the Nursery today . . . Alaina—sweet, smiling child—slugged Hasan. Alaina is young in that way; if she's frustrated, she might hit someone. And Hasan slugged her back. So they had a meeting. They talked. Actually it turned into a series of meetings, with me facilitating.

I knew what had happened, that Alaina had hit Hasan, although Alaina was boo-hooing that Hasan had hit her. So I talked with her and I said, "Well, Alaina, you know"—this was after I had facilitated a lot of meetings between them, and it felt right for me to say this to her—"You know, Alaina, if you hit people, they may hit you back." Her big blue eyes were locked right on me. She was listening. I said, "So you need to think about that." And she did. She thought about it.

After a while she walked over to Hasan and said, "Hasan, Hasan." He looked at her. She said, "I'm sorry I hit you." At that point, then he could talk. And basically what he said was, "You know, Alaina, if you hit me, I won't want to play with you."

And so now Alaina is at a point where she can think about all this, and learn about her feelings, understand herself better, and make the changes she needs to make . . .

You know, Alaina did a lot of work today.

Jeanie: Yes! That is a *lot* of work.

Ann: Real work. I feel good for her. I know she's going to cross this path. And that is always so wonderful, when you see all the work the children are doing, and how they make good use of it.

Don: Jeanie, I think I saw a couple of Kindergarten boys having a meeting today, sitting with you outside on the grass.

Jeanie: Yes. Liam and Brecon got into conflict over the little three-wheeled scooter. Brecon was riding it, then he got off and laid it down and went off somewhere. Liam came along and picked it up and rode it. Brecon came back for it. That's when the confict arose. A push, some yelling, some grabbing and pulling . . . Then Brian stepped in. I was right behind him.

Don: You sure were. It was like you came out of nowhere.

Jeanie: Well, we're always watching them, you know. It's free time, but we're keeping an eye on them.

Don: I heard you say, "It looks like two people need

to talk to each other."

Jeanie: Right. Brian said it looked like Liam had the scooter first. Brecon was wailing, "But I had it first!" He was starting to cry. So they needed to have a meeting.

And it was hard, because Brecon hadn't sorted it out, that when you're riding the scooter and you lay it down, it's no longer yours. That anybody can come along then, and ride it—it's their turn. Liam explained all that to Brecon. He spoke quietly. But Brecon was still upset. He yelled, "I don't care what you say!" and started crying again.

I kept them at it. I knew this was important for both of them. They went back and forth for a while, flip-flop, flip-flop. Liam knew he was right. Brecon couldn't see it. But they kept on talking about it. They really wanted to work it out.

And they worked it out. Liam said to Brecon, "Okay, you can have it." And he set minutes. That's something I do a lot with the children, and it's something the children do among themselves. A useful tool. Liam told Brecon, "You can ride it for three minutes, then bring it back."

Brecon agreed. He jumped up and got on the scooter and rode it for, like, two seconds—no more than that. Then he gave the scooter back to Liam. I think it was just, Brecon couldn't give it back until he had it. Once he had it, he gave it right back.

Don: Was this a good resolution?

Jeanie: Yes, I think it was. Because it's not about who was right. In adult terms, it might not be seen as a good resolution because Liam was right, and yet he gave up the scooter. But what is right in adult terms is not relevant to these two children resolving their conflict.

In the end, they both felt okay about it. Brecon *wanted* to give the scooter back. And Liam took it back. If it hadn't been okay with Liam, he wouldn't have taken it back. So they both felt okay about how they worked it out.

And so did I. Because it's about each of these children learning what they need to learn through this experience.

Don: What do they need to learn?

Jeanie: For Liam, it is important that he learn not to give up what he values, not to let go of what he wants, in order to take care of someone else's feelings. Because Liam is empathetic. He feels others' pain. When Brecon burst into tears, Liam felt that. To see Brecon crying was hard for him. It would have been easy then for Liam to just let Brecon have the scooter, to say "Okay, it's yours." But at the same time, he wanted to ride that scooter. So he had to work with all that. And he came up with a solution that made Brecon feel okay. *And* Liam got to ride the scooter.

For Brecon, it is important that he learn to say how he feels. Brecon is very bright, he's very verbal, he's very articulate—but when it comes to his feelings, he has no words. His words dissolve into tears. That is what he experienced in this situation. So he worked with that, and he worked through it, and he got to the place where his feelings directed him to go. He could give up what at first he wanted, and he felt good about it in the end.

So yes, it was a good resolution. They had a good meeting. I'd say they did it beautifully.

 ## We Need A Meeting

On the porch, Kit and I stand talking for a moment. She's pleased with her Younger Group. "Fifteen girls," she says. "I've never had so many girls." Pause. "It's kind of nice."

As she's talking, Ben G comes running up, out of breath, excited, upset: "Kit! Kit! They took my place on the swing! I need help. I need—we need—we need to have a *meeting*." He reaches out for Kit's hand and takes it, holds it.

"Okay, Ben," Kit says.

Shardé comes up to us, walking briskly in a busy stride, as if she's on her way to somewhere else. She's small, compact, energetic, cute, a round-faced child with big bright eyes. She says to Kit in her husky voice, "He left his place." She presents this as a simple matter of fact: we didn't take it—he left it.

"Okay, Shardé," Kit says.

Ben G says to Shardé, "We need to talk."

Shardé looks at him. She's thinking about it. She knows she has the upper hand, and that it's not to her advantage to have a meeting with him; but that's the way things are done here—and she knows it is the right way—so she agrees.

She goes with Ben G inside the school. They sit down together on the sofa in the hallway, and they talk, earnestly, for a maybe a minute.

They are having a meeting.

Kit and I watch them through the window wall. We can't hear what they're saying. Ben G begins talking, stops, starts again. Shardé is trying to listen, but she loses patience. She sighs. She interrupts. As she speaks she makes beautiful movements with her hands.

Somehow the two of them reach an agreement. The meeting is completed. They go back outside to play . . .

I see them on the swings, side by side, swinging away, another child standing nearby, awaiting her turn.

Ursi and the Reindeer

Eight lively young children—Ursi, Regina, Max, Zakiyah, Allegra, Francesa, Oona, Hypatia—were doing a "play," as they called it, being reindeer, Santa's reindeer, with names for each child's deer-self taken from *The Night Before Christmas,* which Ursi researched and brought to school, along with a Santa Claus suit for herself to wear as she rode in the wagon ("Santa's sled") being drawn by the deer.

Okay. They did that, lining up in an elaborate procession, linked to each other by a long series of strings and knots—all the reindeer in harness, two by two. There was much awkward shuffling about and standing still, limitations imposed by the demands of the harness.

Nobody was very happy with this "play." It began with high hopes and expectations, especially Ursi's. She rushed about arranging everybody in their harness, giving them their deer-names, telling them where to line up.

But gradually the whole thing broke down. There was some bickering and balking at Ursi's commands. Santa's sled never did get pulled, though Santa was suited up and ready to go.

Finally Ursi unharnessed the reindeer, and everyone drifted off . . .

Kit, who watched all this from the hallway windows, asked the children if they needed to have a meeting about it. Hesitantly, then resolutely, they said yes. They gathered together in the little library space of the Younger Group room and began to meet.

Kit and I sat down on the sofa nearby and listened.

At first the children spoke vaguely, tentatively, focusing on the reasons the harness didn't work— the lines kept "snapping," as Regina said. They talked about that as the cause of the failure of their play. But they knew that wasn't it.

After a while Hypatia came out to the sofa and asked Kit to come into the meeting with them. They needed help, she said. So Kit joined the unhappy group.

The children talked some more about the harness trouble. Ursi said she had felt "frustrated." Hypatia said she had felt "disappointed." Ursi said she was frustrated *and* disappointed with the others for not doing what they needed to do to make the reindeer play work.

Then Francesca, the youngest in the group, made a breakthrough. She said she felt the problem was, they should not have been told what roles to play, what names to have, where to line up—they should have been free to choose for themselves who to be and what to do.

That freed the others to speak their minds. Max and Regina said that it wasn't the harness breaking, but Ursi's demand that they *be* in harness, that made doing the play so frustrating. Allegra said she joined the play in the first place because she thought they were going to be horses. She wanted to be a horse galloping, she said, not a deer in harness.

"Maybe we could just play a game," Allega suggested, "and not have it be a play."

"Plays," said Ursi, "are really hard. You have to learn all your lines and memorize your part, and then everybody changes things and it's all different. It's too hard to do it all. It's confusing."

The children kept up their search for what went wrong. A few of them spoke about what kind of play would work better than the kind of play that had not worked.

Then Oona plunged to the heart of the matter.

Tense and shy, looking at Kit, Oona began: "I think that Ursi—"

Kit redirected her, saying: "Oona, this is everyone's meeting. Speak to the group."

Oona faced Ursi, and spoke directly to her. "Ursi," she said. "It's because you were telling everybody what to do. You're not the boss of us."

Ursi nodded, and looked away. She defended herself, but she did so half-heartedly, gazing blankly at the wall as she spoke, and speaking in a flat, emotionless voice. She said she knew the others were unhappy with their roles; she had been waiting for them to tell her so.

But she clearly did not expect this to be accepted by the group. She realized that the others recognized the truth of Oona's statement; she recognized it herself.

"I feel," Ursi said, "really, really tired. I feel like I could just go home and get under the covers and snuggle with Bojangles, and just stay there all day and not come back to school. Not even go to school, just stay home."

The children now turned to the task of healing the wounds of their conflict. Asked by Kit what they wanted to say now, the children began to acknowledge the parts they had played in the failure of their play.

Max went first. "I'm sorry I made the harness break," he said.

Regina said, "I'm sorry I yelled at people about the harness breaking."

Oona said, "I'm sorry at yelled at you, Hypatia."

Allegra said she was sorry she hadn't spoken up in the beginning about wanting to be horses instead of reindeer.

Zakiyah stood up and looked all around the group. Clearly she felt sad about her part in the failure of their play, but she could find no words to express it; and so she just stood there silently, expressing sorrow with her presence.

So did Hypatia. She sat in silence, gazing sadly at her friends.

Ursi, then, speaking carefully, looking up at the ceiling as she spoke, said: "I am sorry that people felt I was bossing them around."

Kit leaned forward. "Ursi," she said, "there's a way to say your words so that we can hear them coming from *you*. From your heart."

Ursi nodded. She was sad, and brave. She turned and faced the other children, and spoke directly into the heart of the group. "I am sorry I bossed people around," she said.

And that was it. The group dispersed . . .

Before Kit and I could rise from the sofa, Oona brought to Kit the Little Book she had been working on. She proudly showed her the last page, full of words written in bold shapes and bright colors, and decorated with flowers. *I love* were the only words I could make out, but Kit could read all of Oona's writing. Together she and Oona read the whole book, and they showed it to Ren, who congratulated Oona and joined in the reading.

Then Kit and I went out into the hall and talked about the meeting.

I said I thought it was remarkable. "They just kept homing in on the truth," I said, "until they got right to the heart of it."

"That's what they *do*," Kit said, in her soft, pleasing voice. Her eyes were bright.

"It's really powerful," she said.

We were both feeling the wonder of it.

"Don, you know what?" Kit said. "I haven't always had faith that they could do that. It took me a long time to really grasp it. To really know it. To really believe."

She laughed at herself. "I used to read this little quote, over and over. I kept reading it to myself for inspiration. Finally I got it. And I hope I never lose it."

Kit recited it: " 'For such is the nature of truth that all it seeks, all it asks, is the liberty of appearing.' "

"It's by Thomas Paine," she said. "From *Common Sense*."

Everyone Can Play

Walking into the Younger Group room, I can tell by their strained, solemn faces that the children feel something serious has happened. They are sitting on the rug in a half-circle, having a meeting of the whole group.

Jade, in tears, is speaking. "I need somebody to tell me what I'm supposed to *do*," she says. "They just *pushed* me. They just pushed me aside . . ."

Quinn rises to speak, his face flushed with emotion: "I have seen Jade on the field. I've seen her out there with a sad face."

Throughout the group there are murmurs of agreement. The children are concerned for Jade. They, too, have seen her on the field with a sad face.

Liana says, "They said girls don't need to play football. But we *do* need to play! I think we need to talk to them. I think the Younger Group football players need to talk to the Older Group football players."

Quinn: "We could practice, and learn to play. Practice among ourselves and learn. "

Richard: "You can learn. When I first started trying to play, I got knocked down, I got hit in the face by the ball. But after a while, I kind of started getting the hang of it."

Kit, in her rocking chair, has been listening closely. Now she says to the group: "I hear two things. One, that you want to learn the game. Two, that you want to have a meeting with the Older Groupers."

Liana says, intensely: "They get real *mad* if people get in their way. Like, Ryan pushed me away. And Richard fell down by accident and Lucas tripped over him, and Lucas got real mad at him."

Kit: "Why is this happening? What is going on here?"

Liana says, thoughtfully: "I don't know. I don't *know* why."

She is silent a moment; then: "For the past two years the Younger Group boys and the Older Group boys have played football. But not everybody gets to play."

"Yeah, like *girls,* for instance!" says Paloma, spitting out the words.

Liana nods. "Right. So—maybe the boys feel weird now, with girls out there. Maybe they're embarrassed. "

Kit says, softly: "People are pushing you and telling you can't play, for certain reasons."

Liana: "Yes."

There is silence for a moment.

Taylor says: "They just want their way. They're not really used to anybody else playing. Like Sharde kept asking them, 'What are we doing?' but they didn't pay any attention to her."

Richard says, "Well, Asa's kind of nice. Stefan's nice."

Taylor nods; he agrees with that. "But some of the others aren't," he says.

Kit shifts in her chair: "Let's get back to the meeting with the Older Groupers who play football and the Younger Groupers who want to learn to play. Let's talk about that. One more turn to speak and then we'll stop."

Taylor: "No, Kit!"

There is a chorus of voices: "No . . . no . . . no . . ."

Kit: "You need more time? Can you hold focus and—?"

Chorus of voices: "Yes . . . yes . . . yes . . ."

"Okay," Kit says. "Paloma, your turn."

Paloma says, "When we try to practice and stuff, they come up and take the ball away from us. That has happened."

Kit: "Then what happened, after that?"

Paloma: "We left. We couldn't get the ball back from them, so we left."

Jade says, waving her arms as she speaks: "They

say to us, 'You can play, but only if you can catch the ball.' They mean, like, catch it every time. *They* can't catch it every time, but they say *we* have to. I did try to catch it, and I got *trashed*."

Jacob has been listening intently. He is one of the Younger Group boys who play football with the Older Group boys. Now he says, "If we're playing and you see us and come ask us if you can play, we'll probably say yes."

"I don't think so," Liana says. "Stefan and Asa might say we can play, but the others—"

Wade says, "Sometimes when we don't catch the ball, it's like Ryan gets super mad. Sometimes *he* can't catch the ball, so I don't think he should get so mad at us when *we* can't."

Zachary stands up and makes a serious, heart-felt statement of fundamental principle and belief: "It doesn't matter *what* happens, nobody should yell at somebody. Never. Not *ever*. It doesn't matter if you're a first grader or a nineteenth grader, you shouldn't yell at somebody. It doesn't matter *what* the reason is."

There's a flurry of hands in the air, kids wanting to speak.

Quinn: "I only got passed to one time. Sometimes I have trouble catching the ball, and they get mad. But if you stay and keep playing, they get used to you. If you keep playing, you might get better."

Taylor: "Whenever you play football, you're probably going to get hit."

Reed: "Not me. I don't really get hit. Because I just watch them and do what they do."

Ben: "I got squashed the first time I played. They really didn't want me to play. They said I was too young to play. That didn't feel good. I'm *not* too young to play! Even a two-year-old can play."

Somebody murmurs, "Even a newborn baby can play," and there are smiles and general laughter, good-natured and welcome—a release—all around the group.

Kit says, "Okay. I have heard us say we need a meeting with the Older Groupers, right?"

A chorus: "Yes . . . yes . . . yes . . ."

"So let's check with the Older Group and see when we can have a meeting," Kit says. "Wade and Jacob, will you go ask Chris when would be a good time for a meeting between the Younger Group and the Older Group?"

Wade and Jacob dart out the door . . .

Kit: "Who wants to be a part of the meeting?"

Many hands go up. Some children—Jade, Zachary, Quinn—stand up to be counted.

"Okay," Kit says. "We have Jade, Richard, Zachary, Ben, Quinn, Paloma, Taylor, Liana, Mary."

Wade and Jacob come back into the room—and following right behind them are the Older Group football players, all in a row: Stefan, Asa, Will, Nicky, Lucas, Ryan . . .

When the Younger Groupers see them coming in, everyone is surprised, impressed, excited—a low sound, an undertone breathy and tense, spreads through the group: "... *wooooooooo* ..."

Wade announces: "We can have the meeting right now!"

The Older Group boys sit down in the circle. The meeting begins.

Liana leads off: "Why do you guys get mad and yell?"

"Okay, okay," Kit says, gently. "Breathe, everybody. Let's take it a little slower ..."

Kit holds the pause for a few moments. Then she says, "Let's talk about this: What happens? Why does it happen? Do you know why?"

Silence.

Then Stefan says, quietly, thoughtfully: "People sometimes have a hard time losing. If they're losing, they think the rules aren't fair. Some people—"

Beside him, Asa cautions: "No names. Don't say any names."

Stefan: "—scream and yell and they get really mad."

Paloma: "Why are they even out there playing?"

Stefan: "Mostly because they're—"

Kit: "Playing to win?"

Stefan: "—yeah, playing to win."

Paloma says: "Not us! We play to have fun."

Jade says: "When we're practicing, the Older Groupers grab the ball and take it away." She looks at Ryan.

Ryan: "I don't know what you're talking about."

Kit says, to Ryan: "I've heard people say you have a hard time losing."

Ryan: "It's not true. People might brag about it when they score a touchdown, they might scream and yell and that might get kind of annoying, but—"

Jade, her eyes flashing dark, says: "You told me and Liana that we couldn't play!"

Ryan and Lucas glare at Stefan. Jade is his sister. Stefan says to them: "I'm not going to say it's her fault."

There is silence for a moment.

Kit says: "Liana, would you tell the Older Group people the two items that came out of our meeting?"

Liana: "We want to practice playing football, so we can learn. If you Older Group people see Younger Group people out on the field practicing, don't come out there, because we have to learn with only ourselves out there."

Ryan: "But if the Older Group wants to play a game, the space is too small, and everybody gets their feelings hurt."

Jade: "That's what happened to me and Paloma. We said, 'Can we play?' You guys said '*No!*'"

Will says, evenly: "We were already playing a game. If you're going to play, then play the whole time. It's better if you come to us in the beginning. If you just get on the field after we're already playing and all, it's not going to work. If you want to say everyone can play, then you need to learn how to play. Try to catch the ball and play—or stay off the field and watch."

All around the circle, all the children are absorbed in this meeting. They are listening intently; and when they speak, they speak meaningfully, with conviction, and they express themselves clearly and directly. They are taking everything in, thinking about it, responding to it, expressing themselves to one another.

And as the meeting goes on, an important shift occurs. The Older Group boys begin instructing the Younger Groupers about how they can best learn to play the game. In the course of this meeting, the older kids have come to accept the younger kids' demand that everyone should be able to play ...

Lucas is saying: "One thing to learn is, 'Follow your players.' Follow your players and it won't be so hard."

There's an echoing chorus of the Older Group voices—Asa's, Will's, Ryan's: "... 'Follow your players', that's right ... 'Follow your players' ..."

Jade is smiling now. The bright light is back in her eyes. She says: "Sometimes I'm trying to play and people tell me 'follow your players, go follow them'—but I don't know who they mean. I don't know what to do."

Lucas begins explaining the basic principles of

playing football. He speaks earnestly, directly at Jade, and the other Older Group boys listen carefully, nodding their support for each point he makes . . .

And the turning point of the meeting has been reached.

Quinn says to the Older Group boys: "Sometimes when some people drop the ball, guys get angry. But when good players drop the ball, they don't get angry. And sometimes when people make a mistake, they go off the field and just say, 'I quit!' Really, there's no need to quit."

Asa says: "Yeah, I get mad. I do."

Will says: "Sometimes if a game gets tense, people get mad and there are fights and stuff. People argue. It gets out of hand sometimes."

Lucas says: "When that happens, we should just stop it, and agree, and quit fighting."

There is a murmur of approval all around the circle.

Kit says, looking around at everyone: "We have done some good work here. You have really done good work."

She pauses.

"Now, can we come up with any agreements?"

The children lean forward—some scoot forward—and the circle tightens a little. The group as a whole seems to take a deep breath.

Asa says: "If you're going to play, come before the game starts."

Lucas: "Or tell us you'll be out there right after you finish your lunch."

Quinn: "There have been times when people do want to play and they tell somebody they will be out there after lunch, and then when they get out there, people say it's too late, they can't play. That has happened."

Kit holds up her hand: "I need to say two things. One is about time—we've got five minutes left. The other is, we always get to this point where we're almost done but we can't quite get there."

Around the circle a murmuring chorus signifies the truth of this: "Yeah. . . yeah . . . yeah. . ."

Kit: "So, what do we do?"

Silence for a moment. Then:

Lucas: "We just agree to what we agreed on."

Another silence. Everyone is waiting for something.

Asa says: "If people tell somebody they want to play, I think they should be allowed to play."

Again the chorus of children's voices, murmuring yet emphatic, one last time: "Yeah . . . yeah . . . yeah . . ."

Agreement has been reached. There is an intense silence throughout the circle. It seems to fill the room.

Kit whispers, "Thank you, everyone."

That releases the meeting. Everyone begins filing out of the room. Jade, Liana, and Ryan sit down together at a table, and begin to talk.

Discovery and Wonder

It's always, How do you help that child

move toward discovery and wonder?

That's my job as a teacher.

—Kit Crawford

Kit Crawford, the Younger Group teacher, is a small, russet-haired woman with a soft voice, big eyes, warm smile. At any moment in the day, any place in the school, children will come up to Kit and hug her, and she'll hug them, and she won't miss a beat in the tempo of what she is doing at the time, be it eating her lunch, talking to someone, reading something or writing something down. It happens all the time. Kit is freely accessible to the children, approachable, available, accepting and welcoming of their attention. That's just the way she is.

Kit grew up in Michigan, a minister's daughter. She and her husband, Jeff, were homesteaders in the Michigan woods, activists for civil rights in inner city Detroit, and, later, graduate school students asking big questions about education and human potential. Kit began teaching at the Antioch School in 1984. Jeff was teaching at Central State University, near Yellow Springs, and their children, Jason and Linda, were enrolled in the Antioch School. One day when the kindergarten teacher was ill Kit volunteered to substitute for her. She subbed some more that year, and the next year the school invited her to teach science, part-time.

Kit, an artist as well as a scientist, soon found herself teaching science *and* art—"a fantastic combination," she says. Inspired, Kit created an art/science program, blending the two supposed opposites. She did this with a confident, capable, girlish

123

enthusiasm: "I thought of myself as an artist/scientist, and I enjoyed the wonder of that." The next year, she became the Antioch School's full-time Art/Science teacher.

"I *loved* being in the Art/Science Room," Kit says, "seeing all the kids coming in feeling free to do what they were coming in for. In that room everything flies around fast. There's a lot of nonverbal learning and synthesizing and knowing and discovering. More than anything, I enjoyed watching the children discover stuff. It was a great feeling."

Kit developed a teaching style that evokes and supports the children's development—and enjoyment—of their own learning energy. "We didn't have many rules," Kit says. "The kids were capable, and they felt capable. I knew they would do what they needed to do."

To the children's questions, Kit would respond by asking them questions: "When they'd ask me how to draw a flower, I wouldn't show them how, or try to tell them how. I'd say, 'Well, what do flowers look like? What do they feel like to you?' Or if we were learning something like 'heat rises' or 'light travels in a straight line', I'd say, 'Okay, you know that. Now what do you do with it? Where do you take that knowledge—where does it lead you?' Then I'd stand aside and let them do the rest."

Kit was the Antioch School's Art/Science teacher for nine years. In 1994 she moved to the Younger Group when its newly hired teacher became seriously ill and Kit was needed to fill in. She has been the Younger Group's teacher ever since.

It was when I went to the Younger Group that I discovered I really was a teacher. I didn't have a strong sense of that before. I knew I was an observer. I liked to talk to the other teachers about the children of the school. I made a point of standing with them in the hallway, looking out the windows at the children playing. We'd talk about what the children were doing, and what we were seeing, and what it all meant. I learned a lot that

way. Things would be revealed to me about how children are. My feelings about being a teacher just kept getting stronger within me, the more I watched the children play . . .

And now, all these years later, I'm still standing at the window watching the children. And I'm always learning more and more. It's just a constant opening up of another layer of seeing and understanding.

And so, as the teacher of the Younger Group, I find that I am really not so far from where I was in the Art/Science Room. It's still about children discovering stuff, and the wonder of that. It's always, How do you help that child move toward discovery and wonder? That's my job as a teacher. And always knowing how really capable the children are, how good they are at doing what they need to do, learning what they need to learn.

That's what I understand about it all. Trust is big. I mean, in this school, we're not teaching to the test here. We're trusting that our children are going to learn everything they need. This school is built on trust.

Kit's personality sets the tone for the Younger Group. The room is open and welcoming, with several comfortable places where the children can choose to locate themselves—the pioneer kitchen, the loft, the pillow-filled rowboat, the sofa in the library space, the cushions on the floor. "I like to have a lot of places where the children can be," Kit says.

Like her, the children are approachable, accessible, available to each other. They have a lavish, buoyant, ever-present sense of humor. They're very sociable. And beyond the lively buzz of social conversation, the children make a point of talking to each other in a serious, meaningful, purposeful way—the way Kit talks to them.

And, like Kit, the children teach. The children teach each other and learn from each other. Kit says she considers the whole school a learning community: the teachers learn from the children, just as the

children learn from the teachers, and the children learn from each other, and the teachers learn from each other. "We all live the day together." Kit says, "and we keep on sharing all we're learning."

There are all kinds of ways that children go through the process of becoming more and more aware of themselves as learners. And a lot of it has to do with the fact that all of us here are excited about learning, and sort of expecting that everyone else will be excited about it.

So the child looks around and sees a room full of children who are excited about the work they are doing. They're sitting at the table writing stories in their free time, they're on the rug playing chess in their free time. Seeing all that going on all around him, the child is getting information about what's possible, and he might want to try it out.

He might need a little encouragement, a little boost. The other children will do that. The group will do a really good job of it. I do my part, too. If I have a child who says he's not really good in math, I say things to that child like, "You're not interested in that yet?" or "Is that a place where you want to do some more work?" I pitch the future to them, because that's where they're going.

And of course they'll get there, of course they'll learn—that's my attitude. That doesn't say anything about whether I'm going to make them

get there, or lead them there, or show them how. Or when they're going to get there. It's just saying, "This is a possibility for you."

They have to take it from there. The real work has got to be theirs. They have to own it. One thing we all know for certain is, the more things that children can do on their own, the more they will learn.

Sometimes the whole group will join together and take on the task of helping a child learn, when one of them needs some special teaching. When Hue arrived as an adopted child from Vietnam, seven years old, knowing no English, the children understood that their role—the role of the group—would be to help her learn to live an entirely new way of life.

And they soon understood that Hue's strong and vivid personality meant that they should not try to take the initiative to teach her things, but wait and respond when Hue made her own initiatives to learn. She started making them right away. From the beginning, Hue would ask questions of the other children. She would question them constantly, often when they weren't expecting it; and, speaking in her native accents and intonation, Hue sometimes sounded abrupt and harsh to the children:

"What your name?"

"What you doing?"

Hue would station herself in the hallway of the Antioch School and fire these questions at every child who passed by.

At first this startled the children. Then, seeing and hearing the way Kit responded to Hue, the children began answering her as Kit did, matter-of-factly giving her the information she asked for:

"What your name?"

"Lucy."

"What you doing?"

"Going outside."

Gradually, Hue's speech became gentler. Her whole demeanor softened. And her questions became more sophisticated. Very soon, it seemed, she was asking the one great question: Why?

"What you doing?"

"Going outside."

"Why?"

"To play."

"Why?"

"It's fun."

"Why?"

"I like to."

"Why?"

"Well, uh, because—"

"Why?"

Relentlessly Hue asked, *Why?* And because she really wanted—really needed—to know the answer, the children knew they must answer her question, as best they could.

Sometimes it was difficult. Hue was asking the children why they lived the way they did. To answer her, the children had to *think* about Hue's question, and ask it of themselves: Why *do* I live this way? Why *do* I do the things I do? These were questions they had never really asked before, and they began to look inside themselves, searching for the answers.

In this way, Hue became an important teacher for the children. And Hue's way of teaching was very much like Kit's way—for Kit's teaching is rooted in the questions she inspires the children to ask and answer for themselves:

I challenge them: "What is your question?" When a child comes to me saying, "I can't do this, I don't get this," I say, "What is your question?" I tell them, "If you can find your question, then you can find your answer. Think about it, find it out, bring it back to me. Tell me what your question is."

It's all about self-responsibility. When a child accepts responsibility for asking her own questions, she discovers she is making her own choices, living her own life.

And that will be the question, at some point: "What will I do with my life?"

They can ask it whenever they need to.

Hue's questions got answered, and she went on to ask more and more. She learned from the children, and they learned from her. By the end of the year, Hue had found a solid place for herself in the group.

She made vast progress toward mastering English. She worked hard. She took responsibility for her learning. She was a demanding taskmaster. When she and Kit worked together on reading and writing English, Kit would say, "Good work, Hue. You're getting it." But Hue would frown and shake her head: "Naw, Kit. I do not have it. I do not know it yet." During free time she would take an armful of books into a quiet corner of the room and read them to herself, slowly sounding out word after word.

One rainy day, Hue came up to Kit and asked her: "Why it raining?"

Kit responded: "What a good question!"

Hue gazed out the window at the rain for a moment. Then she looked at Kit, a thoughtful expression on her face.

"What is rain?" Hue asked.

Kit's eyes sparkled: "Oh what a good question!"

To ask a question, and to feel its meaning for your life; and to explore its possible meanings, seeking to discover your meaning; to own that process, to make it your own—for Kit, this is the very heart of learning:

The experience of learning can happen anywhere: when we're in the garden, or on the sandpile, or in the Quiet Room writing a poem, or at the art table doing stained glass . . . Wherever we are, whatever we're doing, when we are in the process of discovery, we're in the presence of learning.

And some of it is like magic. I'm talking about a kind of feeling that you are doing something that, deep down, you understand. When you watch the children experience that, when you see them come to some big place and smile—that's when they know they have learned.

And that learning is useful. We are going to be able to take what we have learned and use that, again and again and again and again. It's something we have acquired. It is ours, forever. It becomes part of us, and nobody can take it away . . . It will be part of everything we ever do again.

Moments like these are not rare in the children's experience of the Younger Group. Kit achieves an intimate connection with the children, and the children achieve this with each other, empowering them to ask profound questions, and reach deep levels of themselves.

From my notebook:

"They are spiritual people," Kit says, talking about the children. She means all the children, but right now she's talking about two of them, Lucy and Liana. Kit has just had a conversation with them:

"Liana wanted to know what sacrifice means," Kit says. The men who flew the planes into the World Trade Center on 9/11—"They sacrificed their lives," Liana said.

"Maybe they didn't like their lives," Lucy said, "so they didn't care if they died."

"I'll bet they did like their lives," Kit said. "They believed in something bigger than themselves. And so they sacrificed their lives."

"That means they weren't bad people," Liana said.

"Well," Kit said. "Did they have to kill other people?"

Liana thought about that.

"No," she said.

Lucy said her grandmother lives in Pennsylvania near the site of the airliner crash, so near she heard the plane hit the earth. "It went *thump*," Lucy said.

She had thought a lot about what happened. "Some people made that plane crash into the ground so it wouldn't crash into a building where there were people," Lucy said.

She, too, though she didn't use the word, was thinking about the meaning of sacrifice.

"Yes," Kit said. "They sacrificed their lives to save everyone else."

They left it at that. Lucy and Liana were deep in thought, Kit said. So was she . . .

"Kids *care,*" Kit says. "They care so much! They are so bright, and they see so much. And they have no way to process it all. They know they've been born into a crazy world. Of course they're confused. Of course they don't feel safe. They are very vulnerable.

"And they are very brave. They would save the world, if they could."

Ren Smith, a gifted teacher, assists Kit with the Younger Group. He works with Kit for several hours each day, and also helps Ann in the Nursery and Jeanie in the Kindergarten. Then he runs the after-school program in the late afternoon. Ren has been at the Antioch School for five years. He is thirty years old, African American, and, as well as being a teacher, he is a writer. He occasionally teaches at creative-writing conferences and workshops.

Among all the soft voices of the teachers at the Antioch School, Ren's voice is the softest. His whole demeanor expresses the gentle, thoughtful delight he takes in the children; and from them he evokes warm feelings of affection and trust. He shifts in and out of many roles with the children: teacher, tutor, mentor, counselor, friend.

As a student at Antioch College Ren discovered the Antioch School. He had work-study internships at alternative schools and child-care centers in New Mexico, Vermont, California—and at the Antioch School.

He was initially drawn to working with children, Ren says, to prepare himself for perhaps being a father of his own children someday: "I wanted to familiarize myself with other ways, better ways of raising children." He was impressed with the ways adults interacted with children in these child-centered places: "There is no raising your voice to a child. No failure to answer a child's question. No walking away from a child who needs your attention . . ."

After completing an internship at Synergy School, an alternative school in San Francisco, Ren returned there and worked as a member of the staff. "It is a wonderful school," Ren said, "with really good kids. But if I had a child to send to school, the Antioch School would be my choice. There is a realness to the way the children are here. At Synergy, the kids comprised one big group. At the Antioch School, every child emerges as a distinct human being. That's a big difference."

What creates this difference?

"At the Antioch School," Ren said, "the children's social and emotional needs always come first. You're dealing with each child's whole personality. You respect that personality. If there's a conflict, you talk about it with the child. You talk to the child, and you listen to the child. You don't control the process. You don't dominate the child. You're not trying to resolve the conflict in terms of rightness or wrongness, or deciding what should be done. It's about asking a question, instead of making a decision. You're engaging the child in an ongoing process—a process of relationship, and discovery, and understanding."

The quality of the teaching is what really makes the difference, Ren said:

To do this work the way it's done here, to relate to the children the way these teachers relate to them—this takes an incredible amount of energy and dedication. It demands complete honesty and authenticity. It demands complete respect for the child.

The focus always has to be on the child, and what the child's particular issues are at that moment. And that's hard, because people naturally tend to bring their own issues into it, especially control issues. When I started working here, I had control issues around my need to fix the problem, to step in and resolve it. I made the mistake of not allowing the children to resolve it. I would get involved in the rightness and wrongness of it—I'd get attached to the conflict. It was their conflict, but I would tend to jump in and make it mine. I would want to lead them to the conclusion that I thought was best for them.

So, I had a lot to learn. Watching how the teachers here did their work helped me understand. And the children taught me a lot. I admire the ability the children have to resolve a conflict and then let it go. I feel that I've learned to do that now. I learned it from them.

It's an art, really, this way of teaching. I think the children here benefit from it greatly. This is the way it should be done.

 Fractions

In the Younger Group room, Ren is at a table with Lucy, Liana, Chloe, Henry, and Rylie. They're doing math.

Liana asks Ren, "Can I use the calculator?"

Ren: "Why?"

Liana: "I can't figure this out."

Ren, softly: "No."

Liana: "Why, Ren?"

Ren: "We're trying to hear the figures in our heads."

Ren's voice is relaxed, pleasant, friendly. When he's with the children there's a sparkle in his voice, as there is in his eyes.

Kit, walking through the room, passes by the table. She says to Henry: "Stay with it. Just stay with it 'til you get it . . . You are getting it. You do get it."

"I got it!" Henry bursts out. "I knew it! I totally knew it."

They are doing fractions.

Chloe is balanced precariously on the edge of her chair, tense and eager, staring at her worksheet, pencil in hand. "What does this mean?" she says, whispering to herself. She can't figure it out.

Then, suddenly excited, Chloe exclaims: "Oh! I didn't think of that!" She looks around the table, amazed and pleased, her pixie face fresh again . . .

Lucy is conferring with Ren, one on one. She is a good learner, focused, assertive. She shows her worksheet to Ren, asks him a question, stares at him intently, seeking an answer. Ren is the teacher. but it is Lucy who is leading the learning process.

This is just the way Ren wants it to be.

Henry slides his worksheet across the table to Ren, bearing his calculation:

$1/2 + 1/2 = 2/2 = 1$

Lucy points to it, drawing Ren's attention there. "I got that, too," she says, "but it can't be right. It wouldn't be a 1."

Pause.

"Would it?" Lucy says. "Would it be a 1?"

Ren is giving her his full attention, yet he's not saying a word. He's listening.

"Zero," Lucy says. "Yes! It's zero."

But she knows that's not it. She lets her pencil drop, and she puts her head down and closes her eyes.

Quietly, Ren begins to talk to her. As he talks he picks up Lucy's pencil and draws a circle on her worksheet, then cuts it in half.

"Suppose you had something you wanted to share . . ."

Morning Meeting

The Younger Group is having their Morning Meeting. The children are gathered in a circle on the rug.

Mary is taking her turn, speaking in the slow, dreamy, chant-like rhythm that the children somehow speak in for this (and only this) activity. She is saying, "My mother's making pizza tonight, that's a good thing, I like it when she makes pizza . . ."

It's Jade's turn. She's holding a box of shiny marbles on her lap: "These aren't all of my marbles, I just mainly brought the colored ones. Can I pass them around?"

Kit: "You mean one at a time?"

Jade: "Yes."

Kit: "That might take awhile. Is that all right with everybody?"

Everybody: "Yes . . yes . . . yes . . ."

Jade starts passing her marbles around the circle . . .

Morning Meeting continues.

Christina is saying, ". . . and she had the CD in the car, we all wanted to hear it, but we couldn't, it wasn't fair . . ."

Quinn acts out a scene, portraying a person getting angry: "I get mad! I get mad! I get mad!" He hops around the space at the center of the circle, speaking in a parody of an anger-strained voice, a contorted expression of rage on his face—then suddenly he is calm. "Okay," he says amiably, "let's get to the point." He looks puzzled: "The point? The point?—Who scored it?"

The children, and Kit, too, laugh throughout Quinn's act, and they applaud at the end.

Tasha's turn. Solemnly, she holds up a stuffed animal she has brought from home, a little fuzzy bear. "He's special," she says, hugging the bear. "When I was little and I had to go the hospital, I took him with me." She holds her bear up so all can see him.

Zachary's next. He's got news. Yesterday he traded for a baseball card he really wanted. "Sammy Sosa. I really like him."

Now Kit announces that it's time for the Thirds to leave. They are the oldest children in the Younger Group (they're in their third year in the group) and they have to go with the Older Group to practice their parts in the school's spring play. The Thirds—Hana, Paloma, Henry, Mary, Jade, Quinn, Tasha, Zachary—get up and go, leaving just the First and Seconds in the Morning Meeting . . .

There are empty spaces now around the circle, here and there, places where a Third had been sitting and now is gone. Liana says, "We've got to shrink the circle, everyone!" The First and Seconds start scooting themselves closer together, forming a tight, unbroken circle.

Kit watches this from her rocking chair. When the children are all settled, she says to them: "This is the way we'll be next year."

The children look all around their circle, seeing the Younger Group-to-be. It is a significant moment. The children clearly are stirred by it. They recognize what Kit's pointed out as marking a passage in their lives: they're growing, they are changing, their future is coming at them pretty fast . . .

Then the moment passes, and the Morning Meeting is renewed:

Max and Rylie do a skit together, with animal puppets—one Max's, one Rylie's. The animals meet each other and do not know what to say. They dance around awkwardly, making barking sounds, approaching each other, hesitating, hovering in the air, then retreating. Ursi, the designated "timer," intervenes. She brings her animal, a little bear, into the skit, signaling time for the skit to end.

Reed and Richard announce they will do a skit, with Max as the designated "timer." The two boys act out a slapstick comedy scene of mock violent conflict between two big animals—or perhaps they

are men—who are wrestling each other, tackling each other, falling down and flopping about, rolling around on the floor, moaning and grunting mock-angry words. Only a couple of their words are intelligible: "evil darkness." When Reed jumps on Richard's back, Richard, on his hands and knees, starts bucking like a horse, and some of the children sitting in the circle have to scatter quickly out of their way to avoid being hit.

Around the circle there are frowns on the faces of the children. Reed and Richard are laughing, enjoying the wildness of their skit, unaware that it is not being enjoyed by the others.

"Max, you're the timer," Liana says, urging him to call "time" and end the skit; but Max does not respond. So Liana intervenes. She steps into the circle and puts her hands on both boys' shoulders, like a referee in a wrestling match. "Break it up, you guys," Liana says. "Right now!"

And they do. Immediately Reed and Richard back away from each other. They sit still on the floor, looking around the circle. The kids who scattered return to their places, and everything is still for a moment.

Throughout all this, Kit has been watching with a pained expression on her face. Now she says, softly, "Did anyone get hurt?"

Lucy stands up. "I wasn't hurt," she says, looking directly at Reed and Richard, "but I would feel more comfortable if they weren't so rough."

Around the circle, children nod their heads in agreement.

"Okay," Kit says, "let's talk about this. Can we give Reed and Richard some feedback, so they will know how we feel about what they were doing?"

Immediately the children begin to respond.

Chloe says, "Don't be so wild. Don't jump on each other."

Ben G says, in a hushed voice of amazement: "You were so *wild!*"

Erin says, "I don't like it to be so rough and everything."

"I would like it," Liana says, "if you didn't jump on people."

Erin says, "You just could just play with toys instead of—"

"People," Hana says.

"Hurting people," says Lucy.

The children are very serious about this. In this moment all their attention is focused on it; everyone is listening intently to what is being said. And yet each child speaks in a calm and thoughtful, even-toned voice. There is no sense of accusation or blame; rather, there is a strong sense of mutually shared concern. It is clear they regard this as a group problem shared by all, requiring all to share in its resolution.

Richard has been listening closely to what the other children have said. Now he raises his hand, seeking a turn to speak.

"Richard," Kit says, "are you hearing what people are saying?"

"Yes," Richard says. He turns to Reed and says: "I don't want you to pounce on me."

Reed nods. "Okay," he says, firmly. Then: "I don't want you to roll over on me."

Richard nods, and smiles, and looks around the circle.

Kit smiles back. "Okay," she says. "Thank you, everybody."

And the Morning Meeting goes on. The children resume taking turns around the circle.

Christina says, holding up a shiny round object: "I just got this from my mother"—it is a wind-up toy that, winding down, makes a nice, musical buzz—"and I want to pass it around."

Hue, in her turn, tells of her play date yesterday with Ursi. "We fight pillow-pillow!" Hue says, smiling a bright white smile and laughing at the memory. Ursi, sitting next to her, is smiling, too. She leans over and hugs Hue.

Now it's Ben G's turn. He does a solo skit in the center of the circle, acting out a ballet dancer's nightmare: "Oh, I've ripped my pants! Oh, I'm so embarrassed! Oh, please don't look!"

Around the circle everyone laughs . . .

Soon the Morning Meeting ends, and it's time for work. The children are ready for it. Quickly they line up to get their work folders from the folder bin. Because it's Friday, there's a lot of talk about weekend play dates and sleepovers. Waiting in line to use the pencil sharpener, Lucy is talking to Hue:

Lucy: "You're popular, Hue."

Hue: "Why?"

Lucy: "When anybody wants to have a sleepover, they always want you to come."

Hue: "But—but—"

Lucy: "You're popular, Hue!"

Hue: "—why?"

Lessons

The Younger Group room is full of children doing their work. Kit is sitting at a table with Wade. He is working on a math puzzle problem. Henry comes up and interrupts. He's frustrated, impatient. "I doubt that's it," he says, showing Kit his worksheet with his answer underlined. He looks to her for a response. "I'm not answering it for you," Kit says. "You need to sit down and answer it yourself."

Henry turns away, goes back to his worktable. Kit returns her attention to Wade. He says to her: "I don't understand. If this says three dollars, and this is—I don't get it. What answer are they looking for?"

Kit says, "Read it out loud. Listen to what you're reading."

Wade reads the math puzzle question out loud. Ben G hears him and comes up to the table, and watches and listens to the interaction between Kit and Wade. So does Regina, sitting at a table nearby.

Kit says to Wade, speaking slowly, carefully: "What do the words 'and so on' mean?"

Wade makes a puzzled face.

Kit says: "In 'January, February, March, and so on'—what comes next?" Wade thinks for a moment; he says: "April, May, June . . ." He smiles at Kit, and nods. He's got it.

Henry is back, holding out his worksheet so Kit can see his answer. "That's not it," he says, "is it?"

Kit says, "Well, you won't know until you check it."

Henry sighs, and shuffles off . . .

Kit turns back to Wade. He has begun a new puzzle problem. Wade shakes his head, throws up his hands, wordlessly beseeching Kit for help.

She points to a chart on the worksheet: "What do they do to two to get to four?"

Wade starts, stumbles over his words, halts, goes silent, his eyes cast down.

Kit says, "How much did they save in three months?"

Wade concentrates, hard. After several tense seconds, he says: "Fourteen dollars?"

"They're showing it here," Kit says. "Look. It's two dollars here, eight dollars here, and so on— what's the pattern?"

Wade can't get it. He's trying, but he can't break the code.

"You've got to find that pattern," Kit says. Her voice has not wavered in tone or volume; it stays soft, low, even.

In the loft, Zachary and Jacob are playing with a big stuffed bear, laughing and grinning, enjoying themselves. Then they go back to working on the worksheets they've got clipped to their clipboards.

After a few moments, Zachary comes down and reports to Kit, shows her his work, completed.

Kit raises her voice to make an announcement: "Everyone, please listen. Now we're going to make a switch. You know what this means. People move around the room. You put away your folders, pick up new work, meet in new groups . . ."

The children begin moving around the room, putting away their folders, picking up new work to do, arranging themselves in new work-groups. They do it quietly, for the most part. Ben G's excited whisper is the loudest noise in the room. He's telling Rylie something about Passover and "slaves out of Egypt."

Everyone is moving around the room except Henry and Wade, who remain seated, confronting their troublesome math puzzles.

Shardasha, from the Older Group, walks into the room, smiling her big Shardasha smile. "Hey, Kit," she says. "Guess what? It's my birthday."

"Happy birthday!" Kit exclaims, and she rises from her chair and wraps her arms around Shardasha, and holds her in a hug. From all around the room children rush to Shardasha. They gather around her and hug her, two or three of them at a time, giving her birthday hugs.

Wade remains seated, locked in his struggle with the puzzle problem. When Shardasha's visit has ended and Kit is back sitting beside him, Wade says, "It's got to be fourteen dollars."

Kit seems curious. "You mean it's the same every month?"

"No," Wade says. He shakes his head. "No."

"Why?"

Wade starts over.

"Every month," he says, "they made—"

But he stops there. He's stumped.

Someone else—it is Shardé—needs Kit's attention, so she goes to the table where Shardé is working on something. After a minute or two she returns to Wade, and they pick up where they left off:

"They make a different amount of money every month," Wade says.

"A different amount every month," Kit affirms. "So, is there a pattern?"

Wade looks at her. He's thinking.

"What's the pattern? You need to discover the pattern."

Wade stares at the worksheet.

"Oh!" He's excited. "I think I got it."

He writes some figures on the worksheet.

"Here, look. It's four to eight. They double it. It doubles every time."

"You have it!" Kit says. "You've got the pattern!" Big, big smile. She is very pleased. But still, Kit's expression, her manner, the tone of her voice reveal no surprise, no undue elation. She knew all along Wade would solve the puzzle.

"Now," she says, "apply the pattern."

Wade begins charting the money made month by month. "That'd be thirty-two . . . sixty-four . . . one-twenty-eight," he says. He is doing the doubling in his head.

"Your brain's working," Kit says. "Keep going."

"Two times one-twenty-eight—this is hard, Kit . . . That would be two-fifty-six."

"Good job, Wade!" Kit is laughing now, bright-

smiling at Wade. "Look at what you have done!"

Ben G comes up to Kit, whispers in her ear. Across the room, children are making a birthday card for Shardasha. Ben is alerting everyone to come sign it. Kit leaves the table to go sign the card. Wade stays, double-checking his calculations.

As Kit is signing Shardasha's birthday card, Rylie comes up and asks her something, and then Chloe comes up, and she and Kit talk for a moment. "Okay, I get it," Chloe says, and scampers off.

On her way back across the room, Kit goes to the table where Henry is working and looks over his shoulder at his worksheet.

"You've done some good work here," Kit says. "You just need to finish it."

Henry doesn't look up.

"Henry," Kit says, softly. "Why is this so hard?"

Henry shakes his head; he can't find words. He is near tears.

Kit comes back to the table and sits down. At his worktable now, Henry is crying, silently. I point this out to Kit, who nods, solemnly.

"I know," she says, and motions me out of the room. We stand in the hallway and talk.

"I must not go to him," Kit says, her voice a near-whisper. "That would take from him his chance to do what he needs to do. *He* has to do it, because it's his. It's something he has to deal with. And I want him to know that he can do it. There's no question that he can. It's just, he needs to know that. And act on it.

"So, I can't go over there and do it for him. That would be sending him the message that he needs my help. He doesn't. He can do it. He needs to do his work himself."

Kit goes back into the room and sits back down at the table where she and Wade have been working. Wade is still there. He looks up and says, "Is it free time, Kit?"

"Yep," she says. "It's free time," and Wade goes out to play.

Little Brother Bob

Surprise! A sign appears mysteriously on the Younger Group door:

Y. G. Puppet Show—This Way——>>>

Kit laughs when she sees it. "Puppets!" she says. "I knew they were up to something, but I didn't know what."

Inside the room, an audience of Younger Groupers is gathered on the floor in front of the loft. In the front row is Henry, broad-grinning in anticipation . . .

A makeshift curtain hangs from the top of the loft. From behind the curtain the puppeteers, Paloma, Hana and Tasha, work the hand puppets they've created out of paper sacks, elaborately painted and glittered with smiling faces and curly red hair.

Now the curtain is pulled away. Three puppets take the stage. Tasha's puppet opens the show:

"My name is Jessica. I am the mother of all these lovely children."

The audience laughs heartily.

The puppet children—Paloma's and Hana's puppets—begin to quarrel.

"Little Brother Bob," the mother puppet says, "be nice to your sister!"

Little Brother Bob says, "I'm trying to watch a movie and everybody's bugging me!"

The sister puppet: "My brother won't leave me alone!"

The mother puppet: "I'm trying to study and I want you to be quiet!"

The puppet children are quiet.

"Finally," says the mother with a sigh, "I have some time to be by myself. To write in my diary."

The puppet children, too, have their inner thoughts:

"Today is the worst day of my life. I mean, every night we have cabbage. The same menu every night. And I forgot my horseradish . . ."

"I just wish I could trade places with this one enormously beautiful girl. Briana Willington! She's the richest girl in the school and she gets everything she wants. She can have ice cream for her dinner."

Now the puppet children go to school. They huddle together in a tight cluster, protecting each other from the large puppet teacher—who says: "My room is overflowing with your stinking socks!"

The puppet children reply, in chorus: "Your allergies are your problem!"

"That's it!" says Little Brother Bob. "I'm running away."

He scampers behind the curtain.

There is a long pause . . .

The puppet mother appears, lamenting: "I can't find my lovely child. I have looked for him everywhere. Where can he be?"

The audience stirs uneasily. There's no laughing now.

Little Brother Bob appears on the stage. He's bent over, downcast, in despair. "I'm so hungry! I'm feeling very very old . . . I can't believe I'm doing this . . . The only thing I have to eat is—broccoli!"

The audience's laughter revives.

Little Brother Bob stands up straight, and confronts the audience. He asks, in a sad, quavering voice:

"Would you remember me, if I went away forever?"

The audience is very still. All eyes are riveted on Little Brother Bob.

"Stop!" cries Paloma. "We need a break!"

So the puppet show ends.

Partners

In the Younger Group, the older children form reading partnerships with the younger children, mentoring them one on one, as a way to help them learn to read.

Today there are reading partners at work all over the Younger Group room—pairs of children reading books together, sitting together in chairs, lying together on a sofa, sprawled out on the floor with their heads together, bent over a book . . .

Chloe, who is mentoring Christina, guides her to the bookshelves by the window. "We'll find one you like," Chloe tells her in the most kind and encouraging, reassuring way . . .

Henry is Shardé's reading partner. He's nine; she's seven. They are sitting on the sofa together, reading a book that Henry knows by heart.

He seems quite pleased to be doing this, and he's doing it well. He's reading slowly, at Shardé's pace. He's careful to speak clearly as he reads so Shardé can understand the words, take them in, learn how to really read. Henry holds the book so Shardé can see the page, and he points to the words as he reads them, so Shardé can make the connection between what he's reading to her and what she sees printed there on the page. He's a good teacher.

He is a good actor, too. He's entertaining Shardé as he reads to her, intoning the words with great dramatic flair. Dynamic Shardé, a child who is always in motion, sits stock still as Henry reads. She's absorbed in the reading. They both are.

When they finish reading that book, they go to the shelf to get another one. Shardé eagerly picks one out: "What about this one?"

But Henry has another book in mind. "*Yuck Soup*," he says. "Don't you want to read *Yuck Soup?*"

Shardé picks out another book, shows it to Henry. "Oh, yuck," says Henry the punster. "No, no, I can't read that book, it gets so tiring and boring."

Ryan comes walking by. He jostles Henry, smiles at him in a certain way—it's a secret signal they have, to prompt a scene of some slapstick comedy. They begin to act it out:

Ryan knocks a book off the shelf onto the floor. He says accusingly to Henry, "Hey man, you knocked that book on the floor!"

"No way!" Henry says, in a stuffy British accent: "I did no such thing!"

Ryan makes a fist and a mock-angry face. He spins around and acts out leaving in a huff, goes stomping across the room toward the door. Henry acts out a mad pursuit, chasing after the fleeing Ryan, raising his fist in the air, shouting in a stage whisper, "I'm gonna get you!" Ryan's laughing, and right behind him Henry is, too, as they head for the door.

It all happens in a flash. Shardé, caught off guard, is left behind at the bookshelves. Her face goes blank for a moment. Instantly she recovers. She dashes after Henry, grabs his shirttail from behind and pulls on it. It balloons out; Shardé pulls on it some more. Just as Henry gets to the door he reels and staggers backward, dragged back into the room by the irrepressible Shardé . . .

Henry is very pleased—that was a wonderful scene! His face lights up in a delighted grin . . .

They go back to the bookshelves. Shardé picks out a book. Henry shakes his head: "That book? The words don't make any sense."

Shardé picks out another book. Henry says: "No, that book's silly."

From across the room Kit calls out, "There's just two minutes left in reading time."

Now Henry agrees to Shardé's selection of a book. It's about Little Bear and Mama Bear. Shardé and Henry go to the sofa and begin to read. They settle down into the soft cushions, leaning in close together, reading in earnest. Shardé is sitting on Henry's lap, silently saying the words to herself as her partner reads them to her.

Doo Dads

Today is the day for the Toy Store event. For weeks the children have been bringing in all their old toys, stuff they don't want anymore. Today they are selling it all in little stores set up all over the Younger Group room—stores like Doo Dads, run by Chloe, and Beautiful Accessories, run by Hue. They're selling stuffed animals, pink slippers, plastic earrings, cartoon watches . . .

Jade and Paloma have the Yo Gal Store, with a sign saying: "Boys Can Buy Dolls—Don't Be Embarrassed!" At the Food Store, offering cookies and brownies and popcorn, there's a waiting line of eager customers. Zachary is the genial grocer. There's a beauty salon called The Flashy Hair, the brainchild of Ben G, assisted by Regina and Christina. They'll braid your hair in whatever style you choose.

And there is The Bank, where everyone gets their money. They get some money to start the day, and then, after they've clerked for a while in the stores, they get paychecks they can cash at the bank. With their money they can buy and sell, wheel and deal, make a profit, lose it . . .

It is a free-market economy, and the children are busy making it work as best they can. They are a bit perplexed, but undeterred, by the arbitrary vagaries of economics. What's a fair price? What's something worth? Very quickly the children grasp the real issue: What is money worth?

As the event progresses, everyone begins buying more and more stuff. There's an undertone—I feel it—of stress and tension. "How much cookies can I buy for five bucks?" Henry demands of Zachary, who replies: "Chemicals. Don't eat. You'll get poisoned."

Wade swaggers up and says, "Zach, can I buy your store?" "Sure," Zachary says. "Give me one million dollars." Wade—he's one of the bankers—pulls out a wad of bills and hands them over.

Jade proudly announces that "our shop"—the Yo Gal Store—has "sold out!" She promptly spends all the profits. She buys a new car from Chloe at the Doo Dads store. "Keep the change," Jade tells her.

Making change is a bugaboo. At the bank, Jacob and Erin endure a torturous series of mathematical calculations trying to make change for Shardé. Erin finally ends the agony with a baleful, "Whatever, okay?" She tells Shardé to take as much money as she wants.

In the midst of it all, Ben G and Reed have a fight. "He punched me right in the nose!" Ben G cries, red-faced and weeping. Kit tells them to sit down and have a meeting about it. But Reed, breaking the unbreakable rule about meetings, refuses: "I'm not talking to him!" Kit places her hands on Reed's shoulders and looks him in the eyes: "It is your *responsibility*," she tells him. So Reed and Ben have a meeting, right there in the middle of the Toy Store. A minute and a half later, Ben G is smiling.

I watch all this with a certain foreboding. It seems to me this event is taking the children out of themselves, somehow. They just don't seem comfortable with it, really. They're excited and invigorated and all that, and they're having fun; but they're struggling with it, too. They just can't quite make this thing their own—but they keep doing more and more of it, spending more money, buying more stuff; and selling more stuff, making more money . . .

Hue, who has made a fortune selling her Beautiful Accessories, is going around buying everything she sees. So is Shardé—she's got a couple of big shopping bags and she's filling them up with stuff . . .

I have bought my own share of goodies today—a pair of gangsta sunglasses, a Rugrats wristwatch, and a Happy Hamburger, which I sold to Richard for what I paid for it, twenty-five cents. I'm wearing the sunglasses and the funky watch. People notice. Wade gives me a look. "You need some money,

Don?" He holds out a handful of bills. "Here, I've got plenty. Take some of mine." I take a few thousand dollars. "Thanks, Wade." It's the second gift of money I've been given today. At the Doo Dads store Paloma slipped me some spending cash . . .

Toward the end of the Toy Store time, Shardé comes up to me, carrying her shopping bags. She says, speaking in a careful, serious, soft-spoken way: "Don, I would like to give you something."

She stands there, looking thoughtfully at me, for a full moment of time.

"I know you like to write a lot," she says. "So, here—"

She hands me a small, neat box of bright-colored crayons.

It is a lovely gift. I am touched by it, and surprised, and at a loss for how to respond. I am stirred and warmed in some deep place inside me by the wise and generous heart of this wonderful child.

"Bright colors, Shardé!" I hear myself say to her. She is gazing at me solemnly. "Thank you! Thank you so much!"

She lingers for a second, then moves on to the person next to me—it is Rylie—and begins to give another gift. "Rylie," Shardé says, "you have a little brother, right? Here is something you can give him, if you want to . . ."

Little Books

The Younger Group is gathered for a reading of their Little Books. The children are both the authors and the audience; they're sitting on the rug in a kind of formal circle, alert, attentive, expectant.

Paloma's book is the first to be read. Jade does the reading, for Paloma feels too shy this morning to read her writing to the group. As Jade begins, Paloma buries her head inside her shirt. It's a distraction; around the circle there's an rippling of tittering and laughter. Several children, led by Christina, raise their hands in the signal for silence.

In the new quiet, Jade's reading takes on a kind of hypnotic rhythm, as Paloma's story—it's about being lost in the world—turns inward:

I had to face my fears.
How do I find my way home?
How do I get there?
"Follow the black brick road," said the pig.
"Like the yellow brick road," voices murmur.
Other voices go "Sshhhh, sshhhh . . ."
An hour later I was still walking.
I fell through a hole . . .

At the end of the story the children applaud. Quickly the next author—it is Quinn—begins reading his book. Its title is *The Puppy Cat Mouse:*

A cat and a mouse didn't get along.
The cat set a trap . . .

Max starts making cat noises.

Ben says, "Please stop! I can't hear when you're doing that."

Henry: "Yeah, stop!"
Out of nowhere another puppy came.
Now there were ten cats and ten dogs.
"O my god!" whispers Shardé.
Ten more dogs jumped over the fence . . .

As he turns the pages Quinn holds up the book so his audience can see the pictures he has drawn. Around the circle some of the children are laughing and whistling and jostling each other.

"Younger Group," Kit says, "hush!"

It's Ben G's turn to read. He's nervous. His book is a picture book, and he scoots around the center of the circle holding the book open so the children can see his drawings. He provides a running commentary: "They are fighting over who has the best pond . . . They went swimming and they irritated their friends . . ."

Ben G pauses. He seems dazed.

The children wait patiently.

"Need some help, Ben?" Kit asks, from her rocking chair at the edge of the circle.

Ben shakes his head no, and revives himself, and completes his showing of his book.

Regina is next. Her book is *Going to School in Germany:*

This is how it is in Germany on school days.

Kids always have to take a book and a notebook and a pencil to school . . .

Regina's presentation is smooth and poised and elegant. Her speech is clear and when she shows her book she holds it up high so everyone can see the pictures she has drawn—of a school building, children walking on their way to school, a bird in a tree and a "bird on the wing" . . .

My mom used to go to school in Germany. She told me this story. I am glad I go to school here.

When Regina is finished reading, Ursula goes to her and hugs her as the children applaud all around the circle.

Along with the applause, someone is whistling. It irritates Henry: "Please, please don't whistle!" he cries out. Ben G is offended: "We want to congratulate people, Henry."

The last to read is Hana. She comes into the center of the circle and kneels on the rug. The children are silent as Hana begins: "This is *The Snow Book.*" Her voice is light and mellow.

If the snow was eight feet tall, that would be cool and fun!

She holds up her book showing her drawing of a girl running across the page with a snowball tucked under her arm. She's smiling.

You are wondering why I brought it up.

I've been thinking a lot about what I would do.

Hana shows her drawing of a girl with a serious expression, her dark eyes peering out of the book directly at the reader.

I would make a snowman. It is fun, very very fun!

Hana has drawn a big, big snowman, with a little sled nearby, and a child holding a snowball.

But when it's summer I am glad . . .

Hana shows a girl wearing shorts and holding a bunch of flowers. She is smiling, and all around her there are flowers—bright green flowers are everywhere, floating around the girl, overflowing the page . . .

There are good things in the world!

There is quick, sharp applause all around the circle. Hana holds the last page so everyone can see the flowers.

Ben G stands up to get a better look. He says, admiringly: "Why are some of your flowers upside down?"

"I dunno," shrugs Hana, coyly with a grin. She knows Ben G has given her a compliment.

Giving Thanks

Kit, at Thanksgiving time, writes a message to the parents:

We sit down in a big circle often, sometimes to solve a problem, sometimes for Morning Meeting, sometimes for birthday celebrations. This time we were in our circle to make a group poem.

"What's that?" someone asked.

"Oh, it's where we each say a line," someone else said, even though we haven't done this very often. This was to be a group poem about what we are thankful for.

I asked who might be able to start us off. Someone said the first line, I wrote it down, and we proceeded around the circle. The children reached down inside and came up with wonderful things, practical things, truthful things.

And then one of our dear little new kids, overwhelmed in a way, looked at me and proclaimed, "I love you, Kit."

There was a small silence. I grinned real big and showed that I was writing that down. Then I asked the next child in line for a contribution to the poem. I didn't know if there was going to be a tittering, a making fun of, an embarrassment. There could have been. But just to let you know, there wasn't any of it. These children are used to there being all levels of maturity and great breadth of being in their group. They allow for it. They shift slightly in their seats, and accept it.

When we had traveled around the circle to where I was, I paused, looked out over the group and said, "I love YOU, children."

Then I wrote that down, too. Smiles all around.

We went on for some more lines to the poem. Then I read their poem back to them. They applauded themselves.

Happy Thanksgiving, everyone!

Our Thankful Poem
by the Whole Younger Group

I'm thankful for the Earth
Nature, trees, and the big blue sky
I'm thankful for oxygen
I'm thankful for my aunt, and that nobody is dead
I'm thankful for everything we can wear
I'm thankful for everything and everyone
The school and the vegetation
The sun, the earth, the protection
Earth and plants and human beings
I love you, Kit!
I'm thankful for the moon and the sun
At Thanksgiving I eat turkey with my friends
I am happy for every one of us
I am thankful for being in the Younger Group
Thanksgiving is fun for everyone
I love YOU, children!
I'm thankful for life on earth
I'm thankful for me getting a dog
I'm thankful for all the things God has made
And the ground, the sky, the birds
The animals, the trees, the oxygen
The clothes that we wear and the books that we read
And how we learn
Learning and swimming
And the planet we're on
And the state we're in
I'm thankful for God and the USA
I'm thankful I'm here
I'm thankful for my friends and me
And everything in life
I'm thankful for this school
For hamsters and pets
For hard math problems
For my loose tooth

The Wisdom of the Group

A kid crying

is like an underwater volcano erupting,

forming an island of teachers and children coming to help.

—Gabe, Older Group

The teachers:

Brian: I like our Morning Meetings. I know every group has a meeting every morning. I think lots of important stuff goes on there. One thing is, the kids listen to each other talk. They're learning to be listeners. That's a skill that's really good for them to learn, the listening part of talking with people.

[Pause.]

Our kids are usually pretty good at the talking part.

[Everyone smiles.]

Kit: For the Younger Group, our Morning Meeting is a good place for the children to really bring the group together. And keep it together. Make it work.

Chris: In the Older Group, if for some reason we have to skip our Morning Meeting, then we haven't really started the day. It's a way to bridge home and school, and come together into the group. We share things that are important, things that need to be told. If somebody comes in with a problem, or a concern, or something yucky that happened to them, they get a chance to say it, get it out there, share it with the group. Or to share something good, like the day-before's soccer exploits—"we won!" They can bring all these kinds of things to the group, for either the pleasure or catharsis of sharing it. And they have established this—

Brian: It's ritual.

Chris:—as a special time for the group to be together. Yes, that's right, it's like a ritual. I think the kids feel safe in Morning Meeting. It's a safe place for talking about those things that they need to talk about, but maybe have some fears and qualms about.

To be able to do that is very important to them.

Ann: So much of what we all do here is learning how to be together, in a group.

Jeanie: It's probably the hardest work the children do here—the letting go of themselves as the center, understanding themselves as a part of a group, part of a greater whole. Those things are really challenging lessons for the children to learn.

Don: How do they learn them?

Kit: I think it starts with problem solving. Some of the first social things the children do as a group revolve around solving a problem they encounter. At this school, we set it up so that the children are pretty much responsible for solving their own problems. So—how do they move those blocks to the other side of the hallway? Being a group helps them get that job done. It's what works.

So they come together for some common group purpose and they interact socially around that. And then it kind of just keeps going. It starts in Ann's room and it goes on and on, through Jeanie's room and mine and Chris's and Brian's. The work and the play they do, they do socially and together. They're always honing social skills while they're working together trying to get things done.

And the things they are doing are just their size. They are child-size things, and they keep finding good things to do together, projects and activities to refine and actualize. I think that helps them see themselves as confident and capable.

So, that's how it starts. And eventually that's what brings them together as a group.

Chris: I love to see how kids bring other kids into the group.

Kit: My kids have an uncanny sense of how to do that. Ben G was real good with Hue when she first came into the group. I mean, she had just come here from Vietnam, and she had to learn *everything*. He softened the way for her a lot—to the point where we had to have a talk about him doing her work for her. Because that was work *she* needed to do.

And with little Emma Liz—Ben always says something complimentary to Emma Liz in a kind

of public way just at the moment when the room is quiet, and he says it in a tone of voice that everyone will hear, and *it brings her into the group.* That's the kind of social knowledge I have seen some children have. They use it to benefit people who might need some help. And it's intentional, I think.

Jeanie: Oh, yes, I think it is, too. I think they do it to keep the group together, to keep the group functioning. And they know how to do it.

Kit: There's wisdom in it.

Don: Can you folks say a little more about what you mean by "wisdom"? And in what sense is it "intentional"?

Jeanie: Just like today in the Kindergarten. We were having cake for snacks and Johnny noticed that the snack helpers had forgotten to put out forks. He said, "I'll go get them." He said to the snack helpers, "You sit still." Then he went and got forks for everybody. And he's someone people are working with, trying to integrate him into the group. They aren't quite sure about him yet. But every single child he gave a fork to smiled at him and said, "Thank you, Johnny." He got a "thank you" from every single child, and every child said his name—it was "Thank you, Johnny" all around the table.

Now if someone else had been the one who got the forks, that might not have happened. There was a reason they did that. They wanted to give him that positive reinforcement—"This is a great thing you did for us. This is really kind, and thoughtful, and nice. And we appreciate it." They knew how to reinforce that behavior. They knew he'd feel it in a really important way.

Don: So that's what you mean by "intentional"?

Jeanie: Yes. "Intentional" is the right word for it. They have that uncanny awareness of each other. Yes! *Awareness* of each other.

Don: They were aware of his need—

Jeanie: Yes! He *needed* it. He needed to hear that from them, and feel it. As a group they knew that, and as a group they knew what to do. They knew it might bring him closer to them.

Ann [*softly*]: That is the wisdom of the group.

Kit: The other day something happened that really speaks to this. Emma Liz brought a toy to school, a little kitty, very cute and fluffy, and she showed it around the circle at Morning Meeting. Now, with Emma Liz, the children are becoming aware that she is an *outré* child, you know, very distinctive in her responses to things. She doesn't always do the "normal" thing. She is super intelligent, and yet she doesn't have quite the same exact attention to detail that the others have. And the others are beginning to see that.

One of ways she's different is, at Morning Meeting she doesn't come into the circle. She sits outside the circle, even though everyone else is inside the circle. Liana is her partner and she's aware that her task is to bring Emma into the circle—to bring her in with us. And some of the other children are aware that this is their task, too. We want her to come in.

So, a couple of days ago Emma brought in this little toy kitty and she carried it around the circle and showed it to everybody. Okay. But then today she brought in the same kitty, again—and at Morning Meeting she presented it in exactly the same way. She was just walking around the circle carrying the kitty, holding it out so everybody could see it—just as if we had never seen the kitty before.

It was an awkward situation. We were all sort of embarrassed, you know. But nobody said anything. They didn't say, "Yeah, yeah, Emma, you showed us that before . . ."

Well, the third or fourth child she showed the kitty to—it was Izzy—she reached out her hand and touched the kitty, you know, just sort of scratched its fur, very gently. Izzy did that, and then on it went, all around the circle. Every child—and I did it too; all of us who were in the circle did it—we reached out and we touched Emma's little kitty. We all did.

Because it was our way of touching Emma, you see. Of reaching out to her and touching her. We were responding to Emma's way of reaching out to us.

Oh, I just got chills!

I've got them now, thinking about it.

I swear—I swear to you, and you all know it is true—there is an *understanding* that children possess, an awareness, a very deep and special feeling they have.

Because for Emma Liz, given who she is, what the children did in that moment was perhaps the one thing we could have done that she would understand from us. And they knew to do that one thing. They knew what to do, and they knew how to do it.

How *do* they know? It is astonishing to me.

And I just want to say—this kind of wonderful thing, it happens here all the time. It really does. Caring. Reaching out. Being kind. I see it happening constantly, I really do.

And I am overwhelmed by the kindness of these children.

The Adventurous Hamster

One day just before Thanksgiving, Neetahnah's hamster, Junior, missing for a month after escaping from his cage in the Quiet Room, was discovered in the Art/Science Room, alive and well.

In the ensuing excitement, Neetahnah was bitten on the finger, quite painfully, by Junior. He was returned to the Quiet Room, where a group of children were meeting.

Here's what followed, as recorded on tape (the children were already working with a tape recorder):

Tasha, breathlessly: "Neetahnah cried a lot and she was really, really upset!"

Jade: "Because something happened to her hamster."

Tasha: "Yeah, and because Junior never bit anybody before."

Mary: "He turned wild!"

Jade: "He turned from a home hamster into a stray hamster."

Don: "Do you think he's wild?"

Tasha: "Not for good, I think, but he's had a lot of changes, and I think he's really freaked out."

Neetahnah comes in carrying Junior in a box. Didi is with her, bringing a hamster cage. Neetahnah starts to take Junior out of the box, to put him in the cage.

Jade: "Don't! Well, maybe . . ."

Emily: "Don't! He might—"

Mary: "He might attack!"

Junior stays in the box. With Didi's help, the transfer of the hamster to the cage is successful. The children crowd around the cage, peering intently in at Junior.

Tasha: "It's really surprising he's still alive."

Mary: "He survived a lot!"

Didi: "Poor guy."

Jade and Emily, crooning softly: "Hi, Junior . . . Hi, Junior . . ."

Mary, sadly: "Poor Junior."

Neetahnah: "How am I going to give him his water? I'm really scared to put my hand in there."

Tasha: "I don't think he's going to come out, Neetahnah. I think he's scared to death."

Mary: "Poor Junior. Too much like war for Junior."

Tasha: "I can't believe we found him!"

Jade: "I wonder what he *did* all this time?"

Emily: "We don't know *what* all he did."

Tasha: "Oh man, he's been through a lot."

Jade: "He's one adventurous hamster!"

Neetahnah puts some food in the cage, and quickly Junior emerges from the box.

Mary, Tasha: "He's fat! He's fat!"

Jade: "You're not jokin'!"

Emily: "He's really eating now."

Mary: "All that food! He was hungry."

Tasha: "I wonder what he's been eating all this time?"

Emily: "Mary left out a piece of food under her carrel, he probably got that."

Jade: "I bet he found food, like dropped food on the floor."

Neetahnah: "I put out food for him. I put five bowls of food out for him and every time, the next morning it was gone. So he's been eating food."

Don: "So, Neetahnah, you never gave up hope that he might still be alive?"

Neetahnah: "Yeah. I mean, his food was gone, so I knew he probably had to be alive."

Tasha: "I didn't. I really thought he was *lost*. I thought he was *gone*."

Jade: "So did I."

Emily: "So did I."

Mary: "So did I."

Don: "Do you think he's glad to be discovered?"

Mary: "Maybe. Maybe not."

Tasha: "I don't think he knows he's been discovered."

Mary: "He probably doesn't know he was lost. He probably just thought he was in some big, big hamster cage."

Jade: "So, are you happy, Neetahnah?"

Neetahnah is silent.

Jade: "I mean, duh, of course you're happy. But are you feeling a bit nervous with him?"

Neetahnah shrugs.

Tasha: "Are you scared? Happy? Sad? Mad?"

Neetahnah: "I don't *know*!"

Mary, thoughtfully: "I'd feel kind of mad at him, if I were you."

Neetahnah, softly: "Yeah, kind of."

Mary: "And kind of happy he's still alive."

Neetahnah: "Yeah."

Mary: "Kind of mad, and kind of happy."

Neetahnah is waiting for something more.

Mary: "And kind of thankful."

Solemnly, Neetahnah nods Yes.

Everyone is silent.

Jade, with a flourish, turns off the tape.

Everyone Is Together

Kit talks about the Younger Group's Halloween play, The Haunted Lunch Box:

Plays are always good for group building. Especially the Halloween play. It's a school tradition. We always have it in October, so every year it's one of the first things the kids focus on together.

The children create the play. They write it and direct it, act it, stage it. The tradition is: Make it original. Make it from scratch, from your own ideas.

So, we brainstormed it. The children came up with ideas, pages and pages and pages of ideas. They came up with them and I wrote them down. I'd read them to the group and say, "This is what you have so far . . ."

At first their ideas didn't go together. Everybody wanted there to be a kitty in the play. Some people wanted there to be a cave. So there was a kitty in a cave. Then somebody wanted there to be a bunny in the cave, too. And so on . . .

For three days we brainstormed ideas. No cohesion.

Then a moment came when Ben G got a kind of dreamy, gleamy look in his eyes, and he said, "The Haunted Lunch Box." That's all he said, just that. And everyone started to laugh, and we all kept on laughing for a long time—a long buzz of laughter just circled around the room.

So that was a start. We all thought "The Haunted Lunch Box" was funny and we went on from there. They brought up the cave thing again, and someone thought of the Evil Sorceror—Henry came up with the Sorceror—and the whole play really took off from there. Liana said the phrase "sorceror's minions," and Quinn said something about "chase 'em all the way to New York City!"

About then I was saying, "Well, you've got all these good ideas. What's your intention?"

Silence.

Then Hana said, "I think I see how they can fit together."

I knew they had it then . . .

An interesting thing happened with Tasha, as the kids began figuring out what parts everybody was going to have in the play. It's interesting for what it says about the workings of the group.

Tasha is a very capable child, very bright, very aware. She's new this year. Her parents brought her here because she was bored in the school where she was. So Tasha is new, and the Younger Group can be a tough crowd to get into—they've been together here for several years, they know each other very very well, they are bonded, they're a very tight group.

And Tasha has found her way in, very skillfully. She's found her way by watching and waiting for the right time to say things and do things. It's very skilled and careful work she's done.

And she's been treated with a lot of respect and consideration by the kids. She's written three Little Books, and when she read them the kids all applauded and cheered. And they were impressed by her math skills. They'd look at her work and they'd say, "Wow, Tasha, you know how to do that already!"

Then one day she overstepped. They were all talking about the play, and they started talking about taking parts, and Tasha said, "I want to be a piece of candy." And there was silence for a moment or two, and then a couple of the kids said, "Naw, I don't think that's a good idea . . ." It was all very subtle, but when she got that reaction Tasha realized right away what had happened. She had a stricken look on her face for a moment.

She had missed her cue, you see. She'd been very skilled up to now at watching and waiting, but this time she went too fast. And the group was saying, "Hold on. Wait a minute, Tasha. You can't have it all. You're not taking the throne here."

Then a day or so later, another child said, "Maybe I could be a piece of candy . . ." Yes—it was *very* subtle! And the kids didn't consciously understand it; they were just doing what they were doing. But Tasha understood it quite clearly. The group was saying, "This is our process. This is how we do it. We are not going to alter our process for you."

So it was a gentle correction, nothing overt, no confrontation—pure process. It was the process of the group affirming itself.

Stuff like this always happens when we're doing a play.

Later they found a way for there to be more than one piece of candy in the play. Hana came up with that. She said, "Maybe we can have the Evil Sorceror steal all the little kids' candy." Everyone liked that. They all said, "That's a good idea." So there were three or four pieces of candy in the play, and Tasha got to be one of them.

I love this group! This group is *dynamic*. They have great creative energy. And they can also be quiet, and listen. At rehearsal, when there was a problem, they could stop and be quiet and hear feedback about it—so they could fix it. "Sit down and listen" is something they tell each other. All during the time we were working on this play, they would tell each other things to do and not do. They would talk to each other and help each other. They would direct each other.

This is group building. It's a difficult, demanding process. And it's a wonderful process. The children own it. They take it on. They make it happen.

It was difficult, at times. They had some trouble being quiet backstage, and things like that. And trouble with bunching. The kids wrote the play so that there was always a group of children moving around the stage together, all in a group. They *all*

had to move together, they had to stay *together* as they moved—that was the whole point.

And it was difficult. The issue was, it was hard to be constantly moving around without leaving somebody out of the group. They'd all be moving and two or three kids would be left behind. So we'd talk about it, and practice it, and practice it, and practice it . . .

They had to rehearse it again and again. I said to them, "Make sure everybody's with you! When you move, make sure you move together!" And it *is* hard to do. You have to look out for everyone in the group, you have to reach out to them all and make sure you include them. I told the children, "You have to do this. You have to care about this."

You have to care. That's my expectation.

And when the children performed the play, everything went fine. The whole play was just fine! When the group was moving around the stage, they all moved together—not one child ever got left out. Amazing!

There were quite a few lines in the play about not leaving people out. I loved it when the minions said, "Minions are powerful children, too!" They would not be left out of Halloween. The Evil Sorceror says, "All the candy is mine, Halloween is all mine!" But the minions tell him, "You have to share the candy with us, we're part of Halloween, too!"

The children didn't want the Evil Sorceror to be left out. They were very clear about that. The minions tell the sorceror, "You've got to go trick-or-treating with us, because we're part of you." The minions were part of Halloween, and so was the Evil Sorceror. All of them were parts of Halloween; all of them, together, *were* Halloween.

The kids were very clear about what they wanted when they wrote these lines. The resolution of their play is: everyone's together in the end.

Yes! *Everyone is together.* That's the resolution of every play I've ever seen the children put on.

THE WISDOM OF THE GROUP

 # Remember

Jeanie tells this story of her Kindergarten group:

Each year as school ends, I sit down with the children and remind them that our school year is almost over. We reminisce. We marvel at how much each person has changed and grown. Then we make a list of all the things the children would like to do one more time before summer vacation.

This year, high on their list was "Go for another walk in the woods." I asked Chris if the Older Group would like to join us, and on a beautiful day we all headed off for the Pine Forest in the Glen.

Chris took the lead, and I walked at the end. I had the best job, for I had a complete view of the children interacting with each other.

One of my Kindergartners who still lives in a very fantastic world was spinning tales of intrigue and personal heroism. "You live a very exciting life," responded his partner.

Another child, who had recently had an unpleasant encounter with stinging nettle, worried out loud about getting stung. Her partner assured her: "I know how to fix that with jewel weed. And, here—let me give you a piggyback ride so you don't have to worry for a while."

Another child fell and scraped his knee. When we reached a stream his partner said, "I'll get a leaf for you. We can put some water on it and your knee will feel better. That's what I always do."

That's how our walk went. Branches were held for the person coming next down the trail; people checked to make sure they were not walking too fast for their partners. And in many other ways, I was struck by the kindness, thoughtfulness, and acceptance of the children to each other as we walked through the woods.

Later in the week, I asked each child to remember one thing about our Kindergarten year and to draw or write about that memory. Everyone sat at the table together, and the memories started flowing.

One child said, "Remember when we went to the woods, and we had to walk across that big river on those rocks?"

Everyone looked up. We all knew he had been afraid.

Then one of the children said, "We all made it across safe."

"Yep," added another child. "You made it across, too. You just took your time and did it your own way."

Everyone relaxed, and went back to their work.

One child's list of memories covered both sides of her paper. Another child made a list of four memories . . .

One child drew a picture of a smiling girl on a sunny day, and came to me, saying: "Will you write my words? I want to say, 'I remember how it feeled to feel the wind.'"

Growing Up

So many changes they're going through!

It's not easy being a child.

—Chris Powell

Chris Powell, the teacher of the Older Group, is a slender, intense, energetic woman, dark-haired, dark-eyed. She is bird-like in a way, with her bright eyes and sharp, alert gaze; and she loves birds, and has them as pets. She keeps parakeets and parrotlets in her home and at school, where they become the children's pets, loved in the pure and natural way that children love animals. Chris loves them in that way, too.

And so it was striking to witness the response of the Older Group, the children and their teacher, to the death of one of their birds, their parakeet, Woodstock. He died during the summer before the start of the new school year; Chris had to tell the children during the first day of school—indeed, during the first few minutes of the first day, for the children came in expecting to be reunited with Woodstock and found instead his empty cage.

Chris assembled the group and told them of his death; then she broke down weeping. "I loved that bird!" she blurted out through her tears. The children were crying, too. Chris started to leave the room, then stopped and turned around; she stayed with the group, so they could grieve together.

It was, however sad, a powerful beginning for a new school year. It was about emotion deeply felt—and shared—by the children and their teacher, drawn close together in this heartfelt moment.

Chris, in response to a question, describes her path to the Antioch School, starting with her childhood in New York City:

As a child I was shy. Socially, I was always very uncomfortable. In school you had to raise your hand and all that, and it was all very uncomfortable for me. I remember sitting in school looking out the window, wanting to be out there, moving around.

As I grew older I became rebellious and angry. I never saw any teacher as an ally, or someone I could rely on, count on to help me or mentor me, never as someone to have a positive experience with. In high school, I mostly stayed home. Graduated with honors. Went away to college.

At Antioch College I discovered that education could happen in a whole different way. I had my first experience with the Antioch School when I did some volunteer work with the swimming program. I watched what the children were doing, how they were interacting, how they treated each other. As I got to know more about it, I really liked what the Antioch School was doing. That's how I discovered that there really are schools where children are honored and respected.

So I went into education. I became a teacher, I think, because I hated school. My thinking was: I will do whatever I can to allow children's lives to be fuller than mine ever was in school . . .

I taught in elementary school for a while. Then I taught high school kids labeled LD, "learning disabled." I had a multiple-age classroom; my students were in my class for four years, so I got to know them really well. They were burdened with family problems. The pressure of poverty was intense on these kids' families, and on their neighborhoods, on every facet of their lives. I had to learn flexibility. I had to relate in a different way to each individual child, because each one was so different from the norm, and they were so different from each other in age and stage of development. I had

to learn about different learning styles; I had to learn different ways of teaching.

Mostly, I had to know my students, really well. And I did. We got to be close to each other, a really close-knit group. That was the best part of it all. We were like a family. We developed real respect for one another.

Respect, and self-respect. That was the expectation I put forth for these kids, who were the kind of kids nobody thought could learn to do anything. My expectation was: "You *can*. You can learn. You can do stuff. You are capable." We did a lot of really good things together. I loved teaching those kids.

When the Older Group position came open here at the Antioch School, it was really exciting to me that I could possibly teach here, because I knew that at the Antioch School children are treated like whole human beings. I knew, for example, that here they value free time for the children . . . Free time, really, is what stands out as what I knew and really liked about the Antioch School. Free time and all the beliefs about children that go along with that.

So that's how I came to the Antioch School. I came into it with great enthusiasm! And a lot of it was about free time, and what it means for the education of a child.

Chris celebrated the virtues of free time in an article she wrote for the Antioch School newsletter:

Free time and play are not an accidental occurrence at Antioch School, but a planned and valued part of the curriculum. Play and learning go hand in hand. A child at play is a learning child. All five senses are actively engaged—the entire body, the creative and inventive aspects of the intellect, the whole child, heart and soul.

And just what kind of learning has been taking place during free time? Here are just a few of the things the Older Group children have been doing recently:

Emily, new to the Antioch School, is learning to ride the unicycle. It is hard, but she applies all of her concentration and determination to the task. She is learning balance, physical control, poise, confidence, and, as with any difficult new skill, developing new neural connections in her brain that will serve her in many different ways.

Henry is out observing his world. He has an uncanny ability to find the most amazing insects and spiders I have ever seen. "Look what I found, Chris—it's a Hickory Horned Devil!" or "Look at this spider I just found!" With the gentlest touch imaginable, Henry gathers up his living discoveries, and looks for more information about them in books or on the Internet. His interest draws in others, children and adults alike, as he finds close-up photos and reads interesting facts about the insect or spider he has found.

Anna has discovered Mark Twain and is curled up on a couch reading *The Adventures of Huckleberry Finn* . . .

Ben, Luke, and Ryan are working on a video using the school camcorder. They are developing plots, and filming and re-filming to get the desired special effects.

Ryan, Cole, and Wade are building a quarter pipe for stunt skating. They hunt for suitable materials and the necessary tools. Next, they engineer the appropriate slant. Trial and error ends them up with a quarter pipe that will give them a good challenge for their stunt skating . . .

Most of the children in the Older Group have moved up from the Younger Group; some of them have been in the Antioch School since Nursery School. They have been through a lot together. They have played together, they have struggled together to resolve their conflicts, they have experienced themselves learning and growing together as a group. They know each other well, and have formed strong bonds. Even so, moving up to the Older Group is a big step for the children to take.

"The Younger Group kids feel they are making a quantum leap into the Older Group," Chris says. "They see the older kids doing advanced work, middle-school or even high-school level work, and they wonder if they'll ever be able to do all that. I try to gentle them into it. I try to tell them it's okay to move gradually . . .

"So many changes they're going through! They're moving from childhood to adolescence, really shifting in body and mind. It's important that they develop a positive image of themselves to take through these changes. I want them to move forward with the self-confidence to tackle a number of interests. That's what we work toward every day in the Older Group."

Chris pauses for a long moment, gazing pensively out the window at the empty play-yard. Suddenly she says, with emotion:

"It's not easy being a child."

She speaks of one of her Older Group children. The child has excellent skills, Chris says, but lacks self-confidence, lacks self-esteem. "There has been a lot of upheaval," she says, in this child's life, "a lot of transitions, self-doubt, serial parenting, geographical changes . . ."

Many children go through such difficult times in their lives, Chris says. "Some kids in the world suffer poverty, homelessness, hunger, deprivation. In Yellow Springs, other things can cause kids to lose their sense of security. A lot of negative things sometimes come together as the children get older, and it can really be devastating. Things happen that are disappointing, and disturbing. There's a loss of trust in adults. There's a lot of confusion about what goes on in the world. There's a lot of fear out there. It's what children grow up with today."

She speaks of the 9/11 World Trade Center disaster, and the Older Group children's response:

It was interesting what they talked about. The thought of our retaliation, what things could happen, scared them. And some things we were doing confused them. Like in Afghanistan, we were bombing them and feeding them at the same time. Kids at this stage of life see that kind of thing and really take notice of it. There were heated arguments about it in the Older Group, a lot of talk about food versus bombs.

For months the kids were upset. In some of the stories they wrote, they kept repeating the imagery of the twin towers falling. In the Art/Science Room someone made a clay tower with an airplane stuck into it.

And now we are dealing with it again, with this war in Iraq. The kids are thinking about it. Jesse came up and asked me the other day, "Do you think the United States would support Israel if Israel went to war against an Arab nation?" He's searching for an answer to that question. It's bothering him. It's on his mind.

Chris says it again: "It's not easy being a child."

A few of the children in the Older Group, perhaps two or three each year, come to the Antioch School because their previous schools did not serve their needs, or because they encountered difficulties there, or in their families, or with other aspects of their growing-up lives. No one calls them problem children—often they are brilliant, creative, gifted—but sometimes their interactions with the world have shut them down emotionally. These children come to the Antioch School for healing and renewal. Chris says:

I do sometimes get children who come into the group with emotional shutdown. When a child comes in who is fairly shut down, actually it's trust that becomes my curriculum for that child. The goal is to build enough trust for the child to start coming up out of that shutdown place, and start trusting the group, start trusting life again. Any kind of academics would take a back seat to that. The first thing to do is deal with their soul, their being.

So I provide a lot of honesty, a lot of freedom to move around and explore, free from other curriculum. Because a lot of times there is a total and intense fear of failure. So if what a child needs to do is just write random numbers in her journal—that's okay. If what a child needs to do is not go swimming for a whole year, just sit on the bench by the pool and feel really, really uncomfortable—that's okay. It's important to just let them move at their own pace, move into the group in their own way.

In their own way. That's essential.

One thing about this school that's very useful for this, is the kids can flow freely back and forth among the different age groups. They can play with younger children or older children, as they might feel the need to do that. I'm thinking about a particular child who came into the Older Group a number of years ago. He needed—he really *needed*—to go down to the Kindergarten and play with blocks. It was *essential* to him to play with those blocks. He had missed that part of his growing-up process and he needed to fill it in. And he did.

Every day he'd go down the hall to the Kindergarten and play with blocks. He kept going down there for an entire year.

And so that year he didn't really establish much connection with his peers. The following year I weaned him from the blocks, because he'd done that work, he'd filled in that gap. So now he was present in the Older Group all the time. But the other children still weren't interacting with him very much.

Then one day someone asked me, "Chris, how do you spell—?" It was some long, very difficult word. Before I could say what I always say to that question—"Go look it up in the dictionary"—his child said, "That's easy!" He spelled it perfectly. And it was a *difficult* word. Every face in the room turned to me with an expression of disbelief—like, "*What?* Is he *right*?" And he was.

Always after that, whenever somebody would ask me how to spell a word, I'd tell them—against all my rules about "go look it up in the dictionary"—to go ask this child to spell it for them. So they would take their words to him, and he was always able to spell them. Every time. He gained a lot of prestige. His peers were made aware that "Oh, there's more to him than I thought!" And this helped him move forward in his life, toward where he needed to be. Pretty soon he became accepted as a part of the group.

Even before that, I think the children understood him pretty well. All that time when he was leaving the Older Group and going down to the Nursery to play with blocks, the other children didn't make anything of it. They might say, "Um, where is he?" "Oh, he's down in the Kindergarten." They just wanted to be sure where he was. I think they understood that's where he needed to be.

The Older Group "is a place where children of ages nine to twelve can hold on to the magic of childhood," Chris said.

"Children at this age are growing more independent, but they want the security of knowing they are being looked after. They need to be free to be young children and play with toys, free to try out new ideas and responsibilities, without pressure . . .

"The Older Group is a family-like environment, where children can explore and share ideas and social relationships in a safe context. We have tables and couches instead of desks and chairs. The couches allow for a cozy place to read a book, to share ideas, work together on assignments, and for conversation during free time. There's room to move around.

"The journey, the exploration, the pleasure of learning something new—these are factors that develop independent thinkers, and people who enjoy learning and know how to learn."

 Private—Keep Out

One of the ways the Older Group kids express their many-layered lives is via their study carrels, the cubicles—shelf space, desktop, chair—that line the walls of the Older Group room, one for each child.

This is Ryder's carrel, filled with her things:

a blurry snapshot of her dog
a box of crayons
a box of pencils
a small, heart-shaped box of candy
clipboard
notebook
two rulers
a comb
a picture, clipped from a magazine, of four little brown dogs wrapped up in an American flag
a small hand-squeezer exercise ball
calculator
address book
three small notebooks, neatly stacked
The Answer Book for School Survival
three stuffed animals: soft, furry dogs, white, yellow and orange
a neon-green plastic bracelet
a box of sparkly stardust
a sign on the top shelf:
Private—Keep Out

Schoolwork

At the big table in the Older Group room, Chris is leading a lesson on Native American folklore. Grouped around her are Hannah, Jenna, Jesse, and Claire. Claire is reading to the group from a book: "Some scholars say . . . religion . . . stories travel by land . . . folktales . . ."

Nanako, a Japanese exchange student at Antioch College, is visiting the Older Group today. She's sitting at the round table in the middle of the room with Polo, Ben, Pat, and Asa. They've been there three minutes and already they're speaking Japanese, following Nanako's direction. They're all leaning forward toward the center of the table, forming a circle, speaking together, quietly. They are saying *Kyoto,* repeating after Nanako—*Key-oh-toe.* Kyoto, Nanako tells them, is her hometown.

Polo asks how to say "Ohio," and Nanako translates: *Ho-bow-wa,* is how it sounds. Polo is listening intently. They all are. Nanako is smiling and laughing, her eyes sparkle. She's delighted to be here, she's having fun. She is wearing a bright red sweater.

Bill is in the Quiet Room teaching a math lesson, with Crystal, David, Nicky, and Will. Sounds of math-talk can be heard through the door, Bill speaking rapidly, "Okay, that's right, it's 57 degrees. So this is how the triangle will look . . ."

Shardasha's at a computer station, busy doing cyber-art, glancing over her shoulder from time to time to see what's going on with Nanako's group . . . Lucas and Anna and Ryan and Marlee are on the sofa doing math, getting ready for a session with Bill.

At Chris's table, Jesse reads aloud from a book, *Legend of the Flute:* "Once, many generations ago . . . possibly from hearing the wind through the trees,

people figured out how to make a flute." Chris asks the group, "Do you think this is possible?"

Ryder is with Hannah at the computers.
Hannah: "How do I get Music?"
Ryder: "Go into Shop and type Music, it'll tell you what to do."
Ryder's wearing a red and white T-shirt that says on the back:
YES
YES
YES

Chris is saying: "Folktales change a great deal. Different people will tell them differently. So over time, tradition would change . . . mythology . . . coyote stories . . ."

Actually, when you see it close up and read the small print, Ryder's T-shirt says:
YES I'm female
YES I'm an athlete
YES I can kick your butt!

Nanako is telling her group, "This how you say, *I see you. . .*" She says it in Japanese, then repeats it, looking closely at each of them, in turn—Polo, Ben, Pat, Asa—in their little circle there at the table. She says it with a clear, strong meaning. It is a statement of friendship.

David, at his study carrel writing a story, has been listening closely to Nanako's group. Now he gets up and goes over to their table, stands there looking on, observing . . .

Nanako is teaching the kids the Japanese words for Up, Down, Left, Right. She acts the words out, demonstrating with her hands, arms, body language: "This is Up"—she reaches upward: "This is Down"—she bends downward . . . The kids are speaking Japanese words in unison now, sounding like a chorus, speaking their new language in a rhythmic chant.

Bill emerges from his room, his students streaming out behind him. "Okay. New group," Bill says from the doorway. "Right now!" The new group is Anna, Lucas, Ryan, and Marlee . . .

Coming out of Bill's room, Crystal spies an open computer station. *"Yes!"* She goes quickly to it, starts e-mailing her e-pals in Australia . . .

Everything is moving quickly now, things are happening fast all around the room . . .

Asa is talking to Polo in Japanese. Much laughter! Nanako laughs too . . . Then quickly and deftly she calls them to order, invites them to be serious, returns them to the work they are doing.

Nanako is beautiful, charming. She is calm and relaxed—and she is serious. She is *teaching*. She leads the children gracefully, with an easy, natural sense of authority and presence.

Chris is telling her group: "We're going to read about Tecumseh now . . . Tecumseh lived at Old Town, just up the road from here . . . Shawnee . . ."

Nanako places her hand on Polo's neck and says the Japanese word meaning neck. She pats Asa's cheek and says the Japanese word meaning cheek. The boys pronounce the words after her, two or three times. Then they touch their necks and pat their cheeks, and say the Japanese words. This is all done quite solemnly. "Good," says Nanako.

Then Asa reaches over and pats Polo's cheek, and Polo pats Asa's cheek, and the two of them say the Japanese word together—it sounds perfect!—and everyone dissolves in rollicking laughter. Nanako included. She's laughing most merrily of all.

Bill's group is at work in the Quiet Room—not so quietly. You can hear them:

Bill: "What do you do with the known factor?"

Anna: "Divide the product by the known factor."

Bill: "That's right. Very good. Now here's what happens—"

Nanako's teaching them numbers now. They've done one, two, three. She holds up both hands, with all five fingers raised on each. "What's this?"

Stefan has joined the group. He's smiling at the wonder of it—here they are, speaking Japanese . . .

Chris asks her group: "Where is the nearest burial mound, anybody know?"

Nanako's doing names, writing them out on a sheet of paper so everyone can see. Carefully, slowly, she writes out her own name in Japanese. Asa says, "Can you write *my* name?" Nanako begins to write. All heads are bent over Nanako's writing. Asa says, "Is that an A?"—Asa's smile of recognition . . . All is quiet as Nanako writes Polo's name.

Polo: "Wow!"

Nanako's group takes a break. It's free time now.

Shardasha immediately bonds with Nanako, they're hugging each other, Shardasha is overjoyed . . . Shardasha and Nanako play RockPaperScissors in Japanese, as a group gathers around them . . .

Shardasha, happy, relaxing on the sofa now, says to no one in particular: "RockScissorsPaper, wow, that's a hard game to play in Japanese!"

Outside, Ben and Polo are in close communion on the tire swing, swinging together slowly, round and round, occasionally patting each other's cheeks, carefully saying some words in Japanese, breaking up into howls of laughter . . .

Hurly Burly Shakespeare

The Older Groupers are learning *A Midsummer's Night Dream.*

Chris: "Okay, let's read the play. Act I, Scene 1. Nicky, you're on. Read Theseus's part."

Nicky: *Now, fair Hippolyuta, our wedding day*
Draws on apace. Four happy days bring in
Another moon. But O, methinks, how slow
This old moon wanes! I wish the hours had wings.

Caitlin Guthrie-Freeman is visiting the Older Group, to help them work on the Shakespeare play. She is an Antioch School graduate, a trained vocal musician and a Shakespeare scholar (and she is Ann Guthrie's daughter).

Caitlin: "I want to talk to you about Shakespeare's words. He used *so many* words! It's estimated he added three thousand five hundred words to the English language. Shakespeare's words paint wonderful pictures. And they *sound* very wonderful. They are evocative. They are expressive. Some of his words are [she reads from a list]: *hubbub, hurly burly, bubble—*"

Jenna: " 'Bubble'? He made that up?"

Caitlin: "Yes, he did."

Jenna: "Wow! He made Bubble-Up!"

Caitlin passes around the room lists of Shakespearean insults. Immediately the kids start picking favorites and shouting them out: *maggot pie, pigeon egg, wagtail, hugger mugger* . . . The kids are delighted with these words. There's a *hubbub* of *hurly burly* all around the room . . .

Caitlin: "You'll notice that with a lot of the words, even if you don't know exactly what they mean, you can get a sense of what they mean just by the way they sound. For example, *quailing.* Anybody know what it means? Want to take a guess?"

Will: "Scared"?

Caitlin: "That's right. It means you're shaking in your boots."

Ryan: "What's *hell-hated* mean?"

Caitlin: "Anyone have an idea?"

Henry: "Does it mean, like, this guy was so bad that hell spat him out?"

Caitlin: "That's exactly right, Henry."

Many hands are up all around the room.

Jade: "What's *fat kidney*?"

Caitlin: "You ate too much."

Will: "What's *earth vexing*?"

Caitlin: "Let's think it out. What's *vexing* mean?"

Will: "Like, bothering, frustrating . . ."

Caitlin: "Almost . . ."

Will: "Annoying."

Caitlin: "Exactly. So *earth vexing* is—?"

Will: "You're annoying to the earth—because you're so useless and boring."

Caitlin: "That's right, that's it."

Hana: "What's *beetle-headed*?"

Caitlin: "What do you think?"

Hana: "Really, really ugly?"

Cailtin: "Yes, that's right."

Henry: "How about *flap-mouthed*?"

Caitlin: "Talks too much."

Gabe: "What's *lout*?"

Caitlin: "A low-down, no-good person."

Ryan, delighted, strikes an angry pose: "Oh, you lout!"

Now the group's ready to do some Shakespeare. Caitlin has the kids read some lines from the play.

Jenna is the first to read:

Love can transform to grace and excellence.
Love looks not with the eyes, but with the mind;
And therefore is winged Cupid blind . . .

Everyone is still as Jade reads:

A lover, that kills himself most gallantly for love!

And Luke: *That will call for some tears . . .*
I shall cry rivers!

Silence . . .

Then laughter engulfs the room.

Strong Words

The Older Group on Martin Luther King Day:

Chris: What does "power of the pen" mean?

Henry: Somebody can say his true thoughts on paper.

Chris: Have you heard the saying, "The pen is mightier than the sword"?

Chorus of voices: Yes.

Chris: Why is it mightier than the sword?

Anna C: You can create something rather than destroying it.

Marlee: When you write, you can reach many people over time, over many generations.

Emily: It's much more peaceful.

Jade: You can write strong words. And make speeches.

Chris: Martin Luther King gave a speech. He said "I Have A Dream." What was his dream about?

Marlee: He dreamed that one day everybody would become equal.

Chris: Do you think that's where we are now?

Chorus of voices: *No!*

Chris: Where do we need to improve?

Chorus: Iraq!

Henry: I have to say—George Bush, I think he probably has a lot of hate inside him. He's pretty greedy. He wants oil from Iraq, and I think that's the whole point of this war.

Anna C: In Iraq there's no rules, there's just chaos there.

Emily: I think George Bush is a good person and he has a lot on his mind.

Tasha: I'm not saying Bush is a bad person. The only thing is, we should stop sticking our nose into other people's business.

Patrick: George Bush has a lot of anger and he doesn't know any other way to express his anger.

Emily: In the first place, war is bad. The reason there's a war is, he wants the oil. He doesn't *say* that, because then people wouldn't want to have a war. And—he just shouldn't have done it at all.

Henry: George Bush has a lot of thoughts but he can't express his thoughts. When he can't express his thoughts with his words, he uses his swords a lot.

Gabe: He has a whole bunch of money he could use. He should use it to save animals, and plants, and people, too.

Jenna: He could make robot people do the war for him, so he wouldn't have to risk people's lives

Marlee: Soldiers choose to be soliders and go to war.

Chris: How about the people of Iraq?

Jenna: What if both sides were robots?

Chris: What you're saying is, we need a peaceful way to fight war.

Chorus of voices: *Yes!*

Chris: And what way might that be?

Marlee: With words.

Chris: So we're back to words. . . How do we listen to someone's words? What's the difference between hearing and listening?

Ben W: Paying attention.

Luke: Actually taking things in while you're listening.

Henry: Right! Actually taking things *in*.

Chris: You're a better listener if you try to understand other people's point of view. Like, if someone has a very different lifestyle than yours, listening to them. Listen to their ideas—really listen, even if you disagree.

Henry: *Especially* if you disagree.

Chris: Okay. Now let's all think of something that is happening in our world today that you think Martin Luther King, if he were alive, would be working to change. What would Martin Luther King look at and want to change?

Tasha: Everything!

Jade: War—the war in Iraq.

Jenna: Martin Luther King would go against Bush, because he caused the war.

Will: The economy.

Zachary: Destroying habitat for oil.

Mary: Fighting each other at school.

Chris: You mean bullying?

Mary: Yes. Bullies.

Marlee: Drugs. Too many teenagers getting into drugs.

Patrick: There's a lot of drugs going around in a little town like this.

Hannah: Also prescription drugs.

Anna C: Domestic violence.

Emily: What about family arguments? If we want to make a better place of the world, we'd better start in our own homes. If people can't stop a little argument at home, how can they expect people to stop big arguments in the world? Like the war.

Chris: You're saying that conflict solving starts at home?

Emily: Yes, that's what I'm saying.

Chris: What can people your age do to make this a better world, as Martin Luther King wanted? And as you might want.

Jade: Not so much pollution.

Gabe: Not watch so much TV.

Emily: Not use so much water.

Jade: Bike to work. Recycle paper.

Tasha: Plastic bags for trash, so people don't litter.

Henry: Fix the water supply.

Chris: You're saying we need clean water. How could we get that? What can we do?

Emily: I wrote a letter to the editor about cleaning up Massie's Creek, and they printed it.

Chris: That's a good way—the power of the pen. Write letters to the editor.

Gabe: I was on that group trying to help with Massie's Creek.

Chris: There are a lot of things you have the power to help with.

Will: My dad made a sign for Massie's Creek.

Chris: What else can we do?

Luke: No war.

Nicky: Peace on earth.

Ryan: Think a lot harder before we go into war.

Tasha: War shouldn't be something to solve all this country's problems.

Anna C: Find alternatives to war.

Will: Take our troops out of Iraq.

Jacob: Make peace in the Middle East.

Will: Impeach Bush.

Patrick: Plastic.

Chris: What about plastic?

Patrick: I hate it. It doesn't decompose.

Chris: That fits in with what Jade said about pollution.

Tasha: But plastic also saves lives. They use it in IVs in hospitals.

Jade: You can save leftover food with plastic, so you don't waste food.

Anna: You can recycle plastic.

Patrick: The production of plastic pollutes a lot.

Chris: Realistically, what are some things that *we* can do to make the world better?

Gabe: I'm wondering if we could maybe plant some trees.

Jade: Stop cutting down trees for no reason.

Nicky: Write letters to Bush.

Jenna: E-mail Bush.

Nicky: Help fight terrorism by speech.

Chris: How?

Marlee: Talk.

Chris: To whom?

Marlee: Everyone. People. Talk to them about it.

Nicky: Like, ask them, what's the point of killing people?

Cole: Respect other people's religion.

Chris: What else should we respect?

Anna: What other people look like.

Tasha: The color of their skin.

Will: Their gender.

Hannah: Their looks.

Chris: How about if you were sitting next to someone who came from an Arab country. How would you feel? How would you act?

Marlee: I'd want to know more about them. I'd talk to them. I'd ask them about their country, and stuff.

Chris: Let's go back to Martin Luther King. What did he want? What was his dream?

Marlee: For people to be judged by the content of their character, not the color of their skin.

Chris: Do we do that? If we see someone who is dressed differently—do we judge that person by the content of their character?

Chorus of voices: No . . . No . . . No . . .

Ryan: I have a question. What does "content of their character" mean?

[There is a thoughtful pause.]

Anna C: Kindness.

Emily: There's no such thing as an unkind person, there are only unkind acts.

Ryan: What? Like Hitler?

Emily: When a person is born, they're not born good or bad. It's just what they're around. They get it from that.

Tasha: Not always. People who are around nice, kind people don't always be nice and kind.

Anna C: Another condition is where you just don't understand another person's feelings.

Nicky: My mom works with autism. Parents don't treat autistic kids nice, but they are nice.

Chris: So, people can choose not to be influenced by their environment?

Neetahnah: If I'm around people that are screaming and yelling, I don't scream and yell.

Jade: It's like yin-yang. Bad people have some good in them, and good people have some bad in them.

Ryan: What if someone shot you with an M-16— where's the kindness?

Marlee: Maybe he *was* kind, but he's not anymore.

Ryan: Why not?

Marlee: Maybe he was kind until something happened to him.

Chris: So, Marlee, do you think there are kind traits in an unkind person?

Marlee (*nods*): Deep down inside.

169

Integrity

A conflict arose in the Older Group when Chris, responding to an outbreak of boy-girl teasing, took the radical step of separating the boys and girls during free time. She told the children this was necessary because, as she wrote in a message to the school community, posted on the school's website:

> Community-wide in Yellow Springs, there has been a peer-related push toward girlfriend / boyfriend friendships among children in the fifth and sixth grade. It seems we are not immune to this, as this has been a snowballing issue in the Older Group. Unfortunately this has a lot of negative consequences in terms of comfort levels, friendships, and group dynamics. This has resulted in teasing, and in creating situations where people are not comfortable. We are working on this at school . . .

When Chris told the Older Group that boys and girls could no longer play together during free time, the children were furious. They called it "segregation," and angrily vowed to resist it. Five of them—Patrick, Marlee, Hannah, Anna, and Ben—confronted Chris and insisted on having an emergency meeting of the group, so they could demand that she restore their shared free time.

I witnessed the meeting:

"Your stupid rules!" Patrick hissed at Chris, staring coldly at her. They were sitting at the table, face to face. He was staring straight into her eyes. He was enraged, red-faced, choked up, beginning to cry. Hard tears were squeezing out of his eyes. But he did not avert them from her eyes. "We want to have our meeting without you," he told her. "You should go out of the room."

His integrity, Chris said to me once about Patrick. She was describing a strength of his character. His anger, and his inability to restrain it, was a weakness.

"No," said Chris. She stared back at Patrick, unblinking. "I am part of this meeting. I will stay here and participate in it."

I could feel Patrick's anger, verging on rage, threatening to overwhelm him. And yet, at the same time, something strong—*his integrity*—seemed to be rising within him. I felt it. I could tell the children felt it. Hannah, so excited a moment ago, was solemn now, staring at Patrick, fascinated.

"You have to leave," Patrick said to Chris. His voice was steady. Then he spit out these words: "We can't *talk* to you. You won't *listen.*"

And he waited, coiled in his chair, for her to respond.

I was on his side. I could feel how much was at stake for him now. I wanted Chris to back off, leave the room, let him assert his strength in this moment. Let him win. I was a little afraid of what he might lose of himself if she didn't.

And she didn't. "I am going to be in this meeting," Chris said firmly to Patrick. Her eyes were locked on his. "I have something to say, and I am going to say it."

Her eyes were flashing as she held her ground.

We all saw Patrick grow even stronger then. His expression, his whole countenance, seemed to take on a deeper feeling. The tears were dry on his face. His voice was clear and full . . .

I was struck by this. And as I looked at Patrick, this thought came to me: *His integrity is rising as this conflict deepens.*

That's what was happening.

And I realize, now, that Chris was making it happen. She was making this crucial moment possible for Patrick. She knew that he needed—that the angry rage inside him needed—something real to oppose and confront; and she was providing it. By his angry demand he had thrown down a challenge; in the deepest sense, it was a challenge to himself.

They negotiated a resolution of their conflict, and free time, unrestricted, was restored for all.

On the website, they reported the results to the school community:

We in the Older Group have been spending time this week coming up with solutions to the teasing about girlfriends and boyfriends, who likes who, etc. Our discussion today centered around the rules at Antioch School and how they relate to this problem. We talked about which rules addressed this, why those rules are in place, and what we can do to help keep our school a safe and confortable place for everyone.

These are the ideas and recommendations we came up with:

Antioch School rules:

Do not tease about who people like (do not tease at all.)

Don't say things about girlfriend/boyfriend. Don't start rumors. Be respectful.

Reasons for those rules:

People can have friends that are girls and boys without being teased. Teasing can and does hurt people's feelings.

It messes up the games people can play. People end up feeling uncomfortable or in uncomfortable situations.

People can feel jealous, hurt, left out and/or embarrassed.

How we will deal with this problem:

Make only positive comments, don't tease. Keep all other things to yourself. Stop making fun of people.

Just stop!

And Chris stood firm against it, so that he could stand firm against her, and make his own true response.

Chris did this as his *teacher*, helping Patrick learn, in this moment, who he truly is. Her own integrity drew out his intregity from within him.

Integrity.

After that, they worked it out. The children had their meeting, with Chris—and Patrick—participating.

171

Trust

Older Group children serve the school in important ways as teachers of the younger children. They are swimming partners with Kindergarten children, a tremendous responsibility that requires a great deal of skill, attention, gentleness, and patience.

—Older Group Parents Guide

It is Thursday: swimming day. Time for swimming partners. It's an Antioch School tradition. Older Groupers partner up with Kindergartners, one on one: an older child and a younger child become swimming partners for the year. The older child serves as the younger one's mentor, guide, friend, and protector for the half-hour they spend together each week swimming in the Antioch College pool.

Today the children are already paired off and in the water. They're gathered in a bunch near the wall in the shallow end of the pool. They are holding on to each other, bobbing and floating, or just standing still, taking their time getting used to being in the water. Chris and Jeanie and the swimming pool's team of lifeguards monitor the children from the deck around the pool, but only the children are in the water:

Ryan, broad shouldered, strong, solid, holds slender Liam lightly in his arms. Liam's legs are wrapped around Ryan's body. Together they are turning slowly, slowly in the water, Ryan moving in a swaying motion, just holding Liam, letting Liam feel safe.

Ryder, tall, calm, blond, holds Azsa, so tiny and brown. Azsa, with her quick-darting nervous energy, perches like a bird on Ryder's hip.

Polo's partner is Oona; they stand together halfway down the four or five steps that lead from the wall into the pool. He's holding her hand, steadying her, waiting patiently for Oona to decide if she will descend the final steps into the water . . .

Crystal, so at ease in her body, submerges herself in the water to her shoulders, and waits for shy Emma Rose to step into her arms—and Emma does, quite gracefully. Crystal and Emma float smiling in the pool . . .

Jesse is with Morgan, Anna C with Hypatia, Claire with Francesca, David with Brecon, Paloma with Zakiyah, Asa with Danny, Jade with Cecelia—they're all in the water, holding each other and being held . . . There is an abundant animal healthiness and naturalness, and keen, sharp awareness: the children are alert to each other, they are *together* in the water. It feels good to them. They are comfortable and safe . . .

Crystal, with her graceful strength, is effortlessly lifting Emma Rose up and down, in and out of the water. They are joined together in a smooth, rhythmical motion . . . To fear being in the water never occurs to Crystal. Emma Rose senses this, and it gives her strength. She will not be afraid, and is proud of this . . . They are shoulder-deep in the water now, moving together in a circling motion, slowly turning round and round . . .

A steady hum echoes all around the pool . . .

Asa and Danny: Asa calm, steady, playful; Danny busy, struggling a bit, grasping for the wall . . . Now he's loosening up—Asa is showing him how to cup his hands to make a splash. Danny's tiny hands make a tiny splash, and he laughs and laughs, and does it again . . . Danny splashes Asa . . . Danny grinning, wet all over, clasping himself to Asa's broad shoulders. . . Asa grinning too.

Claire and Francesca: Claire is showing her how to do leg kicks off the wall. She holds Francesca steady in the water. Claire, so small, yet so adult-like now, and an excellent teacher: she's scarcely larger than Francesca, yet she's in full, confident, capable control . . .

Liana with little Emma Liz, holding close to the wall. They decide to get out of the water for a while,

rest, take a break . . . Liana's super-careful caretaking: Emma Liz doesn't make a move, in the water or out, without Liana's arm cradled around her, holding her, leaning in close: "I'm right here with you, Emma. Does this feel okay? Are you comfortable?"

Jade is with Cecelia, taking a break, standing on the deck at the edge of the water. Jade sees Cecelia's impish grin. Jade says "*Wait*, Cecelia, you're not allowed to jump in!"—but Cecelia's already jumping in. Right behind her, Jade jumps in, and she holds Cecelia while she shakes water out of her face, and tries to open her eyes. Jade hugs her for a moment, holds her close. She's safe . . .

As their time together in the water lengthens, the older children lead the younger ones in more daring exploits—floating on their backs, bobbing into deeper water, swimming a few strokes free of their swimming partner's grasp . . .

Anna M, jumping off the wall into Hannah's arms. Zakiyah, wearing big round goggles, leaping into Paloma's arms . . .

Time's up. Chris blows her whistle. Swimming is over for today.

On the deck, the children bundle each other in towels. The little kids are shivering; the big kids are rubbing them down with the towels, warming them up . . . Claire hugs Francesca in celebration of what they have accomplished today.

Hand in hand, the swimming partners walk together to the dressing rooms.

Self-portrait

Being Who You Are

If I was a hen I would say COCKADOODLE-DOO! *as loud as I could.*
—Christina, Younger Group

Circles of the past,
recovering everything, loving it again . . .
—Marlee, Older Group

The teachers, at the end of the school year:

Don: Do you ever worry about what happens to the children here when they grow up? I'm thinking of these wonderful kids moving from the child-centered culture of this school into the unreal culture of the "real world," as they call it. Do you sometimes feel concerned about how these kids will do out there?

Chris: I have great confidence in them. What these children bring forth from their experience here—what they've gained in terms of strength and self-knowledge, inner knowledge, their view of themselves in the world and their responsibilities to the world—that piece is timeless, no matter what the culture is, no matter how unreal the "real world" gets.

Jeanie: I think that is really true. What happens here transcends culture. When you strengthen the individual, you give them the strength to do that. It becomes their own integrity, no matter what is going on with the culture out there.

Kit: Yes, because it's not the external forces from the culture that define them. It's coming from within. The children define themselves. Everything that happens here, it's theirs—it's theirs to choose, theirs to decide, theirs to do.

Jeanie: And they become very used to having all the good feelings that go along with that.

Kit: It becomes natural.

Chris: I remember a conversation I had with someone who would not send his children here because he felt this school wouldn't prepare them for the real world. He felt that in order to be strong and fortified it was necessary for his children to experience racism, to experience adversity, so that they would know how to cope with it once they got older. He felt there was too much protection in this school, that it wasn't the real world.

I think the irony is, this *is* the real world. People here really learn from each other how to be with each other, how to keep their personal integrity in the face of adversity. The children get a chance to really experience each other; they deal with each other's mistakes, find ways to resolve conflict, ways to compromise, ways to speak up for themselves.

And that happens here because it is a good place to learn and grow and develop strengths to deal with adversity—because it's safe to make mistakes, it's safe to mess up your personal relationships and still find a way to come around and make them right again, it's safe to try out different ways of being and expressing yourself, trying to be heard, trying to understand.

Ann: They have so many opportunities to take responsibility. That's the key.

Brian: Taking responsibility—there's nothing more real than that.

Chris: The children develop real strengths for life. To me that is a lot of what this is about, gaining the kind of skills that will take you through life. And they can be personal skills, the kind that you need to build your relationships with your family and your spouse and your children, and they can be the kind of strength it takes to stand up against an unjust law. The children bring all that forth. I feel so lucky to have taught here long enough to see these people reach adulthood with those skills in place.

Ann: I think what happens here is real in that it comes from the children. *It comes from them.*

Kit: I'm thinking about the children moving from here into the world. When I see them out there, all grown up, they look the same as they looked when they were here, when they were little. They look like they know who they are. And I think it's true. They are who they are! Now, *that* is real.

Chris: And they will continue to be true to themselves as they live their lives. I feel sure of that. Because when you are a child and you go through many years knowing that it is okay for you to make your own choices and decisions, when you grow up and go out into the world—it's still okay. You *know* it's okay. I don't think you are ambivalent about it. I think you're pretty sure.

Jeanie: Yes! That is the heart of it.

•

Don: Could we apply what we've been talking about to some of our children who are about to graduate from the Antioch School? I'm thinking especially of Angela and Michael. They have been here practically all their school lives. Perhaps we can trace their progression, from where they were when they first came here to where they are now, as they're about to leave. You might talk about some of the things you remember about them, the ways you have seen them grow and develop. In this way we may illuminate the long-term experience of children here at this school.

Does this sound like a good thing to do?

The teachers agree to do this.
We begin with Angela:

Angela

Jeanie: I remember when Angela started here in the Kindergarten. She was having a hard time with her family in transition. She wanted a lot of things, but she had no idea how to go about getting them. She wanted to lead but didn't now how to do it. She was full of ideas, but didn't know how to convince other people to join in her ideas. Very determined, too. A very determined child.

I sent her on to you, Kit, feeling that there was still a lot of work she needed to do. She didn't know how to articulate her anger. She didn't really know what to do with her anger, and what not to do with it. She couldn't put it down and go on.

Don: "Articulate her anger"?

Jeanie: She couldn't say, "I'm angry." I'm not sure she even knew that she was. She knew she was uncomfortable, but without knowing what it was she was really feeling.

Kit: You helped her grasp all that, Jeanie. And you helped her grasp the concept that she had a responsibility. I remember she would push other children, and she couldn't get anywhere with you without having to be responsible for that. I remember that you did some work with her about why she was angry with a friend, and she really heard you when you told her that it was all right to feel that way. She really needed to do that work first, I think.

And then she could consider the possibility that it wasn't just the world that was knocking her around. She needed to learn that she had something she could do with her feelings over that. Especially since her family was going through upheaval. She needed to know she had power, that she was going to have the power to make herself feel more comfortable. When you get those things hooked up, the child can move forward.

I remember when she first came to the Younger Group. She was a little six-year-old in a room full of older girls. I remember her running this way and that way, sort of at loose ends. Being mad. Wanting a lot and not being clear on how to get it. And then going for it.

That first year she was smack dab in the middle of a whole crowd of older, more powerful people. She didn't know where to begin. She cried a lot. She bemoaned the fact that people weren't picking her for things. And it wasn't that they weren't picking her; it's just that they were moving so fast with each other that they forgot to grab her up, snatch her up, take her along. She had to learn to make herself visible to them. She had to teach herself how to do that. And she had to learn that she couldn't do it in unacceptable ways, you know. She couldn't push people, she couldn't hit them. That's unacceptable; it won't work. We had lots and lots of long, long talks about that. She really worked on that.

And she started to modify her ways. She began pulling herself away from that. I'm thinking about her whole three years in the Younger Group now. She made some important changes. She'd go into the Quiet Room and she'd cry. She just had to, because she had to release something that was in her, you know? So when she was having a hard day, she'd just go into the Quiet Room and be by herself for a while, and let everything out. And so, in that way, she kept *owning* that. She just kept on taking responsibility—feeling how she felt, expressing how she felt, being responsible for her feelings in that way.

One day we talked. It was about the time her sister was getting married. She was worried about her sister getting married, because marriage had not been such a great thing for the people she loved. She felt bad about it, you know, and she was supposed to feel good about it. She was supposed to be happy about the wedding. She was supposed to be joyful. But she was just worried to death.

So we talked about those feelings. And as we

talked, she moved from that space of *trying* to get that out, to really *getting* it out. I remember this one moment—I'll always remember it—when she went down this whole long line of pain, all her losses in her life. All of them: when her dog had died, and when her gerbil had died, and when her fish had died, and then on from there. She went down this long list of events in her life that had made her sad— all the things that she had loved that she lost.

And when she was finished with the list she just made a big sigh, and got a drink of water, and she was okay.

Jeanie: Incredible!

Kit: She began going through cycles, repeating this pattern of surviving her losses and starting over, over and over. And I asked myself and worried about it— Would she move beyond it, would she grow beyond it? Or will this be a pattern that she would keep repeating, over and over?

About this time we did a musical in the Younger Group. The children wrote this musical. And Angela, who always loved music, wrote a song. She put a little tune and some words together and she made music, she made this song. And in the play she sang her song. Now, all of us went together and made up the music for our play, but there was this one song that she pretty much put together herself. That was something we didn't know she could do. And she could, and everyone saw that in her, and we knew it was special.

That was just one of the ways she was special among us. She had wonderful skills that we didn't know she had, and once we knew, we could all appreciate. That musical was one of the times when she had the spotlight on her, one of those times that feel good to children, when other people say about something they can do, "Gee, that's good, that's exciting, that's really great." Positive response, and it's genuine, and it's *yours*—nobody can take it away from you. These are some of the pieces children grow by.

And so by the end of her time in the Younger Group, Angela had gained something strong within

herself. She had moved forward and matured and smoothed out as she went. She had kindness. She had a lot of concern for other people. And she had a sense of knowing about herself in a really, really solid way. She was not quite settled in to it yet, but really knowing it.

Chris: All the time she was coming up through the school, Angela was the only girl at her age level. All the other girls she associated with were older. So here Angela was, fairly young herself, scrambling to keep up with the older girls without a lot of social skills to back her up. That's where her social discomfort came from, trying to keep up with children who were older and more sophisticated than she was in the social realm, though they were not necessarily ahead of her intellectually.

When she first came to the Older Group, she was very cerebral. Everything was about her intellect. Her writing was exquisite! She spent a lot of free time reading and writing. She did not like to do anything physical. She just didn't want to do anything at all with her body. She didn't want to play outdoor games. She'd fuss and whine and then she'd find a way to stand off by herself way out in the field and not really participate. If we went for a walk in the Glen, like to the Pine Forest, she was like "Oh no, I can't walk that far," and then she'd just trudge along instead of walking. She'd just trudge along, lagging behind, just not wanting to do this at all.

And yet at that time, I think. she joined the swim team, so she began to be physical with swimming.

Jeanie: Always a good sign!

Chris: Yes. Soon she started taking on swimming as her physical challenge. Then when she was in her second year in the Older Group, she matured quite a bit socially. And the older girls were Ryder, Claire, and Crystal, and they were quite sophisticated intellectually, and so she was more included in that group of girls than she ever had been before. And those girls were also very active physically. I think that pulled Angela out of the strictly cerebral role into a more physical way of being. She was like, "I'm moving, I'm living in my body, I play games, I'm wrestling with these girls." Because that was one of the ways to be with those girls. Which was perfect for Angela—she started developing this other side of herself, the physical side. And the social side of herself, too.

This year it's all coming together. This year everything's jelled, all of those things she was working for. Now she's having girls surround her and want to be with her, and adore her and cuddle up to her when they're working, and sit in her lap—all the things she wanted to have in terms of her social life. She is a role model for all the girls, and a leader, and a mentor. She is looked up to.

Brian: By the boys, too.

Chris: Yes, the boys are really liking her. They seek her out and they have some really good, really beneficial conversations.

Kit: It's all very wonderful, all she has accomplished.

Chris: It really is. And, looking back over it, it's interesting to see how it's come full circle. Angela has always developed well ahead of her peers intellectually, and that's part of what separated her from her peers. Because intellectually she's just way above a lot of other children in terms of her understanding of things, her interest in the broader world. And now, being the oldest girl in the Older Group, that's sort of a natural place to be.

On top of that, she's developed social skills, and she's developed physical skills. She's become quite adept and athletic. She's joined other kinds of activities, besides swimming—soccer, basketball, and all these other things, in school and outside school, too. At school she's out playing football and over-the-bar and everything else—she's in the thick of all the physical activities here at school. That's what Don and I were looking at today, and we remarked about it. We were watching her playing outside at lunch time and we noticed how comfortable she is in her role, and in her body, and her mind, and her feelings about herself.

So, all these things have come together and unified for her. It just doesn't feel that there are any more gaps for her to fill in. She's filled them all. She found the way. With all the challenges she's had growing up, socially and physically and emotionally, she's found a great many ways to strengthen herself. She's leaving here in a wonderful, wonderful place.

Don: She really is. I've noticed how much the other children appreciate her capacity for understanding. She fulfills a role almost like counseling with the other kids. Advising them, commenting wisely about things that are going on with them.

Jeanie: She has a really rich understanding.

Brian: She has gotten kinder.

Chris: Yes, she's gotten kinder, with having people look up to her and being a more of an older, role-model kind of person. She's not separated out anymore. That was part of her anger, when she didn't feel included or understood. She'd snap at people, and some of that snappiness came from her anger. That's not there anymore.

Don: I also noticed, in the Writers Group, that she was important to Michael. He would be restless and fearful about writing maybe, and he'd try to tease Angela and distract her. She'd just absorb it good-naturedly, and give it right back to him, playfully, to the point that he'd end up smiling. Pretty soon he'd be calm again. They did a lot of good work together.

Chris: They've always been good for each other. Angela and Michael have always had a special relationship. They could calm each other, especially a lot of times when Angela felt not supported and not understood. It would be Michael she'd go and talk to.

Don: So, how about Michael—shall we talk about him now?

Self-portrait

Michael

Kit: He started as a first [in the first year of the Younger Group]. And he was *so* shy. When his mom brought him in, his presenting behavior was, he went up into the loft and covered himself up with blankets and a pillow. He just burrowed in, you know. And his mom was telling me how shy he was and he peeked out between the pillows and he said, "I can't read!" And I said, "Well, okay, is that something you want to work on?"

He was kind of a tough kid. And that came from being sort of scared. I tried to treat him well; my feeling was just to be soft with him. He was somebody who was going to leave the moment things got uncomfortable.

And he did do that. He would physically flee a lot. If just in the normal course of relating to the other children Michael was challenged, or talked to in a certain way, he was likely to run away. He would run out of the room and hide. He'd hide in the hallway behind the lost-and-found box, or behind a door, or down in the bathroom or somewhere.

And we'd just kind of go on with what we were doing. I'd go out and check on him. I'd go by where he was hiding and I'd say, "Do you need a little more time?" And he'd say yes, or actually he would nod yes. So I'd give him a little more time. Then when he was ready, he'd come back to the group.

That's what we did to get through those times that were just real painful for him.

The rest of the time, we were just moving along. He wasn't very eager to do things unless he really had a strong foundation of competency and choice. There were some things he could do well. He could construct. He could see how to solve a problem of construction, of building something, putting things together. And he could see how to solve a social problem. He would offer his solution and he would show us the way to go. And he still does that. That was him saying to us, "This is how to do it, this is what I

do. Take it or leave it, this is what I do." He would define himself for us in that way.

He was pretty good at things he chose to do. He would practice building things at home, so at school it wouldn't be too hard for him to show us what he could do. Like if we were doing things with crafts sticks at school, he'd go home and get his dad to get him a bunch of crafts sticks, and he would work with them at home. He'd learn how to work with crafts sticks and he'd practice and get good at it. Then at school, when somebody would say, "Gee, I don't know how to do this," he could say, "Oh, you just do it like this," and he'd be right.

Little by little, he built that kind of persona: he could do stuff, he was capable and knowledgeable. But still, any little confrontation would just throw him out the door. He was just fragile in that way.

I think we built some ability and some stability in our relationship, he and I, in those years we had together in the Younger Group. And he built some stable relationships with the other kids. But I think it was always kind of tentative. And as he got older, sometimes it was pretty hard. I was walking pretty softly around him.

There was one time when I pushed it, because pretty soon he would be going on into the Older Group and I thought, "Well, let's see where you are, how ready you are to move on." So I sort of pushed the situation. And he just cussed me out like a sailor! And one time he really blew up at Lucas. And now I see that he and Lucas are really good friends. And we weathered our difficulty, too, he and I. He had a volatile reaction to having to sit down and talk a problem through and be responsible for his part of it, and yet, still it was possible to sit right there at the table and go through it with him, without his getting up and leaving the room. He was really, really angry at me, but we got through it.

And then he found the perfect way to come into

the Older Group. He brought in a solution the first day, right, Chris?

Chris: Yes, that's exactly right. He certainly did. That first day in the Older Group, Michael didn't want to participate in anything we did. He had his own thing for us to do. He came in with a big piece of paper and he whispered to me, "Can I make an obstacle course for the Older Group?" I said, "Sure." And he drew up this huge map—it took up the whole table—of an obstacle course he had laid out on the play-yards on both sides of the school. Then he asked me if he could make some numbers and tape them to the trees and the jungle gym, and different things on the play-yards. And he went out and did that.

By maybe 1:30 in the afternoon he had this whole thing set up. So we all went out there and he told everyone what the obstacle course was. He had the map and he showed people what to do, like follow the numbers and try to get past all the obstacles he'd set up. And it was fun, it was really a fun thing to do. Everybody had a great time. All the kids really appreciated what he did. It was huge success for Michael.

That was the way he knew to start in. He felt important and like a leader. And all the parts of Michael, his dignity and his integrity and his confidence and his ability to do things, all those parts of him were right there in place. He was saying, "This is who I am. This is what I do."

But he wasn't over his anger. For the next two years he had a number of physical explosions, usually with Luke, with Polo, with David, and with Ben. They were the ones who could really push Michael's buttons. And it was usually about either teasing or feeling left out.

We had many conferences. I would let him cool off, and then we'd have a conference. Because a lot of times, at the height of things, he would go into the Quiet Room by himself, and he'd cry. He'd just be so angry he'd be crying. It was anger crying. He just felt so much anger that he needed to weep.

And the other kids were good about that. They'd just let him do that. He would sit here and pout and

swear and turn bright red and sweat and everything. In a fury! They were pretty good about sitting there and waiting for him to finish that. And then everybody would have his or her say.

Every once in a while there'd be a yelling match between Michael and David. Sometimes they couldn't avoid yelling. But by the middle of his last year in the Older Group, he had a lot of that under control. He really learned a lot about walking away. And he learned more about being able to say to himself, "This is about them, not so much about me. So if they are going to act like idiots and jackasses, that's their problem, and I don't need to be a part of it."

To this day, if he's disgusted with something that Luke and Ben are doing, he'll just come into the Quiet Room and sit down and work it out within himself. Then he'll spend some time with Anna. They'll write a story together, and sit and chat. They'll say things about other people, like, "Oh, they're so immature!" Because it just galls Michael, how immaturely the other children can behave at times. So he's learned to just take some time away from all that. And then he'll work his way back into friendship with them.

Kit: So, he's really found his way of coping with it. And make it work.

Chris: Yes, it's working for him now. And another one of the skills he's really taught himself is to use the appropriate words before he gets to the snapping point.

Don: I've grown to really like Michael and really appreciate him. I wasn't sure that I would in the beginning. I think very highly of him.

Brian: I think he really benefited from your presence here this year. It was really valuable for him to hang out with you and do Writers Group.

Chris: Yes. The conversations you had in Writers Group were so illuminating—they fed his soul. It meant a lot to him to have those discussions. He really feels mature and respected and that his ideas are capable of being discussed.

Don: My impression is that he's extremely bright, extremely intelligent. And he knows a lot. I'm struck with how much he knows about how people are, and why they are that way. He can come up with very insightful, very astute psychological interpretations of why people do certain things.

He really liked the day he and I went downtown to get the material for the darkroom. We walked around town a little bit. His eyes were wide open, you know. He was wanting to know what was going on here and there, like what the hardware store was all about. He was curious about some of the history of the town, what it was like in the old days before there were cars. We had some quite sophisticated conversations, really. I enjoyed being with him on that outing.

Chris: Yes, he's a very special, unique human being. He has so much personal integrity! He really does. He has this core of integrity about him. And all during his time here, he has built up his ability to express that. From hiding it to expressing it—he's come that far.

Don: Integrity—how does that manifest with him?

Chris: Let me get my thoughts together . . . I mean integrity in two different ways, on two different levels. One is his inner core of himself, that he knows to be himself, that he respects and likes and wants other people to see. That is part of his integrity, and it is integrated now.

And he also has moral integrity. This part of him is not quite integrated yet. He has high expectations of other people's behavior, and he can't always hold himself to that same standard. A lot of times something that somebody else will do—for example, an older child being unkind to a younger child—will make him so angry he can hardly stand it. He might go into a rage over that. And yet, on the other hand, he may do the same thing to some younger child who upsets him somehow.

So he's not able yet to manage that himself, but it's in him and it is meaningful to him. He has to keep measuring his own behavior around it, which is the one of the things I've seen him do, particularly this year. That's one of the reasons that it's so important that he's been able to express anger in a

more appropriate way. He's holding on to his own integrity.

When he's been angry recently, most of his anger ends up with Michael just separating himself from the source of his anger. But not running away. He doesn't flee. It's a deliberate separating himself, in a positive way—"I'm going to do something else, I'm going to hang out with Anna, who is there being quiet." Or once with Emily. He spent time with Emily, and she was knitting and he was learning to knit and they sat down and worked together on their knitting. It was quite wonderful to see them.

So he's found his way, using his social skills, and working on anger management. He has achieved a great deal. He's happier.

Brian: He's been way calmer. More confident. More humorous, too.

Chris: He's more relaxed. He's not so tied up inside with anger. And he is a wonderful, wonderful swim partner. He just really is. He is so good with Henry P! Henry was scared to come in the water, you know. And Jeanie had told me about Henry needing very special attention, so I paired him with Michael. And Michael was just the right person. He was *so* patient with Henry! He would sit half in the water—and you know the water in that pool is *cold* in the winter—and he would sit there waiting while Henry stood on top of the ladder, not coming in, not coming in, not coming in . . . Michael would just be talking to him and playing games. He'd swim underneath the ladder and he'd quietly come up close and talk to him. He'd pretend that he was different kinds of animals and make Henry laugh. He'd do all kinds of stuff, and gradually Henry would start coming down the ladder. He'd come down two steps and get a little wet, and then he'd stop. Then he'd come another step and stop. Finally he'd get down into the water.

Jeanie: It took *forever* sometimes.

Chris: But he really didn't want Michael to pick him up or touch him. And eventually Michael was able to pick him up and hold him.

[Chris makes a gentle cradling motion.]

And then he was able to play with him in the pool. But it took months—months of very slow, very patient work.

Jeanie: Michael invented the game where Henry would splash him and Michael would fall away from the splashing and dive down in the water. And Henry would laugh and laugh. That was one way Henry could relax.

[*She laughs at her memory of this.*]

Michael was so creative! So gentle. It was truly remarkable.

Chris: And he wouldn't go into it thinking, "Oh, I'm going to have so much fun helping Henry." Every time it was, "Do you think Henry's going to get in the water today?" Like he was dreading it. And then he'd be just wonderful with him.

Jeanie: He wouldn't let any of that impatience show. Not at all. He was wonderful.

Kit: He was showing real respect. He was giving what he wanted for himself.

Chris: Exactly. He knows who he was at all his stages, and that gives him a lot of patience for children who are intimidated by new things and need to find their own way. Just like he used to be.

Jeanie: I think it's very touching when children gain the gift of self-recognition that Michael has, how they can give it back to another child. It doesn't just stay with them; it circles back as a gift to another child. This is very touching to me.

Brian: He is very gentle with the younger children.

Kit: Instrumental in all of this is Sophie.

[*Sophie is Michael's sister; she's in the Nursery.*]

Kit: She provided a place for Michael's gentleness.

Ann: Yes! He is the *best* older brother.

Jeanie: He really is.

Chris: He is!

Kit: Sophie is being such an important part of his life. I remember when she was just a baby and his mom first brought her to school. Michael held her and was showing her around, letting people see her. And he was just so present to that. He was so much his true self, so careful and gentle, caring for that little baby. Michael couldn't help but be his true self with that baby . . . And now Sophie is—

Ann: She's four and a half.

Kit: Michael's had that many years to feel that part of him grow.

Chris: Yes, the nurturing part.

Kit: Michael came out of himself with Sophie.

Ann: I love it when he comes down to the Nursery to tell me something about Sophie. He's standing there telling it to me and it's almost as if she's right there with him. I don't know how else to put it—I just feel her presence there with him. He'll just be giving me a message, like she'll be coming late or she's got a cold or something. And you can feel the presence of Sophie inside Michael. You feel that softness.

Kit: Yes. Yes . . . You know, I'm thinking now: it took him just the right amount of time to go through the school.

Ann: Yes. It feels just right.

Kit: Because this is what happens by the time you leave us. Finding out who you are, and finding ways to be who you are—these are the things that happen to children here.

And watching it happen, with child after child . . . Oh, it gives me chills now, thinking about it! Because this is what trust does. This is our process. It's what happens here. It's what the children *do* . . .

Child after child, finding ways to be who you are.